Gallica

Volume 45

THE FACE AND FACIALITY IN MEDIEVAL FRENCH LITERATURE, 1170–1390

Gallica

ISSN 1749–091X

Founding Editor: Sarah Kay

Series Editors: Simon Gaunt and Peggy McCracken

Gallica aims to provide a forum for the best current work in medieval and early modern French studies. Literary studies are particularly welcome and preference is given to works written in English, although publication in French is not excluded.

Proposals or queries should be sent in the first instance to the editor, or to the publisher, at the addresses given below; all submissions receive prompt and informed consideration.

Professor Simon Gaunt (simon.gaunt@kcl.ac.uk)

Professor Peggy McCracken (peggymcc@umich.edu)

The Editorial Director, Gallica, Boydell & Brewer Ltd., PO Box 9, Woodbridge, Suffolk IP12 3DF, UK

Previously published volumes in this series are listed at the end of this volume.

THE FACE AND FACIALITY IN MEDIEVAL FRENCH LITERATURE, 1170–1390

ALICE HAZARD

D. S. BREWER

© Alice Hazard 2021

All Rights Reserved. Except as permitted under current legislation no part of this work may be photocopied, stored in a retrieval system, published, performed in public, adapted, broadcast, transmitted, recorded or reproduced in any form or by any means, without the prior permission of the copyright owner

First published 2021
D. S. Brewer, Cambridge

ISBN 978-1-84384-587-4

D. S. Brewer is an imprint of Boydell & Brewer Ltd
PO Box 9, Woodbridge, Suffolk IP12 3DF, UK
and of Boydell & Brewer Inc.
668 Mt Hope Avenue, Rochester, NY 14620-2731, USA
website: www.boydellandbrewer.com

A CIP catalogue record for this book is available
from the British Library

The publisher has no responsibility for the continued existence or accuracy of URLs for external or third-party internet websites referred to in this book, and does not guarantee that any content on such websites is, or will remain, accurate or appropriate

This publication is printed on acid-free paper

Printed and bound in Great Britain by
TJ Books Ltd, Padstow, Cornwall

Contents

List of Illustrations	vii
Acknowledgements	ix
Author's Note	xi
Introduction	1
1 Levinasian Faces in Arthurian Verse	28
Emmanuel Levinas and the Middle Ages	36
Le Chevalier au lion	43
Le Chevalier as deus espees	57
La Vengeance Raguidel	67
2 Marginal Faces	80
Sources	83
The Picture-face and the *sainte face*	91
Letter-faces	96
Affect and the Real: Tomkins and Lacan	98
3 The *visagéité* of the *Roman de la rose*	116
The Vice Portraits	121
The Garden Wall	141
4 Faces and Genitals in the *fabliaux*	160
Trubert	164
Le Chevalier qui fist parler les cons	179
Conclusion	203
Bibliography	211
Index	225

Illustrations

1	Bibliothèque nationale de France (BnF fr. 5716 p. 461 (detail)	85
2	BnF fr. 343 fol. 60r (detail)	86
3	BnF fr. 343 fol. 60v (detail)	87
4	BnF fr. 343 fol. 60v (detail)	87
5	BnF fr. 343 fol. 78v (detail)	87
6	BnF fr. 5716, p. 348 (detail)	89
7	BnF fr. 5716 p. 350 (detail)	89
8	BnF fr. 5716 p. 157 (detail)	89
9	BnF fr. 13568 p. 354 (detail)	90
10	BnF fr. 13568 p. 361 (detail)	90
11	BnF fr. 13568, p. 359 (detail)	90
12	BnF fr. 343 fol. 82r (detail)	99
13	BnF fr. 343 fol. 90v (detail)	99
14	BnF fr. 343 fol. 86v (detail)	102
15	BnF fr. 343 fol. 87r (detail)	102
16	BnF fr. 343 fol. 81v (detail)	102
17	BnF fr. 343 fol. 95v (detail)	102
18	BnF fr. 343 fol. 86v (detail)	102
19	BnF fr. 343 fol. 82v (detail)	113
20	BnF fr. 343 fol. 88v (detail)	113
21	BnF fr. 343 fol. 88v (detail)	113
22	BnF fr. 343 fol. 91r (detail)	114
23	BnF fr. 343 fol 97r (detail)	114

24	Bodleian, MS Douce 371 fol. 4v (detail) Amant and Oiseuse at the garden gate	122
25	BnF fr. 12595, fol. 3v (detail), Tritesce	127
26	Bodleian, MS Douce 195, fol. 2v (detail) Covoitise and Avarice	127
27	BnF fr. 19153, fol. 5v (detail), Amant and Oiseuse at the garden gate	147
28	Arsénal, MS 5226, fol. 6v (detail), Amant and Oiseuse at the garden gate	148
29	Bodleian, MS Douce 195, fol. 5r (detail), Amant and Oiseuse at the garden gate	151
30	British Library, MS Harley 4425 fol. 39r (detail), Jalousie's castle, with Dangier. © The British Library Board	156

Acknowledgements

I would first like to thank the Department of French at King's College, London, for providing such a supportive, stimulating and enjoyable environment in which to work, and the AHRC for providing me with the means with which to undertake this project. As mentors, both official and unofficial, as well as friends, Ros Murray, Soizick Solman and Sanja Perovic have gone out of their way to help and guide me. I would also like in particular to thank Siobhán McIlvanney, who could not have been a more generous and supportive Head of Department while I have been working on this book.

I extend my grateful thanks to the imaging and reproduction departments at the British Library, the Bodleian Libraries and the Bibliothèque nationale de France for their patient help with obtaining permissions and images during the difficult summer of 2020. I also thank these institutions for kindly agreeing to let me reproduce images from their collections.

My friends have been wonderful throughout the lifespan of this project and, indeed, beyond. I would like especially to extend my sincerest gratitude, for many and various reasons, to: Anna Brown (and family), Kate Brook, Megan Friedman, Ellie Whiteside, Lydia Gaunt, Elliot Evans, Hannah Morcos, Morgan Daniels and James and Laura Simmonds-Read. I owe debts which cannot be repaid to Saraid McIlvride, David Boldrin, Kathryn Maude and Fuad Musallam and would like to acknowledge my deepest gratitude. Lucy Dawkins has been my ardent supporter and chief confidence-booster and I give her my love and thanks.

Jane Gilbert has given my work more time than it deserves and I am truly thankful. As the person who, many years ago, introduced me to medieval French, Jane is also owed my particular thanks. I would also like wholeheartedly to thank Sarah Kay and Miranda Griffin, who provided me with hugely helpful feedback on this project, as well as Peggy McCracken whose support, encouragement and advice have been invaluable.

I must extend my warmest thanks to Simon Gaunt, who will always be an inspiration to me and whose generosity of time, spirit and encouragement is still boundless, long after his official supervisory duty has expired.

Writing this book has, at times, felt like an unending task. Elizabeth

McDonald and Caroline Palmer at Boydell & Brewer have, correspondingly, been endlessly patient, kind, helpful and encouraging and I cannot thank them enough.

Finally, I pay tribute to my family. My parents, Catherine and Jeff, have picked up the pieces countless times, and to know that they would do so again is a gift I am lucky to have. My brother-in-law, Nathan, is a source of endless warmth and kindness that I often call upon. My sister, Florence, has taught me what it means to consider somebody a 'rock' and it is to her that, for what it's worth, I dedicate this book.

Author's Note

The key common factor that unites all the theorists that I have used in this book is that, in one way or another, they have all engaged substantially with the concept of the face, and it is this part of their work that I focus on in this book and which is given the most detailed explanation.

One thing that I hope comes out of a reading of this book is a sense not just of the power and complexity of the face as a multifarious, shifting and enigmatic concept, but also of its historical, social and philosophical importance as a cipher for how we understand the world around us. The theoretical writings that I call upon here are also, in part, a testament to this.

I have chosen to focus on a set of theorists most of whom were writing in the same half of the twentieth century and among whose works there was and is significant dialogue and often disagreement. Readers do not need to be well versed in deconstruction, psychoanalysis and post-structuralism in order to engage fully with this book. What is worth stating here is that each of the theorists I turn to is concerned with unravelling and remapping how we encounter and interpret meaning, and each, in their work, adopts an acceptance of that meaning's plurality and slippage.

Introduction

In the late twelfth- or early thirteenth-century romance *Le Bel Inconnu*, the hero takes his helmet off, revealing his face and, he assumes, himself, to the *Pucelle aux Mains Blanches*:

> Guinglains l'avoit bien coneüe
> De si lonc con il l'ot veüe.
> Son cief et son vis desarma;
> Errant vint, si le salua.

> [Guinglain had known her for a very long time when he saw her. He uncovered his head and face; she immediately came and greeted him.][1]

When, somewhat anticlimactically, she fails to make the association between his face and his identity, the knight is forced to explain. There is, in this scene, a crucial and, to modern readers, startling disjunction between the characters' expectations placed on the face as a marker of individual identity. Guinglain assumes that because the *pucelle* has already seen his face and already knows him, she will have made a clear association between the two, such that his face will suffice as a sign of his identity and presence. She, on the other hand, seems to have made no such connection and requires an altogether different guarantee. We witness the converse situation in the slightly later *Hunbaut*: the *chastelaine* of the castle of Gaudestroit is in love with Gauvain, having never seen him. She has a statue made of her would-be lover which is, nonetheless, so realistic that Kay, Yder and Giflet, who all know Gauvain well, believe it to be Gauvain himself and are persuaded otherwise only when the *dame* tells them that it is just a statue. Here, the connection between the visual sign of a face and the identity and presence of its 'owner' is so strong as to overreach the reality of the situation. Neither episode is central to its respective narrative, and each seems very casually and yet profoundly disruptive of the connection

---

[1] Renaud de Beaujeu, *Le Bel Inconnu*, ed. by Michèle Perret, Champion Classiques: Moyen Âge, 4 (Paris: Champion, 2003), lines 3995–8. Translation is my own.

between face and essence, either over- or understating its status. The same thing occurs in other motifs and guises of the broader period: in narratives of resemblance, such as the twelfth-century *conte*, *Floire et Blanchefleur*, Marie de France's *Fresne*, or the thirteenth-century *Roman de la Manekine*, characters' physical similarities often give rise to uncanny recognition, to surprising misrecognition or to willing substitution. The relationship between the face and its human in medieval literature is widely, and often surprisingly, variable, sometimes to the extent that it breaks down entirely, and yet the fact of this connection is one of the least contested and most enduring principles in literature and, indeed, beyond. Jean-Paul Sartre described the human face as 'la limite extrême du corps humain' [the furthest limit of the human body], in the sense that it is at once the locus of all that it is to be human, both socially and psychologically, and, at the same time, the vanguard of humans and of humanity, leading the rest of the body inexorably into the future. In this book I want to investigate the possibility, raised repeatedly and yet subtly in medieval narrative and textual culture, that the face is neither of these things.[2]

My goal is not limited to a discussion of medieval texts, however. As far as anything can be universal, across both time and space, the face is a universal phenomenon and any discussion of it in context necessarily has much broader implications. Kelly Gates explains that the face

> has been a special object of attention in the organisation of visual practices and the development of visual media technologies, and technologies designed for representing and analyzing the face have played a special role in defining and redefining what it means to be human.[3]

In this book I explore how medieval French literature plays a role in this phenomenon and how its own faces play 'a special role in defining and redefining what it means to be human'. This project came about from the observation that the face in medieval narrative seems to enact and dramatise contradictions that we see in contemporary, specifically Western European, society. The rise and rise of biometrics and the normalisation of facial recognition technology in particular has relocated, or perhaps simply highlighted, the place of the face at the heart of our understanding of what it means not just to be human but to be individual, consistent and readable subjects in society. At the same time, popular society and culture are becoming increasingly accepting of the notion that an individual's identity

---

[2] *Les Écrits de Sartre*, ed. by Michel Contat and Michel Rybalka (Paris: Gallimard, 1969), p. 562. Translation is my own.
[3] Kelly A. Gates, *Our Biometric Future: Facial Recognition Technology and the Culture of Surveillance* (New York: New York University Press, 2011), p. 194.

is not necessarily consistent, nor is it always readable. This seems to me a curious echo of the role that the face plays in the medieval narrative examples noted above: the face is at once overtly signalled as *the* indicator of identity according to certain conventions, and yet at the same time moves in and out of line with those conventions, sometimes obeying them, sometimes not, and thus always undermining them. In this book I analyse the face as a medieval literary phenomenon and, by extension, as a motif in and of itself. The face is not a stable phenomenon, but part of the literary, cultural and social work that it does is based on the assumption that it is, and part of the work of this book is to follow the face around various medieval textual incarnations in order to understand it as expansively as possible. Here I refer again to Gates's work, in which she urgently spells out the contemporary political and social implications of certain ways of seeing the face, and in which she powerfully reminds us of three key points: that the face is a culturally and historically constructed phenomenon, that its appropriation and use is often politically and ideologically inflected and that the methods we use to read and interpret faces then in turn become the criteria and values by which we judge them. The final two sentences of her book offer a neat starting point for my own:

> Faces and their representations are never stable, standardized objects. Instead, they are hybrid assemblages of material and meaning, markers of identity and sites of affect to be sure, but always situated somewhere, on their way from somewhere and to somewhere else.[4]

In the texts I analyse, the face plays various and contradictory roles; it appears in different visual guises, is used and understood in different ways and, as often as not, is explicitly illegible. Indeed, one of the key tenets of this book is that what we consider to be a face is in fact much, much broader, and much more malleable, than simply the 'eyes-nose-mouth' configuration that we usually find on the front of a human's head. Equally, the qualities of faciality are, as we shall see, more than just legibility, surface, communication and identification.

To try to get to grips with the specificities of the phenomenon of the face, it is helpful briefly to consider one of its most influential literary incarnations, before moving to a discussion of its role in the current moment. The literary examples I evoke at the beginning of this Introduction have inherited the problems set out in Ovid's telling of the story of Narcissus. Here, the antihero is tormented by the beautiful image that he sees so clearly in front of him but which, as he also sees, is impossible to reach. Gazing at his own

---

[4] Gates, p. 200.

reflection, Narcissus is enchanted by the features of the face he sees there and yearns to be united with what he believes to be another person. The fact that this 'other' appears to be demonstrating exactly the same desire to be with Narcissus serves to enhance his own yearning and, of course, his frustration at how an apparently insubstantial barrier can so effectively separate the would-be lovers. Eventually realising that the image he sees is his own reflection – 'iste ego sum' – Narcissus experiences a new level of frustration.[5] No longer bemused by the lovers' division, he now laments their proximity and wishes for their separation, knowing it to be impossible. The bind he finds himself in is too much, and Narcissus dies.

Whatever the moral of the tale is understood to be, the face is the focal point for its central issues. It is the particular beauty of the face in the pool which lures Narcissus; the first frustration he feels is caused by not being able to reach the face behind what he imagines to be an insubstantial barrier; it is the shift in Narcissus's perception of the face he sees in front him which is the turning point in the narrative and which precipitates its ultimate tragic *dénouement*. The narrative, in other words, revolves around how the face is read or, rather, around the fact that the face *is* read. The mistake Narcissus makes can, from this point of view, be characterised as his believing that the face he sees in the pool represents the existence and qualities of something behind itself. He fatally underestimates the complexity of the face as a visual phenomenon, and, like many literary protagonists and commentators since, he automatically imagines it as essentially tied to and representative of a single, discrete subject. Jane Gilbert writes about the many romance figures in medieval French who are compared, or who compare themselves, to Narcissus, and notes that an equally frequent motif is the repudiation of that comparison; both affirmation and negation, she argues, underpin the loving subject's identification with the mythical lover.[6] Gilbert points out that when the literary trope of Narcissus is used to figure the lover in medieval French literature, it incorporates both the positive and negative aspects of the mirror motif: on the one hand, the mirror's capacity to reveal truth and, on the other hand, its dangerous propensity for distortion and illusion.[7] What is important in this book is that it is specifically the face that incarnates this tension between revelation and distortion and which enacts what Gilbert describes as 'a source both of irony and of complex and varied interplay around such notions as truth, reality, and subjectivity'.[8]

---

[5] Ovid, *Metamorphoses*, trans. by Frank Justus Miller, 3rd edn, rev. by G. P. Goold, 2 vols (Cambridge, MA: Harvard University Press, 1977), I, p. 156.
[6] Jane Gilbert, '"I am Not He": Narcissus and Ironic Performativity in Medieval French Literature', *MLR*, 100 (2005), 940–53.
[7] Ibid., pp. 941–2.
[8] Ibid., p. 942.

In some respects, then, Narcissus is caught in a version of the snare in which, as I outline below, more explicit, and more modern, discussions of the phenomenon of the face also find themselves. That is, they all assume the face to be an outer surface with a corresponding inside, and assume that its enigma can be solved through correct decoding. The questions raised by the story of Narcissus are questions not just of how to read or misread faces and surfaces, but of what they are: the face Narcissus sees in the pool is firstly someone else's, then it is his own; the surface he sees is both the surface of his face and the surface of the pool. To put this differently, we might say that the surface Narcissus sees has a number of different, and ostensibly mutually exclusive, depths.

The story of Narcissus feeds directly into French literature of the High Middle Ages – the period under investigation in this book – and is retold in several different guises. Narcissus turns up as himself in a number of places: the *Roman de la Rose*, the *Lai de Narcisse* and the *Ovide moralisé*, among others; the problems raised by the story, of the status and coherence of the link between outer appearance and inner essence, are also, as noted above, transposed onto different situations and motifs, and proliferate widely.[9] It is this repeated engagement with questions of interiority and representation that I investigate in this book. On the one hand, then, I explore medieval literature and follow the motif of the face as it engages with and demonstrates these questions. On the other hand, the book asks questions of the face itself, as a physiological, aesthetic and philosophical concept. Rather than use a stable modern notion as a foil against which to test the instability of the medieval, or vice versa, I aim to read the two side by side and to explore the limits, dimensions, metamorphoses, inadequacies and versatilities of the face in medieval literature and modern theory.

The face as a literary motif does not exist in a vacuum – much as literature itself does not. Indeed, as this Introduction will go on to demonstrate, the face is an object of investigation for sociology, psychology, linguistics and history before it is for literary studies. It is also a topic covered in great breadth and depth from an art-historical point of view, which traces pictorial representations of faces according to their symbolic schemes, historical style, their explicit purposes and their implicit effects. Our understanding of the face and our reaction to it as modern readers and interlocutors are not just influenced by, but are an integral part of, our understanding of 'face' as a 'real life' phenomenon. I investigate the idea of face *as* representation through

---

[9] For a discussion of French medieval rewriting of Ovid's *Metamorphoses*, see chapters 1 and 2 in Miranda Griffin, *Transforming Tales: Rewriting Metamorphosis in Medieval French Literature* (Oxford: Oxford University Press, 2015). Griffin's second chapter focuses on Echo's role in the story of Narcissus and Echo.

looking at literary representations of the face. My book is not linear, however, and uses what I refer to as 'face theories' – modern deconstructions of the idea of face as purely and simply representative – as tools with which to unpack the literary faces I encounter. As such, my book touches upon broader philosophical concerns; not only how we read literary faces but how we read faces that we encounter outside of texts. Not only am I concerned with the question of the legibility of medieval representations of the face, of what can viably be read into them, but I am also concerned with the legibility of face and faces in a more general sense. What, I ask, is at stake when we think we can read an other's face? Is the link between inner character and outer expression a viable one? I examine the legibility of medieval representations of the face in order to explore how we can read them, why 'read' may not always be the most appropriate term and what these different encounters with medieval faces tell us about the conceptual link between an inner essence and its outer expression.

Furthermore, I investigate the observation that our relationship with the face seems to be curiously immune from the broad dissemination of the implications of an arbitrary relation between signifier and signified, following the linguistic turn of mid-twentieth-century critical theory. I suggest that the face has the capacity to function not only as different kinds of sign (conventional, indexical, connotative, metonymic etc.) but also as a non-sign, and that the implications of this – both literary and social – are hidden in plain sight. In this book, then, I subscribe to Paul de Man's iconic position in 'The Resistance to Theory', and start my investigation from his assertion that

> By allowing for the necessity of a non-phenomenal linguistics, one frees the discourse on literature from naive oppositions between fiction and reality, which are themselves an offspring of an uncritically mimetic conception of art.[10]

In other words, my book works on the basis that the face is a phenomenon that transcends the idea of an accessible, attainable truth, not only by operating between literature and 'non-literature', but by oscillating between symbolic and non-symbolic.

What became clear over the course of my preliminary research is that it is somewhat disingenuous to consider the face a static object of study and that, in fact, it is better thought of as a particular structure of thought. The overarching concept of face as a hinge between two distinct but related domains is universally mapped onto 'real' faces and, in turn, representations

---

[10] Paul de Man, 'The Resistance to Theory', *Yale French Studies*, 63 (1982), 3–20 (p. 11).

of faces. Aside from the more recent theoretical use made of the face, to which I will turn shortly, a brief overview of a number of key historical ways of thinking about and studying the face also leads to this conclusion. The terms with which the face is evoked remain consistent, regardless of the discipline within which it is being examined; it seems it always has been, and is still, understood as the hinge between inner and outer, as an access point between the visible and the invisible, and as a readable surface by which we can know an implied or inferred depth.

In an illuminating article in which she considers the use of the term 'vultus' in Hildebert of Lavardin's c. 1100 'Rome Elegy', Monika Otter notes the different implications of Latin terms used to refer to the face.[11] She explains that 'there is some slippage [in classical sources] between your face as quintessentially you, that by which we can stably recognize you; and your face as mobile, adaptable, consciously manipulable, therefore also able to conceal or deceive'.[12] She then goes on to suggest that, while the distinction is 'far from absolute', to a certain degree these two meanings can be seen to be reflected in the respective use of 'facies' and 'vultus'.[13] Etymologically, Otter explains, 'facies' derives from 'facere' meaning 'to make' and is thus more inclined towards expressing the idea of the permanent features of the face, as if sculpted.[14] 'Vultus', on the other hand, implies the expression on a face, and therefore the possibility that it can be manipulated by the bearer in order deliberately to convey a particular, and potentially deceitful, message to observers.[15] In the texts I examine in this book, *face*, *visage* and *vis* are all used to refer specifically to the human face. The first is derived from *facere*, and the latter two from *visus*, meaning 'a seeing, looking; a look, glance; the faculty or act of seeing, sight, vision'.[16] An etymological discussion is not the concern of this book, but it is important to note the expectations inherent in an anatomical feature the language of which is so closely linked to the concept of appearance.

It seems less important to more recent studies of the face to consider it a way of reading permanent characteristics than to think of it as a marker

---

[11] Monika Otter, '*Vultus Adest* (The Face Helps): Performance, Expressivity and Interiority', in *Rhetoric Beyond Words: Delight and Persuasion in the Arts of the Middle Ages*, ed. by Mary Carruthers (Cambridge: Cambridge University Press, 2010), pp. 151–72.
[12] Ibid., p. 156.
[13] Ibid., p. 157.
[14] Ibid.
[15] Ibid.
[16] *Französisches Etymologisches Wörterbuch*, ed. by Walther von Wartburg, 25 vols (Basel: Zbinden, 1925–2002), XIV (1961), pp. 537–40; *A Latin Dictionary*, ed. by Charlton T. Lewis and Charles Short (Oxford: Clarendon Press, 1879; repr. 1955), p. 1998.

either of transient emotions and moods or of a particular relation; marking a mother out to a new-born baby, for instance. David Perrett, director of the Perception Lab at the University of St Andrews, has outlined the many and varied ways in which humans interpret – whether knowingly or not – each other's faces, and touches on the enormous importance of this interpretative activity in human interaction, development and communication.[17] Perrett's book includes a fascinating discussion of how human beings appear to possess the innate ability to recognise face-like patterns, and how the face-recognition process, when working properly, includes two components: firstly, the logical memory that tells us that we already know a particular face, and secondly, the emotional response that a particular face generates.[18] Equally, Perrett outlines experiments that suggest that humans possess an innate ability to recognise face-like patterns, and that the criteria for being considered 'face-like' are relatively meagre.[19] He explains that human brain cells 'respond to the general characteristics of faces for a wide range of species, so long as the faces are round and have a mouth and eyes'.[20] He later outlines the extraordinary discovery that babies less than a minute old respond more overtly to patterns that have a top-heavy bias, and that this corresponds with the organisation of facial features of 'virtually all animals with a backbone'.[21] The implication is, of course, that faces are a crucial component in human communication to the extent that the capacity to read a pattern as 'facial' appears to be present even before birth. Face, in an evolutionary sense, is much less a marker of character than of identity and, in particular, identity as a relational category: who the possessor of a face is in the world of the viewer. It is also a crucial tool in communicating emotion and mood, as attested by the abundance of literature dedicated to decoding the precise ways in which the face expresses both conscious and unconscious messages.[22] Later in his study, David Perrett examines the well-known hypothesis that symmetrical faces are more

---

[17] David Perrett, *In Your Face: The New Science of Human Attraction* (New York: Palgrave Macmillan, 2010).
[18] Ibid., pp. 39–40.
[19] Ibid., pp. 34–5, 51.
[20] Ibid., p. 35.
[21] Ibid., p. 53.
[22] See *Darwin and Facial Expression: A Century of Research in Review*, ed. by Paul Ekman (New York: Academic Press, 1973) for a broad overview of the topic up until the 1970s, and for the thirty subsequent years in review see *Emotions Inside Out: 130 Years After Darwin's 'The Expression of the Emotions in Man and Animals'*, ed. by Paul Ekman and others, Annals of the New York Academy of Sciences, 1000 (New York: The New York Academy of Sciences, 2003). See also Ekman's own edition of Darwin's commentary on facial expression: Charles Darwin, *The Expression of the Emotions in Man and Animals*, ed. by Paul Ekman, 4th edn (Oxford: Oxford University Press, 2009).

attractive to other humans.[23] It is, he points out, indeed the case that human females are more attracted to human males with symmetrical faces, and one of the main reasons for this is thought to be that symmetry signals good-quality genes.[24] Symmetry, in other words, cannot simply be a matter of aesthetics but must communicate something about the nature of the person which is particularly attractive. We have perhaps come full circle in our overview of facial thinking and investigations of the face: physiological features, it seems, are ultimately considered as external clues to internal attributes, whether this interior be a person's soul, their social status or their genetic make-up. I would like, in this book, to depart from this straightforward concept of the face and, to paraphrase de Man, to focus on its reference more than on its referents.[25]

I end this section, therefore, with the hint of this approach. In a 1998 study of the face from a cross-disciplinary point of view, the consultant in clinical neurophysiology, Jonathan Cole, discusses an alarming meeting he had with a patient who had lost the ability to move her face, and explains that 'Her disease had opened up a seam between the face and self I had not realized was there'.[26] Although Cole's is also a comment on the abnormal circumstances that prevent the face reflecting the person when normally it would, he couches it in such a way as to suggest less that he is disturbed by not being able to read someone's face and more that the source of his alarm is the realisation that there is a structural difference between inner and outer – between person and face – that, whether it works to reveal or to conceal, is always there. In other words, instead of simply investigating the possibility that the face is not always an accurate expression of inner character, I will now turn to the possibility that the 'seam' between face and self is indicative of both rupture and suture, and that face is therefore not only a symbol of inferred interiority.

Some thinkers have taken what, given the history outlined above, is a rather radical view of the role of the face and, indirectly, of the structure of thought that it has so consistently signalled. While much of this, as I will discuss below, ties in with modes of critical theory after the rupture of signifier and signified, some of it emerges from different considerations. Max Picard's 1930 work, *The Human Face* (translated into English a year later), explicitly interrogates the kind of thinking that takes the face as a sign of inner essence.[27] He offers a way of thinking about the face that places it in a different relation not only to an individual's interior, but also to the idea of the face as a reflection of individual identity. Picard looks at how the face mediates and reflects not a person's

---

[23] Perrett, pp. 74–82.
[24] Ibid., p. 77.
[25] de Man, 'The Resistance to Theory', p. 8.
[26] Jonathan Cole, *About Face* (Cambridge, MA: MIT Press, 1998), p. 2.
[27] Max Picard, *The Human Face*, trans. by Guy Endore (London: Cassell, 1931).

individual qualities but, rather, their relation to God and their position within humanity. He suggests that the face is indeed capable of expressing the nature of a person's soul, but that it is capable of doing so only when that soul exists in relation to other souls; the face of an isolated person cannot perform this expressive function.[28] In other words, the face is not merely the hinge between the interior and exterior of a single, discrete person, but exists at the nexus of many other influences. Indeed, he goes so far as to say that the erstwhile closeness of humanity was such that the evil of one person's soul could be manifest on another's face.[29] Picard laments what he sees as a degradation of the spiritual state of humanity, whereby the face that once held something of the interplay between clarity and mystery of the Divine is now 'nothing but foreground'.[30] For Picard, the ideal state of the human face is one in which it is both expressive and mysterious, following the paradox of God that the more He reveals Himself, the more inscrutable He is.[31] Not only does the face work to express the individual, the collective and the Divine, but it also works to express a non-linear temporality, in direct contrast to, for instance, Georg Simmel's idea, expounded in his 1908 sociological investigation into the role of the senses in human interaction, that the face is the manifestation of a man's past.[32] Picard explains: 'A human face is more than a mere memento of that which once was there. The very last human face is still a sign of something that is and always will be.'[33]

A key interlocutor of Picard's was Emmanuel Levinas, who examined the divine properties of the human face and moved its discussion into the realm of ethics. Levinas's thinking forms the backbone of my first chapter, in which I look at the possibilities of mobile and multiple faces in the context of an anonymous encounter between two knights. Here I want to position his work in what I have characterised as a branch of 'face philosophy' that thinks of face as something other than a marker of interiority. Levinas's position was also, like Picard's, that the human face held a trace of the divine. Specifically for my purposes, Levinas developed the concept of the face as something the primary purpose of which was not to reveal something about an individual's identity, but simply to express their very existence and presence. For Levinas, an encounter with the face of an other is an encounter across an infinite distance;

[28] Ibid., pp. 87–92.
[29] Ibid., p. 91.
[30] Ibid., p. 25.
[31] Ibid., p. 6.
[32] Georg Simmel, 'Sociology of the Senses: Visual Interaction', in *Introduction to the Science of Sociology*, ed. by Robert E. Park and Ernest W. Burgess, 3rd edn (Chicago: University of Chicago Press, 1972), pp. 356–61.
[33] Picard, p. 21.

the encounter has nothing to do with the accumulation of knowledge, or indeed with diminishing the distance between the self and the other. The face-to-face encounter, therefore, is one in which the self assumes total responsibility for the other, and for which this fundamental inequality is a condition. While I examine his thought in more detail in Chapter 1, Levinas is important here inasmuch as his work is explicitly framed as a reaction to what he perceived as the danger of the pervasive thought structure of Western philosophy whereby all encounters with 'others' were concerned with the accumulation of knowledge of that other and, therefore, with the broader project of gathering all 'others' closer towards the 'same', thereby performing a grand totalising movement which diminished all difference. Levinas thus sought to develop a way of thinking that would describe encounters between two persons while upholding their fundamental difference and distance. He recognised that the face was both the symbol and mechanism of this appropriative movement that he wanted to avoid, and so Levinas reformulated the face, after Picard, into a surface whose role is not to infer, reveal or conceal a depth behind it but to signal its own presence. Michael Taussig expresses this eloquently: 'This is not a question of symbols, of the face as a symbol, but of the face defacing itself as guarantor of the symbolic in a flurry of the infinite.'[34]

Taussig considers Levinas's face in the context of a discussion much more explicitly concerned with the possibilities of faciality as a departure from the straightforwardly symbolic.[35] Taussig notes Sergei Eisenstein's observation that the invention of cinema meant that, 'far from dying out as Lavater's and Aristotle's defunct science, physiognomy was boosted by modernity', and that 'reading the face was here to stay as a type of irreducible folk wisdom of popular culture'.[36] He goes on to unpack the face as an object to be read, and explores the ways in which 'face' as a sociocultural phenomenon in fact plays a role in what he characterises as 'a discharge of the powers of representation'.[37] In other words, the face, for Taussig, both invites and refuses reading.

In a similar vein, Paul de Man has made significant use of the face as a way of thinking about literature which oscillates between discursive and non-discursive and which, he claims, raises the question: 'How are we to reconcile the *meaning* of face, with its promise of sense and of filial preservation, with

[34] Michael Taussig, *Defacement: Public Secrecy and the Labor of the Negative* (Stanford CA: Stanford University Press, 1999), p. 224.
[35] Throughout this book, I use 'faciality' to talk about the quality of being a face, or of being face-like. The two, as I go on to explore, are not entirely distinct. Equally, 'faciality' is not a static concept; part of the goal of this book is to explore many, and sometimes contradictory, incarnations. To refer specifically to the Deleuzo-Guattarian concept I use the original French term *visagéité*.
[36] Taussig, p. 230.
[37] Taussig, p. 256.

its *function* as the relentless undoer of its own claims?'[38] Again, face is figured as something that only partially works within a symbolic framework, and which invites a symbolic reading at the same time as it refuses to complete the symbolic circuit between sign and meaning. De Man's appropriation of the face as a tool for literary analysis is couched in terms of a response to the constrictions of thinking of face as a purely symbolic, representative and signifying model. His face is therefore a face the signifying power of which is not natural to it but is, rather, the expression of 'the figure-making properties of the linguistic system itself'.[39] While not denying the symbolic capacity of face, de Man nonetheless characterises it as a figurative overlay and not an essential component of faciality.

The final face philosophy that I want to note here as foundational to this book is that of Gilles Deleuze and Félix Guattari as expounded in *Mille plateaux*.[40] Like Levinas's work, this particular face theory is examined in much more detail in a following chapter, in which I use it as the basis for an interrogation of the face as marker of subjectivity in the *Roman de la Rose*. Here, however, I want to speak of it in slightly broader terms within the context of this theoretical overview in order to set up what follows. Conforming to the theme of the face theories I have just outlined, Deleuze and Guattari's exists within a broader critique of organisational structures that have as their model and therefore facilitate the relentless movement towards accrual of knowledge. In *Mille plateaux*, Deleuze and Guattari formulate a way of thinking that departs radically from what they conceive of as the constrictive and disingenuous thought that came before and which privileged both the subject as object of investigation and the binary structure of linguistics as a way of accessing meaning. As such, they posit a decentred view of both subjectivity and signification, the most iconic symbol of which is the rhizome, a structure whereby multiple points connect to one another in a non-hierarchical and heterogeneous mode.[41] In a later chapter, Deleuze and Guattari turn to the face, and use this as a tool with which to perform and to explain their project of decentring, of multiplying and of dismantling the hegemony of both subject and meaning. For Deleuze and Guattari, *visagéité* is a regime of organisation and structuration that codifies meaning through the interplay of the 'mur blanc' upon which meaning is visible and the

---

[38] Paul de Man, *The Rhetoric of Romanticism* (New York: Columbia University Press, 1984), p. 92 (original emphasis).

[39] Lee Edelman, *Homographesis: Essays in Gay Literary and Cultural Theory* (New York: Routledge, 1994), p. 193.

[40] Gilles Deleuze and Félix Guattari, *Capitalisme et schizophrénie 2: mille plateaux* (Paris: Minuit, 1980).

[41] Ibid., p. 13.

'trou noir' within which subjectification keeps 'sa conscience, sa passion, ses redondances' [its consciousness, its passion, its redundancies].[42] They argue for face as a way of understanding what is essentially an imperialist codification of meaning and subjectivity which masks the multiplicity of real experience and which presents itself as natural and essential. Face, therefore, is a distorting structure that forces experience into a binary logic. Crucially, *visagéité* is a system that works precisely on the basis of surface and depth and on the mutually sustainable dynamic of inside/outside that forms the basis for *all* meaning. Much as Paul de Man claimed that recognising face is the first totalising discursive act, Deleuze and Guattari see the face as the primary model for signification and subjectivity.[43] In other words, all meaning works according to this overlay of visible surface and inferred depth or, to use their term, volume. It may at first sight appear naive to claim Levinas alongside Deleuze and Guattari as the twin theoretical pillars of this book, since it is broadly acknowledged that the kind of faciality that the latter were critiquing implicitly included Levinas's. Indeed, Levinas offers a concept of face that he sees as a way of overcoming shortcomings in Western thought that are precisely what Deleuze and Guattari characterise *as* face. In other words, on the face of it Levinas sees as a solution what Deleuze and Guattari consider to be the problem. Nonetheless, the theoretical work they do in elaborating its mechanisms is what I use to frame this book. Deleuze and Guattari prise the face away from a conception of it as natural or essential, and use it as a way to describe modes of signification that have been imposed on culture and society. They dismantle face, not to eradicate it but to expose its workings, and, in turn, they allow us to conceive of what else face can do and what space is created within the concept once its boundaries have been rent apart. From this point of view I pair their work with Levinas: each of these face theories examines the *possibility* that face works in a way other than signifying inside via visible outside, and opens the face up as a way of interrogating rather than sustaining the assumption of an accessible interior.

No study of the face, in any guise or historical period, would be complete without a discussion of physiognomy. Although now widely (although not universally) considered erroneous and outdated, its role in shaping how we read faces is unquestionable. There are many studies of the history of physiognomy, all of which are more detailed and comprehensive than what

---

[42] *Mille plateaux*, p. 205; *A Thousand Plateaus: Capitalism and Schizophrenia*, trans. by Brian Massumi (London: The Athlone Press, 1988), p. 167. All translations are from this edition.

[43] de Man, *The Rhetoric of Romanticism*, pp. 90–1.

I offer here.[44] Nonetheless, I wish to highlight certain features of this history that are especially pertinent for the present study. In his anthropological study of the face, David Le Breton explains that physiognomy came about because of the shift in values and perspective characterised as the move from medieval to Renaissance society in Western Europe:

> Transition logique, peut-être, entre une société de structure plutôt communautaire qui ne fait du visage un principe essential d'identité, et une société qui abrite en son sein une structure individualiste qui prend peu à peu de l'ampleur.

> [A logical transition, perhaps, from a society with a mostly communal structure, in which the face is not considered an essential principle of identity, to a society that has at its heart a growing individualistic structure.][45]

Once the notion of the human being as a microcosm of a sacred, cosmic whole ends, and the uniqueness of each individual human being becomes the dominant idea, the human body plays a new role: demarcating the limits of each of these individuals. Instead of marking a person's connection and consistency with the universe, the visible body marks its difference, and the face is its 'couronne'.[46] Furthermore, the face now becomes not just the marker of the presence of a unique individual but also the indicator of the qualities of that individual. Le Breton notes that 'la géographie du visage se transforme. La bouche [...] devient maintenant tributaire de significations psychologiques, expressive' [the geography of the face is changing. The mouth [...] now becomes expressive, highly dependent on psychological meaning].[47] It is this shift that opens the doors for the perhaps paradoxical undertaking of using the face to classify individuals according to a set of types. As Le Breton explains, '[le visage] appelle la ressemblance autant que la différence infinitésimale – à la fois identifiant et distinguant l'individu, signant sa singularité tout en l'apparentant aux autres' [[the face] denotes resemblance as much as it does infintesimal difference – at once identifying and singling out the individual, marking his or her uniqueness while also connecting him or her to others].[48]

---

[44] The Leverhulme Trust International Network, 'Physiognomy: The Arts and Sciences of the Face, 1500–1850', which ran until 2010 and was based at Queen Mary University of London, has an excellent website with a comprehensive bibliography: <http://physiognomy.history.qmul.ac.uk/secondarysources.html.> [accessed 25 June 2015].
[45] David Le Breton, *Des visages: Essai d'anthropologie* (Paris: Métailié, 2003), pp. 28–9. Translations are my own.
[46] Ibid., p. 27.
[47] Ibid., p. 28.
[48] Ibid., p. 54.

In 1866, Jean-Baptiste Delestre took up the baton from the pre-eminent eighteenth-century proponent of physiognomy, Johannes Caspar Lavater, and declared his own goal thus:

> Introduire la physiognomonie dans le domaine des sciences; la débarrasser des vieux langes du passé; lui donner la valeur réelle d'un travail sérieux, au lieu d'en faire un motif de curiosité stérile, tel est notre but.

> [To introduce physiognomy into the scientific domain, to release it from its old swaddling clothes, to bestow upon it the real value of serious endeavours; such is our goal, rather than making of it a motif of sterile curiosity.][49]

Whereas, Delestre claimed, Lavater's study lacked evidence, his was a purely scientific pursuit, based only on evidence and admitting no conjecture. Delestre vigorously claimed to have moved away from what he saw as a long history of physiognomic study which had been propped up by 'deux béquilles vermoulues, l'astrologie et l'art devinatoire' [two dilapidated crutches: astrology and divination].[50] His work, on the other hand, he characterised as simply an act of reading, where the human body is the text, and the human character its meaning: 'La physiognomonie apprend à lire sur la forme corporelle le caractère moral, dont elle est l'enveloppe et l'agent.' [Physiognomy teaches how to read the body as an indication of moral character, of which it is both the vessel and the agent].[51] This clear-cut method and observational rigour allowed Delestre to fill hundreds of pages with the results of his unambiguous reading of the human body, arriving at such conclusions as: 'L'œil avancé, gros et injecté de sang, signale la force et la brutalité des passions abdominales.' [A large, protruding, bloodshot eye indicates the strength and brutality of abdominal passions.][52] The consequent merging of physiognomy and criminology is now infamous.[53] For nineteenth-century physiognomy, the human body was the outer expression of inner character and the face, densely packed with features, was the most expressive and readable part of all.

Martin Porter traces precisely the history of physiognomy that Delestre tried to distance himself from, and his survey provides a useful account

---

[49] J.-B. Delestre, *De la physiognomonie: Texte-Dessin-Gravure* (Paris: Vᵉ Jules Renouard, 1866), p. 20. Translations are my own.

[50] Ibid., p. 19.

[51] Ibid., p. 109.

[52] Ibid., p. 210.

[53] The most well-known practitioners being Francis Galton (1822–1911) and Hugh Diamond (1809–86). Indeed, the connection between this and twenty-first-century facial recognition has not gone unnoticed. See Gates pp. 19–24.

of how the idea of the human body as something to be read is a consistent foundation for this kind of pursuit, whether the framework for it be astrological, magical, theological or scientific.[54] Indeed, Porter's thesis is that the medico-scientific aspect of the study of human appearance has never been, and should therefore not be considered, distinct from its magical and hermetic elements: 'physiognomy is a subject that has to be understood in terms of the coexistence and the reciprocal relationship of the rational and the magical'.[55] Porter's is a history of physiognomy as visual reading and of its reception and development throughout the Renaissance and early modern period. He notes that the physiognomic history from which Delestre sought to distinguish his scientific rigour was understood by its own practitioners as 'a way of looking and listening that was theoretically underpinned by an entire physics'.[56] He goes on to explain that

> despite its much misunderstood reputation both then and now as a 'pseudo-science' or a 'natural magic', physiognomy, be it in its Neoplatonic or its Christian Aristotelian form, was in fact one of the most sophisticated of sign theories of the early modern period.[57]

The implication of Porter's work is crucial: physiognomy is a sign theory, and his observation that it perpetually straddles disciplinary boundaries suggests that the face is an emblem for a particular way of thinking about signs. Face, here, seems to stand for the possibility of access to an interior, and, therefore, for the possibility that there is an interior in the first place. Valentin Groebner's book on violence inflicted on the face in the late Middle Ages offers an interesting counterpart to Porter's recognition of a 'sophisticated' sign theory by suggesting that signs in the Middle Ages held a 'dubious status' and that this was the case in both legal, social and literary domains.[58] Indeed, Le Breton sounds a similar note of caution when discussing the semiotic reading of the face:

---

[54] Martin Porter, *Windows of the Soul: Physiognomy in European Culture, 1470–1780* (Oxford: Clarendon Press, 2005).

[55] Ibid., p. 32. In the course of his very useful overview of the long and complex history of physiognomy, Christopher Rivers makes a similar observation about the convergence, on the face, of scientific and 'supernatural' approaches to enquiry. See chapter 1 of *Face Value: Physiognomical Thought and the Legible Body in Marivaux, Lavater, Balzac, Gautier, and Zola* (Madison: University of Wisconsin Press, 1994), pp. 18–32.

[56] Porter, p. 25.

[57] Ibid.

[58] Valentin Groebner, *Defaced: The Visual Culture of Violence in the Late Middle Ages* (New York: Zone Books, 2004), p. 56.

Le visage est un mi-dire, un chuchotement de l'identité personnelle, non une affirmation caractérologique à l'abri de toute ambiguïté […] La lecture sémiologique opérée sur lui a quelque apparence d'un jeu d'hasard.

[The face is a half-saying, a whisper of individual identity, not an unambiguous affirmation of character […] The semiological reading that we perform on the face is not dissimilar to a game of chance.][59]

Groebner does, however, study how the face was targeted in the late Middle Ages as a particularly visible and eloquent site for inflicting 'private vengeance' in an especially public manner.[60] He notes that the reasoning behind this was condensed and codified in a fifteenth-century Venetian law: 'The face, the law stated, was the noblest part of the body and expressed a person's honor; when the face was damaged, the entire person was dishonored.'[61]

While many of the conclusions drawn by physiognomy appear laughable now – that a certain length of nose indicates a particular kind of character, for instance – the same facial thought is alive and well in more modern times. In the 1970s John Liggett wrote a history of the human face, focusing on its anthropological and sociological aspects and charting the different things that faces have meant to different human societies across time and in different parts of the world.[62] Fifteen years later, the sociologist Anthony Synnott wrote an article in which he outlined the historical persistence of what he called the 'beauty mystique', whereby there is understood to be a definite correlation between inner goodness and external beauty.[63] He traces this idea back to Plato 'and perhaps to Homer', and shows that its continued existence in the late twentieth century is demonstrated not only by phenomena such as beauty pageants but also through convincing experimental data.[64] The relative beauty of the human face, Synnott shows, has hugely important social ramifications and this is itself clearly an effect of the ubiquity of the idea that beauty and goodness coincide. After a whirlwind tour through several centuries of musings on beauty and the human face, Synnott concludes: 'The consensus within European cultural history has been impressive', and states that 'The significance of beauty and the pre-eminence of the face are therefore secure in Western culture, with roots deep and strong in both the Judaeo-Christian and

---

[59] Le Breton, p. 53.
[60] Groebner, p. 72.
[61] Ibid., p. 76.
[62] John Liggett, *The Human Face* (London: Constable, 1974).
[63] Anthony Synnott, 'Truth and Goodness, Mirrors and Masks – Part I: A Sociology of Beauty and the Face', *The British Journal of Sociology*, 40 (1989), 607–36.
[64] Ibid., pp. 608, 609.

Graeco-Roman traditions'.[65] The kind of thinking that understands the face as an external marker of inner qualities has, therefore, a long and remarkably consistent history. In 1908 Simmel eloquently restated the assertion that fuelled the practice of physiognomy: 'What I see, hear, feel of him [the other person] is only the bridge over which I reach his real self.'[66] He goes on to explain that the face is 'the symbol of all that which the individual has brought with him as the pre-condition of his life', and claims that this 'substratum of his life' becomes 'crystallized into the permanent features of his face'.[67]

The face as a mediator between inside and outside is also at issue in work that uses face as a way of thinking through other phenomena. Erving Goffman analysed face-to-face interactions and discussed how we use our faces in these moments 'whenever persons come into one another's immediate presence'.[68] He also used 'face' metonymically, as a term to describe certain kinds of small social interactions, famously describing it thus:

> The term *face* may be defined as the positive social value a person effectively claims for himself by the line others assume he has taken during a particular contact. Face is an image of self delineated in terms of approved social attributes.[69]

In Goffman's formulation, face is both social value and the physiological instrument with which that value is communicated. While he stresses that the two are distinct, they nonetheless both rely on a conception of the face as an external marker of internal or social features, albeit a sometimes-fallible marker:

> A person may be said to *have*, or *be in*, or *maintain* face when the line he effectively takes presents an image of him that is internally consistent, that is supported by judgments and evidence conveyed by other participants, and that is confirmed by evidence conveyed through impersonal agencies in the situation. At such times the person's face clearly is something that is not lodged in or on his body but rather something that is diffusely located in the flow of events in the encounter [...].[70]

---

[65] Synnott, pp. 625, 628.
[66] Simmel, p. 357.
[67] Ibid., p. 359.
[68] Erving Goffman, *Interaction Ritual: Essays in Face-to-Face Behaviour* (Chicago: Aldine Publishing Company, 1967), p. 2.
[69] Ibid., p. 5.
[70] Ibid., pp. 6–7.

In a 1987 sociolinguistic study of politeness, Penelope Brown and Stephen C. Levinson adapted the folk usage of the term face (face as a kind of social dignity), and used it to designate 'the public self-image that every member [of a society] wants to claim for himself'.[71] While not directly exploring the idea of the physical face as a window into the 'essence' of an interlocutor, they nonetheless use it as a way of describing a universally readable interactive experience:

> while the content of face will differ in different cultures (what the exact limits are to personal territories, and what the publicly relevant content of personality consists in), we are assuming that the mutual knowledge of members' public self-image or face, and the social necessity to orient oneself to it in interaction, are universal.[72]

Here, then, as with Goffman, face is taken to mean something that reflects the particular status of an individual, whether that be a permanent status or a temporary one; the importance of the face for Brown and Levinson is that it can be lost, and that it is therefore something that individuals fight to maintain during the course of a linguistic exchange. In this usage, 'face' stands for something like the integrity of a person's appearance. If 'to lose face' means humiliation, loss of dignity and loss of reputation, then face – 'to save face' – means the upholding of a coherence between a person's public presentation and an inner truth. The loss of face therefore signals a profoundly unwanted rupture between inner and outer, the disgrace of which comes from the realisation that a previously hidden undesirable quality has become visible on an outer surface that previously expressed desirable qualities. Brown and Levinson make use of this kind of 'face' as an idea that implicitly facilitates a link between the 'content of personality' and its expression in public. This sociolinguistic face is also revealing, inasmuch as it deals as much with temporary as it does with permanent features; not only the personality is known through the face, but, since face can be threatened and lost, it is also a representation of transient and figurative qualities. Qualities, that is, that may not always, and may not faithfully, be expressed on a person's visible surface. Furthermore, the possibility remains that face can not only express an inner truth but also project a false image. In both examples of formulations of the social face, while it is acknowledged that the face is not exclusively a physiological phenomenon, it is one that is nonetheless always tethered to the

---

[71] Penelope Brown and Stephen C. Levinson, *Politeness: Some Universals in Language Usage*, Studies in Interactional Sociolinguistics, 4 (Cambridge: Cambridge University Press, 1987; repr. 1996), p. 61.

[72] Ibid., pp. 61–2.

role of expressing qualities that lie elsewhere, whether in a person's character or in their social existence.

One very clear way in which the face and the problems it raises have re-emerged as a matter of public debate and anxiety is the development of facial recognition technology. Although its claims to objectivity and scientific rigour might make facial recognition technology appear not to be implicated in the face's role as a marker of anything other than identity, it is in fact precisely the dissonance between its apparent neutrality and its deeper implications that make this technology such a useful illustration of the powerful and productive contradictions of the face. In this section I will use facial recognition technology as a way of explaining and exploring the face as a phenomenon. In doing so, I also hope to make a strong case for the wider importance of the issues I explore as they are played out in medieval French literature.

There are many reasons to be wary of the mass roll-out of facial recognition technology that we have witnessed in recent years. This is not the forum in which to address political concerns, but there are other, perhaps both more subtle and more profound, implications of this phenomenon. This book is, in part, about the relationship between the face and what it is supposed to represent, and one of its key claims is that the face is a highly unstable sign that is, nonetheless, understood and used as if it were consistently readable. What I explore is not simply that this is a contradiction, but that this contradiction is fundamental to the functioning of the face. Le Breton's observation that physiognomy – sorting into types according to facial features – came about as a result of the sociocultural understanding that the face is the mark of the outer limit of a unique individual recalls the classic paradox at the heart of the idea of identity: 'the tension [...] between identity "as the *self-same*, in an individualizing, subjective sense, and 'identity' as *sameness with another*, in a classifying, objective sense"'.[73] On the surface, facial recognition technology has little do to with physiognomy: the former is aimed at using facial features to identify an individual *as* that individual, while the latter claims to read characteristics of any given individual, via their face. Two pertinent problems arise from this apparent distinction, however, and both are painstakingly worked through by Kelly Gates. The first problem is that facial recognition technology cannot, in fact, be neutral, because it is contingent upon so much human infrastructure, in the forms of political will, financial investment and the engineering of the systems themselves.[74] As Gates argues, there is no

---

[73] Jane Caplan, quoted in Gates, p. 16.
[74] This is a perhaps more widely investigated issue in the context of Artificially Intelligent Communications Technology (AICT). For instance, there is widespread debate surrounding the reproduction of various different social biases in commercial AI technology such as Amazon's Echo and Apple's Siri interfaces. The corpora used to train

single way of seeing the face and so the apparently neutral 'eye' of facial recognition technology is in fact just one of many socially, culturally and politically contingent ways of seeing the face.[75]

The second problem, arguably more sinister and certainly more pertinent for this book, is that the technology rests on the assumption that identity is a simple, stable and definitively knowable construct. Not only is this assumption false but, by having it as its central premise, facial recognition technology propagates it and reinforces it as truthful. Gates discusses both facial recognition technology, which seeks only to identify individuals, and Automated Facial Expression Analysis, which seeks to identify particular emotions from facial expressions, but she notes that the two are based on many of the same assumptions, a crucial one being that humans are stable and measurable. Indeed, Gates notes that the two really differ substantially only in the purposes for which they were designed, and not in the ways in which they perform those tasks, and that the automated technologies of facial recognition and facial *expression* recognition are, while often discussed as distinct operations, in fact deeply technologically intertwined, even to the extent that 'computer scientists have investigated individual differences in facial expressiveness as a means of augmenting the accuracy of facial identification algorithms'.[76] What all kinds of facial recognition technology have in common is their more or less acknowledged reliance on the concept of stable human identity. This has serious implications for our understanding of human subjectivity and for our understanding of the role that faces play in society, but also, as the figure of representation *par excellence*, in art and literature. By reproducing the idea that human subjectivity is stable, by reducing ourselves to 'standardized code', we do not account for much of human existence, for the 'dynamic states of the individual'.[77] For Gates, this is no less than 'a reconfiguration of identity', whereby we become, to all intents and purposes, simply collections of discrete data that can be read, classified and manipulated.

In a disturbing 2019 article, Olga Goriunova explores these implications for our broader concept of subjectivity, specifically focusing on how it impacts on

---

these systems are riddled with human bias. In another example, it is acknowledged that the automatic systems used to detect hate speech are at serious risk of reproducing racial bias because they are designed with limited capacity to take into account different linguistic contexts and dialects, according to which certain terms may be considered more or less offensive. In the case of language, the distinction between the purpose of a technology and the infrastructure and technologies that enable it is as striking and yet subtle as in the case of facial recognition technology. All of these technologies rely on what Gates calls a 'preprogrammed script' (Gates p. 153.)

[75] Gates, pp. 9–11, 20–4, 192–3.
[76] Gates, pp. 9, 21.
[77] Gates, pp. 174, 17.

our understanding of how face and subjectivity work together. She argues, like Gates, that much of our contemporary digital infrastructure seeks to stabilise what is in fact an inherently unstable phenomenon: the face. Biometrics, she tells us, attempt to 'affirm the face as the mark of a rich subjectivity that must be unique and true because it is linked to a particular, identifiable, and in this sense, truthful, biologically inspired identity recorded as data'.[78] What Goriunova draws our attention to is the peculiarly disingenuous, and at worst impossible, expectations that we have of the image of a face. Not only do we, in modern, digital societies, see the face as a stable, unique marker, we also see it as the marker of a stable, unique subjectivity. Goriunova does not limit her discussion to facial recognition technology, but sees this concern in a variety of applications where the face features prominently, such as passport photographs and, more perniciously, social media. What these technologies have provoked, she argues, is the false but ubiquitous expectation that the face is 'an index of the truth of fixed identity'.[79] By putting these examples of how faces are used (and abused) in the hyper-facial twenty-first century into the spotlight, Goriunova lays bare the mechanisms by which faces are made to appear as if they were a window to the soul. This might sound like a defence of the innocent face, but my intention here is to shine a spotlight on its contingency and on the serious risks associated with not doing so; my intention for the rest of this book is to explore how this same face works in a particular literary context, and to ask what it can tell us about that context.[80]

This book is an investigation of problems of interiority as performed in a selection of texts, and, taking my cue from these textual faces via modern face theories, a challenge to the ubiquity and universality of face as representation. My argument is that some pertinent examples of literature from the Middle Ages exhibit an illusion of the priority of interiority; that is to say, that they work within the paradigm by which the inside is prioritised over its outer expression, and by which that inner kernel is accessed via the visible exterior. What draws together all the texts I study in this book is their overt engagement with questions of representation, as well as the prominent role played by the visual and narrative motif of the face. Each text leans heavily on the face as an

---

[78] Olga Goriunova, 'Face Abstraction! Biometric Identities and Authentic Subjectivities in the Truth Practices of Data', *Subjectivity*, 12.1 (2019), 12–26.

[79] Ibid., p. 14.

[80] The very real risks of facial recognition technology as a necessarily political tool were highlighted when a series of large tech firms took the decision not to sell their own facial recognition software to US law enforcement in the wake of protests against systemic racism: Jonathan Vanian, 'Microsoft Follows IBM and Amazon in Barring Police from Using Its Facial-recognition Technology', *Fortune*, 11 June 2020 < https://fortune.com/2020/06/11/microsoft-ibm-amazon-facial-recognition-police/> [accessed 11 June 2020].

index of how it deals with signification and subjectivity. These texts are also, by and large, popular and well-known examples of French literature from the High Middle Ages. In unpacking in detail the contradictions, limitations and vast possibilities of the face as a motif, I hope to shed some new light both on this most ubiquitous of signifiers and on some of the most studied and analysed medieval texts.

As the final piece in this introductory puzzle, let us turn, at last, to the Middle Ages and give some sense of key questions being asked about the role of signs and the possibilities and limitations of representation. Stephen Perkinson's study of medieval portraiture provides a useful overview of the development of medieval attitudes towards image and representation. Instead, however, of offering literary evidence for particular social or cultural attitudes, I interrogate how the motif of the face carries with it the complexities of the problem, not of any given solution. Perkinson notes that Western medieval concepts of images and their capacity to represent moved from an early medieval suspicion of 'fundamentally insignificant' surface appearance to a later interest in the possibility that surface appearance can refer to a stable individual.[81] He explains that this 'new, thirteenth-century artistic attentiveness to surface appearances constituted a response to societal interests in the significance of the visible world, including the human bodies that inhabited it'.[82] Brigitte Miriam Bedos-Rezak reaches into the philosophical considerations surrounding medieval concepts of representation and explains that 'Concern about mediation, signification, and representation pervaded the eleventh century'.[83] She traces medieval concepts of sign theory, linking them to theological and political debate, especially on the part of prescholastic churchmen, and shows that their particular innovation was 'to recognize presence and representation as essential to the structure governing the generation of identity'.[84] In other words, these heated debates turned not only on if, and how, a person's or a thing's essence can be represented and communicated, but also on the interrelation of that representation and the ontological status of the essence. As I have discussed above, the most clearly discernible and defined result of these discussions was the re-emergence of physiognomy in the Middle Ages; in the terms of the debate over surface appearance, the human face – the physiological face – was considered an image. Willibald Sauerländer notes that the face was a site of discipline before the medieval re-emergence of physiognomic writings, and he reasonably

---

[81] Ibid., p. 23.
[82] Ibid., pp. 62–3.
[83] Brigitte Miriam Bedos-Rezak, 'Medieval Identity: A Sign and a Concept', *The American Historical Review*, 105 (2000), 1489–533 (p. 1492).
[84] Ibid., p. 1497.

suggests that this was because it has long been considered a surface upon which sin or virtue can be read.[85] Nonetheless, the face embodied the most critical concerns over surface, depth, interiority and identity that were so profoundly debated in the early to High Middle Ages.

Alice Colby's 1965 study engages with these debates through exploring the literary stylistics of portraiture in the work of Chrétien de Troyes and his contemporaries.[86] The study is based on a systematic breakdown of the meaning of individual physiological features as described in Chrétien's works and those of his contemporaries, as well as of the frequency of their occurrence and the language used in the portraits. It thus clearly outlines the system by which literary portraits of bodies and faces are employed in the service of communication, and the data that Colby collects and collates unequivocally show that this communicative function works in the chosen corpus: characters with virtue and status exhibit certain features, and those with dubious moral or social worth exhibit certain other features. This book, then, asks what happens when we approach medieval texts bearing the following in mind: that the face is at the heart of hotly contested contemporary ideas about both the possibility of representation and its ontological implications; that the face has since been consistently, but not unproblematically, understood as a mediator between inner essence and outer visibility; that a handful of twentieth-century theorists have developed ways of thinking about face and faciality from a non-representational, non-symbolic point of view. This book is not about moments when the inside and the outside don't match but, rather, it is about the kind of literary face that works outside or disrupts the whole foundation of this dichotomy and which, therefore, helps to throw into relief and subject to scrutiny not only the function but also the concept of the face, or of 'face'.

I begin this book with an exploration of interiority and surface in the context of duelling knights in Chrétien de Troyes's *Le Chevalier au lion*. Levinas is the theoretical engine for this chapter, and his formulation of the idea of a non-representational face – a face that tells us nothing about the subject behind it beyond its presence – plays out in the anonymous encounter between Gauvain and Yvain. Suspending their individual identities for the moment of the duel, the two knights' facing surfaces become their faces. Following Gauvain into two thirteenth-century incarnations – *Le Chevalier as deus espees* and *La Vengeance Raguidel* – the chapter then explores how surface appearance and individuality interact in a series of anonymous encounters involving Gauvain.

---

[85] Willibald Sauerländer, 'The Fate of the Face in Medieval Art', in *Set in Stone: The Face in Medieval Sculpture*, ed. by Charles T. Little (New Haven: Metropolitan Museum of Art and Yale University Press, 2006), pp. 2–17 (p. 4).

[86] Alice M. Colby, *The Portrait in Twelfth-Century French Literature: An Example of the Stylistic Originality of Chrétien de Troyes* (Geneva: Droz, 1965).

The argument of the chapter is that the texts in question display a complex faciality through a rhythm of loosening and tightening the connection between surface appearance and individuality. The illusion of interiority is thus manifest in this movement in and out of focus of different kinds of faces; those that represent an individual, and those that do not. Specifically, this dynamic brings to bear on the evolving status of the knight as an individual in the movement from the twelfth into the thirteenth century.

The second chapter moves away from narrative and examines the illusion of interiority from the point of view of the graphic mark of the face on the manuscript page. Taking as case studies three fourteenth-century manuscripts (one containing the *Vie et Miracles* of Saint Louis by Guillaume de Saint-Pathus, one containing a *Vie* of Saint Louis by Jean de Joinville and the third containing a series of post-Vulgate texts), I explore the implications of the reader's encounter with a series of small 'doodles' of faces attached, to greater or lesser degrees, to letter forms in the body of the text. Anonymous, at least to the modern reader, these faces draw attention to the signifying power of the alphabetic letter and confront the reader with the challenge of distinguishing the two marks. I first consider the tradition of the *Sainte Face* and the particular power of the graphic face on a manuscript page to work at the intersection of signification and direct communion. I then compare the face doodles to the medieval practice of inhabited letters, and argue that, while there are similarities, ultimately the doodles refuse the reassuring path of animation. Finally, I turn to Silvan Tomkins and then to Lacan, and argue that the faces are both pre-subjective (as opposed to the notion of bodily 'trace' implied in inhabited letters) and, ultimately, non-subjective.[87] Crucially, I argue that, situated as they are at the nexus of a heavily implied and yet alarmingly absent subjectivity, the doodles display the disturbing face of the illusion of interiority.

In the third chapter I return to narrative, but also retain the emphasis on the visual image. Having used Lacan in the previous chapter, here the argument centres instead on the non-representational, non-symbolic work of Gilles Deleuze and Félix Guattari in their collaborative project, *Capitalisme et schizophrénie*. However, I read their notion of *visagéité*, outlined in

---

[87] For the section on Tomkins and Lacan I have drawn on the following works: Eve Kosofsky Sedgwick and Adam Frank, eds, *Shame and Its Sisters: A Silvan Tomkins Reader* (Durham, NC: Duke University Press, 1995); Silvan Tomkins, 'The Phantasy Behind the Face' and 'What and Where Are the Primary Affects? Some Evidence for a Theory', in *Exploring Affect: The Selected Writings of Silvan S. Tomkins*, ed. by E. Virginia Demos (Cambridge: Cambridge University Press, 1995), pp. 263–78 and pp. 217–62, respectively; Jacques Lacan, *Écrits* (Paris: Seuil, 1966); Lacan, *Le Séminaire, livre xi: les quatre concepts fondamentaux de la psychanalyse*, ed. by Jacques-Alain Miller (Paris: Seuil, 1973).

Mille plateaux, as a call not to destroy representational paradigms but to recognise them and to trace their limits, the better to launch a 'fuite' from their restrictions. I read this idea in conjunction with Guillaume de Lorris's section of the thirteenth-century composite verse *Roman de la Rose*, and argue that a similar kind of faciality is at work here. The chapter explores how the garden wall at the start of Guillaume's text, which both marks out the outer edges of the garden of Deduit and facilitates Amant's access to it (and thus his becoming Amant), is a fine rendering of precisely the kind of coexistence between representational and non-representational that Deleuze and Guattari ask us to recognise. Clearly working within a structural dynamic of exterior representation of a more valued interior, as part of which it must regulate access, maintain the distinction between desirable and undesirable attributes and uphold the spatial difference, the wall nonetheless also exhibits an undercurrent of instability and permeability. This chapter argues, then, that the *Rose* demonstrates in spatial terms an illusion of prior interiority: as with the *visage* of Deleuze and Guattari, the wall is a signifying, codified, legible surface that incorporates its own continual and repetitious undoing.

Finally, I turn to the body and its incarnations in a selection of *fabliaux*. I look first at *Trubert*, and at an episode in which a vagina and anus are presented, and accepted, as the mouth and nostrils of a different person. I then explore *Le Chevalier qui fist parler les cons*, and think not in terms of visual correlation but of the mimicry of speech. I then examine two shorter texts in which genitals are afforded 'full' autonomy: in *Du vit et de la coille*, the two named protagonists walk and talk, independently of a 'fully human' subject. In *Do con, do vet et de la soriz*, the three protagonists are similarly independent, and sign up to work in the grape harvest. Each of these texts raises questions about the status of the face and of faciality. In the first instance, the question of inversion is raised: mixing the genitals and the face appears on the one hand to be a subversive act, bringing together two symbolic poles of humanity in their bodily incarnations. I argue, however, with Bloch that the *fabliaux* do not invert but, rather, that they reveal the absence of a solid structure to be inverted.[88] I go on to discuss how these texts question the stability of the body and come to a similar conclusion as I do in the other three chapters: the face in these texts is a motif not of stable signification, nor of its subversion, but of the interdependent coexistence of both. In the case of the *fabliaux* I look at in this final chapter, interiority is both maintained and debunked through bodily metamorphosis.

The face has been the topic of a large number of recent studies and projects, perhaps due in part to the creeping ubiquity of facial recognition technology

---

[88] An argument outlined in R. Howard Bloch, *The Scandal of the Fabliaux* (Chicago: University of Chicago Press, 1986).

and the serious questions this raises about privacy, identity, power and citizenship.[89] Although this book is about texts from the Middle Ages, it is also in large part about how the face has been used as an instrument of both power and liberation, and about how, after all, it is perhaps the most complex and enduring symbol of what it means to be human.

---

[89] In 2004–5 the Science Museum in London held an exhibition entitled 'Future Face'. This, and the accompanying book, set out to explore the role of faces in society, art and science. See Sandra Kemp, *Future Face: Image, Identity, Innovation* (London: Profile Books, 2004). For an example of artistic engagement with the issues raised by facial recognition technology, see Zach Blas's 2013–16 work 'Face Cages', in which he explores the biometric face as an instrument of repression: < https://zachblas.info/works/face-cages/> [accessed 5 January 2020]. Noa Steimatsky has written a book exploring not only how the face works within cinema but also how the cinema has changed faces: Noa Steimatsky, *The Face on Film* (Oxford: Oxford University Press, 2017). Finally, the most recent work of 'face scholarship' that has come to my attention is Jessica Helfand's beautifully produced book, *Face: A Visual Odyssey*, in which the author explores in detail many of the often startling ways in which the face has operated as part of our visual landscape (Cambridge, MA: MIT Press, 2019).

1

Levinasian Faces in Arthurian Verse

This chapter looks at the face as the marker of an assumed interiority in encounters between knights in twelfth- and thirteenth-century Arthurian romance, and uses the work of Emmanuel Levinas to offer an alternative, non-representational reading. Beginning with the judicial duel between Yvain and Gauvain towards the end of Chrétien de Troyes's *Le Chevalier au lion*, and then looking at scenes from two thirteenth-century texts, the chapter charts the problem of representation as dealt with in French Arthurian verse. It is through the figure of the masked knight that the problem is traced; caught somewhere in between his individual identity and social and institutional status, the literary knight finds himself at the convergence of powerful forces.[1]

The goal of this chapter is to analyse these texts while couching the figure of the knight in terms of representation: on the one hand, he is a figure that can be read, and whose surface appearance relates to an inferred inner essence. On the other hand, there are moments in the texts when the knight's appearance frustrates this kind of representational reading. This is not, however, a chapter about disguise and misrecognition as such. My concern is less with when appearance is misread and more with when it is unreadable. Often the two coincide in the narrative, and it can be difficult to distinguish them. But the aim of my analysis is to single out the unreadable face, specifically, to throw it into relief and to put it into dialogue with faces that are read – whether successfully or not. Equally, I do not go so far as to claim that all faces are fundamentally unreadable. Rather, the primary observation of this chapter is that the face is a motif that is *both* representational – and therefore readable – *and* non-representational. To describe this I also refer in the chapter to faces that are 'symbolic' and 'non-symbolic'; in all cases I am describing the difference between faces that refer to and/or imply an interiority, and those that don't. A crucial part of my argument is that these multiple faces are not oppositional; to be 'two-faced' in this sense is not to show one thing and mean another but

---

[1] By 'masked' I refer both to the knight's helmet and also to the more abstract mask assumed when the knight's identity is not hidden but unknown.

to operate both within and without a semiotic. To talk of the knight's face(s) in these terms is, then, to look differently at him, and to articulate him in language other than that of either contradiction or reconciliation (of personal and social forces).

It must be established from the outset that all the texts I look at in this chapter incorporate a clear and readable facial semiotic, within which faces are more or less successfully used as markers of stable identity and characteristics, momentary moods or feelings, as well as different kinds of status and, in some cases, externally originating events or indeed sometimes familial ties. As Alice Colby explained with specific reference to portraits in Chrétien's romances:

> The principal subject matter of a portrait is the person's physical appearance, which serves as a well-defined nucleus around which can be grouped other significant details such as: identity, lineage, age, wealth, education, character traits, talents, popularity, clothing, armor, weapons, and the animal which the person is riding.[2]

Broadly speaking, people with beautiful faces are, with few exceptions, good and noble, and those who depart from the standards of beauty (exhaustively enumerated by Colby) have less than desirable characteristics. Equally, the face is relied upon as an important marker of individual identity. In *Le Chevalier au lion*, Yvain's recovery from a period of physical and mental exile begins when, asleep and naked, he is discovered on the forest floor by a group of women from a nearby castle. The text explains that had he been dressed in his usual attire he would have been instantly recognisable. As it is, however, it is only a scar on his face that allows them to determine beyond doubt who he is:

> Au reconnoistre mout tarda;
> Et nepourquant bien l'esgarda,
> Quë en la fin li fu avis,
> D'une plaie qu'il ot el vis,
> C'une tel plaie el vis avoit
> Mesire Yvains; bien le savoit,
> Qu'ele l'avoit souvent veüe. (lines 2901–7)

---

[2] Colby, p. 4. It is worth noting that Colby's work, as is clear in this brief citation, uses 'physical appearance' to refer exclusively to what might more accurately be termed 'physiological appearance', that is to say, she does not consider clothing, for instance, part of the 'portrait'. While clothing does, of course, have a certain role to play, it is not the primary object of Colby's study, nor of the present one.

[She was slow to recognize him, but she kept looking until in the end she realized that a scar he had on his face was like a scar that my lord Yvain had on his; she was sure of this, for she had often noticed it.][3]

This is not to say that the face is always reliable but, rather, that it is expected to be so. Sometimes the face works apparently automatically, as the externally visible result of inner biological processes; in *Cligès*, for instance, when the hero feels shame, his blood rises and changes the appearance of his face:

> Li sans en la face li monte
> Si que tot vergunnier le voient.

[the blood rose to his face, and they could see his embarassment][4]

Again when he sees Fenice, they both involuntarily reveal their love:

> Et quant Fenice le salue,
> Li uns por l'autre color mue. (lines 5061–2)

[And when Fenice greeted him they both blushed][5]

Later, however, we are told of Cligès's very deliberate and *effective* attempt at preventing his true feelings from showing on his face:

> Cligés, qui ce molt atalente,
> S'en vait fesant chiere dolente,
> Qu'einz si dolente ne veï[s]tes.
> Molt pert estre par defors tristes,
> Mais ses cuers est molt liez dedenz
> Qui a sa joie est atendanz. (lines 5613–8)

---

[3] All references to this text are to Chrétien de Troyes, *Le Chevalier au lion; ou, Le Roman d'Yvain*, ed. by David F. Hult (Paris: Livre de Poche, 1994), unless otherwise stated, and appear in parentheses after quotations; Chrétien de Troyes, *Arthurian Romances*, translated and with an Introduction and Notes by William W. Kibler (London: Penguin, 1991), p. 331. All English translations of Chrétien's works are from this edition.
[4] Chrétien de Troyes, *Cligès*, ed. by Charles Méla and Olivier Collet (Paris: Livre de Poche, 1994), lines 4956–7. Subsequent references in parentheses are to this edition. *Arthurian Romances*, p. 184.
[5] *Arthurian Romances*, p. 185.

[Cligès, though pleased to hear this, went away looking more upset than anyone you have ever seen. He looked very sad outwardly, but his heart was happy within, in anticipation of his joy][6]

Similarly, in *Yvain*, while effecting a ruse that will allow for Yvain and Laudine to marry, Laudine's *damoisele*, Lunete, approaches the knight but deliberately hides her feelings in order that her deceit be maintained:

Mez ne montre mie en sa chiere
La joie qu'en son cuer avoit. (lines 1908–9)

[but [she] did not betray on her face the joy that her heart felt][7]

It is the expectation that the face does reveal an inner truth that allows for it to be manipulated like this. The high stakes involved in facial signification in romance are illustrated in *Yvain* by the figure of the herdsman, whom Calogrenant meets in the course of his failed quest. The herdsman is famously described using a series of animalistic images ('Oreilles moussues et grans | Aussi com a .i. oliffans', for instance, lines 297–8 [his ears were as hairy and as huge as an elephant's]), prompting the knight to aim his enquiry at the herdsman's very essence:

Toutes voies tant m'enhardi
Que je li dis: 'Va, cor me di
Se tu es boine chose ou non!' (lines 325–7)

[None the less I summoned enough nerve to say to him: 'Come now, tell me if you are a good creature or not?'][8]

To which the herdsman responds: '"Je sui uns hom"' ['I am a man'] (line 328)[9]. His interest for the present study lies in the fact that the man's (I take him at his word) very humanity is questioned on the basis of his appearance.[10]

---

[6] Ibid., p. 192.
[7] Ibid., p. 318.
[8] Ibid., pp. 298, 385.
[9] Ibid., p. 385.
[10] Helmut Bonheim suggests that the herdsman is absolutely human, but that his striking appearance is due to a specific medical condition: 'The Acromegalic in Chrétien's *Yvain*', *French Studies*, 44 (1990), 1–9. The same kind of animalistic description is taken up again in the 'loathly lady' episode in the *Conte du graal*. This time, the woman's status is not questioned: Chrétien de Troyes, *Le Conte du graal; ou, Le Roman de Perceval*, ed. by Charles Méla (Paris: Livre de Poche, 1990), lines 4540–73.

The face as a signifier of humanity is taken up again in an episode in the thirteenth-century *Roman d'Yder* in which the eponymous hero is temporarily disfigured as the result of a trick played by Kay. He becomes unrecognisable not only as himself, but also as a man (for which we read 'human being'). It is the lack of mouth and face that is made directly responsible for this particular problem:

> Li ainez fiz au rei de Irlaunde
> S'est del cors Yder merveillié,
> Car li mal est apparaillié
> Qu'il n'a menbre que de home pere.
> Miroez apele i son frere.
> 'Il n'a,' dit il, 'gaires de tens
> Que cist iert vifs, si com jo pens.'
> Kamelins dist: 'Quidez vos donc
> Que ço seit home? mielz semble un tronc:
> Il n'a boche ne il n'a vis'.

> [The King of Ireland's eldest son marvelled at Yder's body, which was so covered in disease that it no longer resembled that of a man. Miroez addresses his brother: 'Not much time has passed since this was alive, I think.' Kamelin says: 'Do you think this is a man? It looks more like a tree-trunk; it has neither a mouth nor a face.'][11]

In another thirteenth-century romance, the motif again combines the physiological and the emotional as the distraught hero's mouth stops working because of the grief he feels in his heart: 'Li cuers li clot la bouche' [His heart closes up his mouth].[12]

It is against this background of ubiquitous expectation that certain moments can be picked out when the face not only fails to represent correctly, but fails to engage altogether with this semiotic. The first of these moments that this chapter will explore is when Yvain and Gauvain fight one another anonymously towards the end of *Yvain*. Here the two friends are engaged by feuding sisters to fight on their behalves. In this instance I argue that the non-semiotic face emerges since the identity of each knight is removed from the equation. Instead of saying that the face is hidden underneath the knights' helmets, I explore what happens if we say that the helmet becomes

---

[11] *The Romance of Yder*, ed. by Alison Adams, Arthurian Studies, 8 (Cambridge: Brewer, 1983), lines 5860–9. Translations of this text are my own.

[12] Raoul de Houdenc, *Meraugis de Portlesguez*, ed. by Michelle Szkilnik, Champion Classiques: Moyen Âge, 12 (Paris: Champion, 2004), l. 3549. Translation is my own.

a non-representational face for the duration of the duel. The second and third sequences come from later texts that, as I will demonstrate, offer a slightly different context for the consideration of the face and its relation to the individual. In the anonymous thirteenth-century *Chevalier as deus espees*, Gauvain is once again the incognito opponent in a duel.[13] A knight named Bleheris – the father of the titular chevalier – is engaged in a duel with Briens de la Gastine. Wanting to ensure the death of his opponent, at the last minute Briens switches armour with Gauvain. Gauvain proceeds to kill Bleheris, who, with good reason, thought he was fighting an inferior opponent. Here the facial semiotic is crucial to the outcome: Briens plays on Bleheris's expectation that the man underneath Briens's armour is Briens. The non-representational face emerges in this scenario when we consider Gauvain himself: from his point of view the identity of his opponent is known but meaningless. Finally, the chapter ends with a series of further encounters with Gauvain, this time in the *Vengeance Raguidel*, also from the thirteenth century. In this text Gauvain meets two figures, independently, who explain to him precisely how they would kill Gauvain if they were to come across him. Since they both admit to not knowing what Gauvain looks like, his death at their hands remains hypothetical, and he is free to show his face. Importantly, neither prospective murderer sees their lack of knowledge of Gauvain's face as a hindrance (although they specifically acknowledge it), and each claims to have devised a way of achieving their goal without recourse to a facial semiotic.[14]

The literary-historical background to this analysis is what Colin Morris called the 'discovery' of the individual in the twelfth century, and the emergence of a courtly and chivalric literary culture that places the individual knight centre

[13] Beate Schmolke-Hasselmann notes that only very few motifs from Chrétien's *romans* were cited or imitated in post-Chrétien Arthurian verse, and that one of those few motifs is the hero's fight with Gauvain, a motif that has its origin specifically in *Yvain*: *The Evolution of Arthurian Romance: The Verse Tradition from Chrétien to Froissart*, trans. by Margaret and Roger Middleton, Cambridge Studies in Medieval Literature, 35 (Cambridge: Cambridge University Press, 1998), p. 202.

[14] Gauvain is a useful focus for my investigation for several reasons: he is a relatively consistent figure across two centuries of Arthurian verse, albeit consistent in what Peter Haidu calls his being 'the sometimes ridiculous other of all knightly adventure'; the hero's fight with Gauvain is one of few features that are directly imitated post-Chrétien (see note 13, above); his being always 'other', as well as his often incognito appearance, is offset by his unique compulsion to name himself and, finally, his reputation is curiously unaffected by what is, especially in later texts, less than ideal behaviour. He is, therefore, a figure whose entrance consistently invokes the question of identity in both individual narratives and generic intertextuality. See Peter Haidu, *The Subject Medieval/Modern: Text and Governance in the Middle Ages* (Stanford, CA: Stanford University Press, 2004), p. 100; Schmolke-Hasselmann, *The Evolution of Arthurian Romance* and Keith Busby, *Gauvain in Old French Literature*, Degré Second, 2 (Amsterdam: Rodopi, 1980).

stage.[15] Whether it is indeed possible to talk of the historical emergence of something approaching the modern notion of the individual in the twelfth century is not my concern. What is certain is that the romances of Chrétien de Troyes departed from vernacular texts that came before (principally the epic *chansons de geste*) as well as their contemporaries (the *romans antiques*) in examining the individual in terms that evoke what we would now consider a psychology, or an inner life, and that the incorporation of this scheme in later texts provides a useful point of dialogue across the genre.[16] Arthurian romance is, from Chrétien onwards, the unfurling of a personal journey for a knight, or several knights. Broadly speaking, the knight in question errs from the right way and gradually, through a process of self-reflection and knowledge gathering, redeems himself and fulfils his own chivalric potential. Donald Maddox thus describes Chrétien de Troyes's narratives as 'vehicles of exemplary ethical development'.[17] Maddox claims to show that this progressive accretion of knowledge occurs through the narrative motif of the 'specular encounter', whereby the individual consciousness of the protagonist is awakened and enlightened through a series of encounters with (not necessarily human) others who impart knowledge to the increasingly receptive knight. Writing shortly after Maddox, Saul Brody examines the question of Yvain's inner life in particular, and clarifies his position on the matter first of all by stating that 'Chrétien is surely closer to Prudentius than to Freud', and subsequently by summarising previous critics' discussion of the extent to which the author reveals Yvain's psyche.[18] Brody's point is that *Yvain* is a text in which the central character undergoes an inner struggle and this is made visible in the text through external symbolism. Taking his cue from Helen Laurie's 1991 article in which she claims that Chrétien's *Le Chevalier au lion* is closely modelled on Prudentius's *Psychomachia*, Brody shores up the twofold notion that the inner life of an Arthurian knight exists, and that it can indeed be known through external observations.[19] To a large extent, this is the case in Chrétien;

---

[15] Colin Morris, *The Discovery of the Individual 1050–1200* (London: SPCK, 1972).

[16] I follow Schmolke-Hasselmann in reading post-Chrétien romance not as imitation but as reaction, and as part of a dialogue among Chrétien, the expectations he sets up, the authors and readers of later texts, as well as modern readers of both. Schmolke-Hasselmann, pp. 21–3.

[17] Donald Maddox, *Fictions of Identity in Medieval France*, Cambridge Studies in Medieval Literature, 43 (Cambridge: Cambridge University Press, 2000), p. 97.

[18] Saul N. Brody, 'Reflections of Yvain's Inner Life', *Romance Philology*, 54 (2001), 277–98 (pp. 277, 278).

[19] See Helen C. R. Laurie, 'The Psychomachia of *Yvain*', *Nottingham French Studies*, 30 (1991), 13–23. It is worth noting with reference to Brody's comparison that Freudian psychoanalysis in fact also proceeds by decoding external symptoms and not, as Brody seems to be suggesting, by introspection.

as demonstrated above, his characters do often have an inner existence that is expressed externally via their faces. The symbolic aspect of Chrétien's texts extends beyond individual characters and motifs and has consistently been the topic of analyses of the Arthurian genre, and of Chrétien both within it and as its progenitor. The famous distinction made between *matiere, san* and the work of the author in the prologue to *Le Chevalier de la charrette* makes it clear that the text works through a structure whereby meaning and appearance are linked but not identical; one will lead the reader to the other.[20] There is, however, another side to this assessment whereby this kind of classical symbolism doesn't quite work, to put it crudely. *Yvain* in particular has been held up as a text in which the symbolic circuit doesn't always complete; as such, it is an especially useful commentary on both Chrétien and his later interlocutors. Paul Rockwell, the most recent editor of the *Chevalier as deus espees*, has argued that this thirteenth-century text takes some of the unresolved tension in Chrétien's *Le Conte du graal* and resolves it through the symbol of the father's sword.[21] Calling the sword 'an anchor of certainty in a world for which interpretation has become problematic', Rockwell makes the case for a resolution via symbolism in the later text.[22] I argue that the face, positioned as it is at the nexus of various symbolic functions (disguise, misrecognition, identification),[23] in fact casts serious doubt on symbolism as resolution to the extent that it, as I will demonstrate, indicates the existence of a non-symbolic plane in both Chrétien and these later texts. The two thirteenth-century texts under discussion here appear to conform to what Baumgartner called a lack of the 'pseudo-realism' that was found in Chrétien's works, and exhibit a 'suspension of the natural and moral laws governing the "real" world'.[24]

---

[20] Chrétien de Troyes, *Le Chevalier de la charrette; ou, Le Roman de Lancelot*, ed. by Charles Méla (Paris: Livre de Poche, 1992), lines 1–40.

[21] A series of articles make this point: the most in-depth treatment is to be found in Paul V. Rockwell, '*Appellation Contrôlée*: Motif Transfer and the Adaptation of Names in the *Chevalier as deus espees*', in '*Por Le Soie Amisté*': *Essays in Honor of Norris J. Lacy*, ed. by Keith Busby and Catherine M. Jones (Amsterdam: Rodopi, 2000), pp. 435–52. See also Rockwell's 'The Failed Embrace of the Father: Historical Continuity in *Le Chevalier as deus espees* and *Le roman d'Eneas*', *Romance Quarterly*, 51 (2004), 2–14 and 'The Promise of Laughter: Irony and Allegory in *Le conte dou graal* and *Li chevaliers as deus espees*', in *Courtly Arts and the Art of Courtliness*, ed. by Keith Busby and Christopher Kleinhenz (Cambridge: Brewer, 2006), pp. 573–85.

[22] Rockwell, '*Appellation Contrôlée*', p. 446.

[23] Here I refer to Lacy's useful distinction between 'identity' and 'identification' in 'On Armor and Identity: Chrétien and Beyond', in '*De Sens Rassis*': *Essays in Honor of Rupert T. Pickens*, ed. by Keith Busby, Bernard Guidot and Logan E. Whalen, Faux Titre, 259 (Amsterdam: Rodopi, 2005), pp. 365–74. It is, for Lacy, identification rather than identity which refers to how an individual appears to others.

[24] Emmanuèle Baumgartner, 'Chrétien's Medieval Influence: From the Grail Quest to

Couching this in slightly different terms, the present project characterises the relationship between Chrétien and his later interlocutors as one that exhibits a perennial acceptance of and engagement with not just the possibility of symbolic breakdown but also the non-symbolic. The 'suspension' of laws and the apparent narrative illogic exhibited in the two post-Chrétien romances in fact to some extent disguise a profound similarity in the three texts' treatment of the individual's 'inner life' and its legibility. These are all, therefore, texts which undercut the process of knowing oneself (in *Yvain*) and knowing others (in *Le Chevalier as deus espees* and *La Vengeance Raguidel*) with a distinct thread of intersubjective encounters that work outside the symbolic system of knowledge gathering.

Emmanuel Levinas and the Middle Ages

In his chapter on Levinas and *Piers Plowman*, James Paxson describes the Levinasian face as 'the icon of the vulnerability of basic need that must unite me with the other before spiritual discovery can take place'.[25] In these few words, Paxson touches upon what is both the interest and the difficulty of thinking about Levinasian faces in medieval literature. Paxson's formulation is a useful prop for expounding, as far as possible, three key aspects of Levinas's work of which I make most use in mine: the face, the Other and the encounter. It is, of course, impossible to separate these concepts fully, but it is useful nonetheless to outline some of the notions that they each introduce into our discussion. Indeed, this section will end by positing the importance of the circularity of Levinas's arguments – the fact that each of his notions, and each of their non-Levinasian counterparts, both supports and is supported by each other notion – and by claiming this as one of the key structural bases of my subsequent analysis. In 2003, Kathryn Banks published a comparative article examining the similarities and differences in how Chrétien's *Conte du graal* and Levinas's *Totalité et infini* deal with the question of enigma and its interpretation. In the course of the article, she enumerates the specific narrative, symbolic and ethical ways in which each text exhibits a kind of oscillation between inviting and foreclosing the interpretation of enigma. I see in her article a compelling recognition of the coexistence of ostensibly contradictory phenomena, although my concern is less with unpacking the

---

the Joy of the Court', in *A Companion to Chrétien de Troyes*, ed. by Norris J. Lacy and Joan Tasker Grimbert, Arthurian Studies, 63 (Cambridge: Brewer, 2005), pp. 214–27 (p. 221).

[25] James J. Paxson, 'The Personificational Face: *Piers Plowman* Rethought through Levinas and Bronowski', in *Levinas and Medieval Literature: The 'Difficult Reading' of English and Rabbinic Texts*, ed. by Ann W. Astell and J. A. Jackson (Pittsburgh: Duquesne University Press, 2009), pp. 137–56 (p. 141).

enigma of contradiction than with seeing in it different signifying modes operating simultaneously.[26]

One of the main tenets of Levinas's thought is that the face of a human being is not the expression of a particular character or personality, nor is it, in fact, the expression of anything other than its own existence, its own status as something that *is not me*. It is therefore tempting to consider the Levinasian face as absolutely distinct from the face as an image or an 'icon', to use Paxson's word. Stephen Perkinson traces the development of the artistic and theological ways in which the depiction of faces in the Middle Ages developed, and his findings corroborate the common-sense assumption that the depiction of faces is intimately connected with the depiction of a character or a meaning behind or beyond the face. Even, he says, when the link between the image of a face and the qualities it represents is ambiguous, slight or the object of scepticism, it is difficult to dissociate the two entirely.[27] For Perkinson, the resurgence of interest in physiognomy in the thirteenth century consolidated the parallelism between what a 'real' face does and what an image of a face does: they both have the capacity to reveal not only something *beyond* themselves but also something *other than* themselves. In other words, deeply embedded in medieval thought is the idea that a face is always an image, in the sense that it reflects, to a greater or lesser extent, something else. However, far from claiming a misreading of Levinas on the part of Paxson, what I in fact see in his formulation is an evocation of the necessary and inextricable relationship between a Levinasian face and a non-Levinasian, classically representational face.[28] Colin Davis points out that Levinasian notions are *both* real and conceptual: '[*visage*] both does and does not refer to real human faces'.[29] Levinas himself starkly evokes the polyvalence of his terms when he explains them in apparently paradoxical ways: 'la relation entre l'être ici-bas et l'être transcendant qui n'aboutit à aucune communauté de concept ni à aucune totalité – relation sans relation' [the relation between the being here below and the transcendent being that results in no community of concept or totality – a relation without relation].[30] In other words, Levinas does not

---

[26] Kathryn Banks, 'The Ethics of "Writing" Enigma: A Reading of Chrétien de Troyes' Conte du Graal and of Lévinas's Totalité et infini', *Comparative Literature*, 55 (2003), 95–111.

[27] Perkinson, pp. 44–5.

[28] Part of my point is that Levinas's ideas – and his writing of those ideas – admit both of these kinds of faces. It might, therefore, seem disingenuous to call one of them 'non-Levinasian', but I use this terminology in order to preserve the sense that Levinas focuses on one kind, even though he recognises both.

[29] Colin Davis, *Levinas: An Introduction* (Cambridge: Polity, 1996), p. 46.

[30] Emmanuel Levinas, *Totalité et infini: essai sur l'extériorité* (Paris: Livre de poche, 1990; repr. 2012), pp. 78–9; *Totality and Infinity: An Essay on Exteriority*, trans. by

claim that the face, the Other (of which more below) or the relation are solely and uniquely structuring concepts that cannot be acted out, but, rather, that they are at once this *and* real-life events and phenomena.[31] When Paxson explains that the Levinasian face is an 'icon', he evokes both the notion that it is representational and that it is a surface that elicits a response from a perceiving subject: Perkinson notes the medieval emergence of the idea that apprehension of a religious image can almost be as powerful either as seeing the 'thing itself' or as, in the case of the Host, consuming it.[32] Indeed, the Levinasian face is as much the site of experience of the obstinately human as it is of the divine; neither is knowable, but both can be experienced. As Michael Edward Moore explains: 'the face of the other is a terrain where we experience an ultimate encounter with human value and meaning (rather than in the self)'.[33] The face as icon is perhaps compatible with the Levinasian non-representational face, inasmuch as it expresses the very inaccessibility and unrepresentability of that which it – in full knowledge of its inadequacy – purports to represent, rather than representing positive characteristics. The Levinasian face is precisely 'cette expression même' [the expression itself].[34]

Levinas opens up a distinction between the non-representational and the representational face, and simultaneously evokes the close relation between the two. Jill Robbins points out that Levinas opposes the '*droiture* of the face-to-face' to the obfuscating effect of representational art that is necessarily viewed '*from an angle*', and, therefore, 'with an agenda'.[35] Levinas, according to Robbins, thus opposes 'face' and 'figure':

> Pour nous [Juifs], le monde de la Bible n'est pas un monde de figures, mais de visages. Ils sont entièrement là et en relation avec nous. Le visage de l'homme – c'est ce par quoi l'invisible en lui est visible et en commerce avec nous.
>
> [For us, the world of the Bible is a world not of figures, but of faces. They are entirely here and related to us. The face of man is the medium

---

Alphonso Lingis (The Hague: Martinus Nijhoff, 1979), p. 80. Subsequent translations are from this edition.

[31] Of course, when I say 'real' or 'real-life', I also refer to the 'real' within a literary narrative; the 'real' for the protagonists.

[32] Perkinson, pp. 80–1.

[33] Michael Edward Moore, 'Meditations on the Face in the Middle Ages (with Levinas and Picard)', *Literature & Theology*, 24 (2010), 19–37 (p. 21).

[34] Levinas, *Totalité et infini*, p. 43; *Totality and Infinity*, p. 51.

[35] Jill Robbins, *Altered Reading: Levinas and Literature* (Chicago: University of Chicago Press, 1999), p. 39 (original emphasis).

through which the invisible in him becomes visible and enters into commerce with us.]³⁶

Robbins quotes the English translation in her book and, in doing so, misses out some of the nuance of the original. It is worth pausing briefly to examine this quotation and its implications in light of what I have been discussing. Levinas does indeed oppose *figures* and *visages*, but also suggests a *rapprochement* between the two. The English translation of the last few words of this passage – 'the invisible in him *becomes* visible and *enters* into commerce with us' – introduces the sense of passing time that is not found in the original. In the French, the invisible *is* visible, and the relation of commerce is *already* entered into. My point is that Levinas's own words allow specifically for the simultaneity and coexistence of the visible and the invisible; the face is not perhaps as unequivocally revelatory as the opposition to 'figure' might lead us to believe, since it is not how the invisible becomes visible, but the site at which both are present. What the face reveals, in accordance with what we have been discussing above, is precisely that it cannot reveal anything other than its own presence. The opposition between the obfuscating *figure* and the clarifying *visage* is somewhat muddied if one of the terms manages to encompass the meanings of both. Indeed, the syntax tells us that it is a relation with the invisible, rather than the visible, that the face facilitates. Although somewhat outmoded, Georg Simmel's discussion of the face offers a perfect counterpoint to Levinas and helps to illustrate precisely the limitations that Levinas's concept of the face seeks to avoid. Explaining how he understands the apprehension of an other through their face, Simmel tells us: 'What I see, hear, feel of him is *only* the bridge over which I reach his real self.'³⁷ He goes on to tell us that the other's face is 'the symbol of all that which the individual has brought with him as the pre-condition of his life' and claims that *within* it 'is deposited what has been precipitated from past experience as the substratum of his life, which has become crystallized into the permanent features of his face'.³⁸ In other words, Simmel's face is both a bridge to and a symbol of something other than itself; crucially, it is *only* a means to another end. Levinas's face spans the means and the end, prioritising neither.

When Bernard Waldenfels explains that, for Levinas, '[t]he "face" is no *mere* metaphor transporting a figurative sense into a higher sphere', he

---

³⁶ Emmanuel Levinas, *Difficile liberté: essais sur le judaïsme* (Paris: Albin Michel, 1963), p. 170; Emmanuel Levinas, *Difficult Freedom: Essays on Judaism*, trans. by Seán Hand (Baltimore: Johns Hopkins University Press, 1990), p. 140.
³⁷ Simmel, p. 357 (my emphasis).
³⁸ Ibid., p. 359.

perceptively and subtly leaves space for the face to play the role of metaphor.[39] What I have tried to demonstrate is that the Levinasian face is indeed 'no mere metaphor', but nor is it absolutely distinct from this function. Levinas's unease with classical representation manifests itself in an alternative that opens up a gap between this and his alternative, rather than eliminating one in favour of the other; the face is the site of *both*. One particular manifestation of Levinas's concern with upholding the tension between different kinds of face is his admission of the physical face into his thought and writing. Indeed, the physical face is not only the model for the conceptual face, but it provides the physical support for the face-to-face encounter. While Levinas's conceptual face is not identical to the embodied face (a term I will use from here on in to refer to the physical face – the eyes–nose–mouth, etc.), they can, and do, coincide. In his relatively early work, *Le Temps et l'autre*, Levinas explains that an erotic encounter is one whereby a relation occurs without any kind of assimilation or *retour à soi*: '[L'éros] n'est ni une lutte, ni une fusion, ni une connaissance. Il faut reconnaître sa place exceptionnelle parmi les relations.' [It is neither a struggle, nor a fusion, nor a knowledge. One must recognise its exceptional place among relationships.][40] While in the context of a somewhat dubious claim that 'la contrariété qui permet au terme de demeurer absolument autre, c'est le *féminin*' [the contrareity that permits its terms to remain absolutely other is the *feminine*], Levinas nonetheless clearly evokes the possibility of a relation that retains alterity, and this concept is calqued on the physical:

> La caresse est un mode d'être du sujet, où le sujet dans le contact d'un autre va au-delà de ce contact. Le contact en tant que sensation fait partie du monde de la lumière. Mais ce qui est caressé n'est pas touché à proprement parler.
>
> [The caress is a mode of the subject's being, where the subject who is in contact with another goes beyond this contact. Contact as sensation is part of the world of light. But what is caressed is not touched, properly speaking.][41]

While the face is '[l]a manière dont se présente l'Autre' [the way in which the other presents himself], it is also what happens when an other's *real* face, specifically, is perceived.[42]

---

[39] Bernhard Waldenfels, 'Levinas and the Face of the Other', in *The Cambridge Companion to Levinas*, ed. by Simon Critchley and Robert Bernasconi (Cambridge: Cambridge University Press, 2002), pp. 63–81 (p. 65, my emphasis).
[40] Emmanuel Levinas, *Le Temps et l'autre* (Paris: Presses Universitaires de France, 1983; repr. 2012), p. 81;*Time and the Other*, trans. by Richard A. Cohen (Pittsburgh: Duquesne University Press, 1987), p. 88.
[41] *Le Temps et l'autre*, pp. 77, 82; *Time and the Other*, pp. 85, 89 (original emphasis).
[42] Levinas, *Totalité et infini*, p. 43; *Totality and Infinity*, p. 50.

A further curiosity in Paxson's formulation is the idea that recognition of their vulnerability unites me with the other. The genesis of Levinas's concept of the Other is his deep suspicion of the basic framework of Western thought that serves always, ultimately, to unite the Same and the Other. The Levinasian Other is precisely that which is *always* inassimilable, *always* at a distance, *always* unknowable. What we perceive of this Other, and that which tells us that it is Other, is its face. In other words, recognition of the vulnerability of the Other is, on this level, absolutely not a way of uniting me with the Other, nor even a way of diminishing the eternal gap between me and the Other. The Other is that which defies any and all possibilities of being assimilated with the self, either though similarity or, indeed, through opposition, since this itself implies a relation of comparable terms. What we must remember, however, is that Levinas does not deny the existence of the kind of other that *can* be assimilated into the subject, that *can* be known and appropriated, and with which I *can* be united. This is the other that sustains the self without troubling it and without disturbing it. The other is assimilable, the Other is not, to put it (necessarily) crudely. Levinas's whole theoretical problem is how to conceive of a relation with an Other that maintains its Otherness; this kind of relation is not identical to every interaction between human beings, but it can be played out in this arena. In which case, there is always something of both the other and the Other in a physical encounter. The Other can be mapped onto an interlocutor, but never eclipses it, and cannot exist independently. Equally, the other can be killed, but the Other cannot. In which case, the faces of the Other and of the other can exist in the same moment, in the same place, and yet be far from identical.

In the later work, *Totalité et infini*, Levinas meditates upon and develops the ideas outlined in *Le Temps et l'autre*. He continues to think along the lines of what he characterises as an opposition between 'une tyrannie de l'universel et de l'impersonnel' and 'l'homme comme singularité irréductible' [a tyrannie of the universal and of the impersonal; man affirms himself as an irreducible singularity].[43] The Other, inassimilable to the Same, is and remains unique and thus absolutely personal. Indeed, the Other is 'pas seulement un alter ego; il est ce que moi, je ne suis pas' [not only an alter ego: the Other is what I myself am not].[44] What is crucial is that this Other is not considered as such because of any physical or psychological characteristic; it is the fact that they are in front of me and not me. In the moment of perceiving the Other, therefore, their identity disappears. Or, rather, it plays no part in the encounter that Levinas constructs as an alternative to the universalising effect of knowledge.

---

[43] Levinas, *Totalité et infini*, p. 271; *Totality and Infinity*, p. 242.
[44] Levinas, *Le Temps et l'autre*, p. 75; *Time and the Other*, p. 83.

While much of what the encounter entails has been discussed above, a certain number of points must be mentioned independently in order to complete this survey of the key theoretical aspects of this chapter and to make it clear later on why the literary episodes I examine are of particular relevance to this exploration of faciality. For Levinas, the face-to-face encounter is the moment at which the Other's face is apprehended; recall that the Other's face is precisely its presentation as *not me*. What is of crucial importance to our investigation is, once again, the relationship between the face-to-face as expounded by Levinas and the physical face-to-face encounter upon which it is based. Colin Davis once again is helpful in drawing out the key implications of Levinas's sometimes impenetrable prose:

> the encounter with the Other is an experience which is not an experience, establishing a relationship which is not a relationship; and anyway this *encounter* is not an event which can be located in time or the history of the subject.[45]

The Levinasian encounter is atemporal and ahistorical, but, as Davis goes on to explain, 'the encounter is [...] not an empirical event (though it may be enacted in any number of empirical events)'.[46] Levinas has been criticised for his persistent use of language and metaphors that evoke ideas that he explicitly denounces as part of the universalising, totalising regime to which he is trying to provide an alternative.[47] The undeniable effect of this is, however, to draw attention to precisely the kind of dual aspect of the face-to-face encounter that Davis so clearly expresses. Levinas tells us that, in the encounter, the Other's face is 'Ni vu, ni touché' [neither seen, nor touched], instead explaining the precise nature of the encounter in terms of linguistic discourse, which is better able to uphold distance without the appropriation of one term by another: 'Mieux que la compréhension, le *discours* met en relation avec ce qui demeure essentiellement transcendant.' [Better than comprehension, *discourse* relates with what remains essentially transcendent.][48] The face-to-face encounter, however, must happen on a certain level through the visual apprehension of the other, which must, in turn, happen at the same time as the linguistic, non-appropriative, relation with the Other. We now approach

---

[45] Davis, p. 35 (original emphasis).

[46] Ibid., p. 48.

[47] The most famous example of this is of course Derrida's 'Violence et métaphysique: Essai sur la pensée d'Emmanuel Levinas' (*Revue de Métaphysique et de Morale*, 69 (1964), 322–54), in implicit response to which Levinas radically re-examined his vocabulary in his later work, *Autrement qu'être ou au-delà de l'essence* (1974).

[48] Levinas, *Totalité et infini*, pp. 211, 212; *Totality and Infinity*, p. 195 (original emphasis).

the particular circularity of Levinas's thought that is such a compelling aspect of his theories. In each of the three key terms I have noted – the face, the Other, the encounter – there is a distinct relation between the 'real', empirical, embodied term and the conceptual overlay that Levinas adds to each. By no means identical, the two layers nonetheless coincide. The Other must also be the other; the non-representational, non-appropriative face must also be the embodied face by which an other is known – is *recognised* – as someone or something beyond simply the brute fact of being something or someone. It is the conceptual gap opened up between two kinds of face – symbolic and non-symbolic – that, I argue, structures a series of encounters in the three texts I examine here, and which thus reveals a particular engagement with the relation between interiority and external appearance.

Le Chevalier au lion

Yvain is an idiosyncratic text within a genre of which it is also considered paradigmatic. It plays with conventional symbolism to the extent that it evokes a highly symbolic order at the same time as it frustrates its resolution, and it is in this context of the text's fundamental interrogation of the imperfect functioning of signification that I examine the role of the face as it appears to exemplify the possibility of both upholding and subverting a text's symbolic backbone. Jean Frappier hints at this when he claims the lion as an illustration of Chrétien's mixture of reason and 'les arabesques de l'imagination, des *caprices* de l'auteur en marge de l'action principale' [the arabesques of the imagination, the author's whims outside of the main action], and explains that the lion's tail being cut off is, for the otherwise noble beast, a 'triste nécessité que le poète s'amuse à souligner' [a sad necessity that the poet highlights for his amusement].[49] A few years later, Peter Haidu develops this notion in *Lion-queue-coupée: l'écart symbolique chez Chrétien de Troyes*. He suggests that Chrétien's *Erec et Enide* is a fully functioning, complete, symbolic text, but that *Yvain* enacts a fractured and incomplete symbolic. Taking the example of the feudal gesture of homage as it appears in the text, Haidu remarks that there is: 'un décalage fondamental entre l'acception normale du symbole et l'utilisation qui en est faite' [a fundamental gap between the usual meaning of the symbol and how it is being used].[50] He goes on to discuss the lion as, once again, the

---

[49] Jean Frappier, *Étude sur 'Yvain ou le chevalier au lion' de Chrétien de Troyes* (Paris: Société d'Édition d'Enseignement Supérieur, 1969), pp. 19–20. Translations are my own.

[50] Peter Haidu, *Lion-queue-coupée: l'écart symbolique chez Chrétien de Troyes*, Histoires des idées et critique littéraire, 123 (Geneva: Droz, 1972), p. 43. Translations are my own.

ultimate symbol of this discrepancy: 'la difficulté vient de l'effort de réduire à l'univocité la polyvalence du symbole' [the difficulty comes from the effort of reducing the polyvalence of this symbol to a single meaning].[51] Finally, Joan Grimbert adds to this discussion by examining precisely this kind of ambiguity and symbolic fracture and seeing in it an incitement to reflection. She explains that Chrétien very deliberately explores the gap between signified and signifier in order to interrogate the effectiveness of language, ritual and text itself. Grimbert sees in the text Chrétien's own awareness that

> Les gestes comme les paroles peuvent venir d'une courtoisie rituelle dont la pratique habile n'implique pas nécessairement la congruence de signifiant et de signifié.

> [As with words, gestures may arise from a ritual courtliness the practice of which does not necessarily indicate the congruence of signifier and signified][52]

The duel sequence can be read as a narrative climax, precipitating eventual reconciliation: Yvain reaches the end of his journey of self-improvement as he takes up arms on the side of good, this time choosing to leave his lion behind, where in previous fights he has been requested to do so (lines 5918–20), indicating that the knight has now reached a stage of self-sufficiency.[53] Gauvain plays his role as the 'cardboard figure', against which the hero proves himself.[54] No lasting damage is done to either knight, nor to their friendship. Arthur demonstrates his cunning, authority and the correct functioning of his moral compass by causing the elder sister to admit that she is indeed in the wrong. Once recovered from the fight, Yvain returns to the fountain in order to provoke Laudine into reconciliation.[55] Finally, Yvain's two identities – as Yvain and as 'le chevalier au leon' – are reconciled as Laudine, not realising that they are one and the same person (or, therefore, that she is in fact his 'dame'),

---

[51] Ibid., p. 52.

[52] Joan Tasker Grimbert, *'Yvain' dans le miroir: une poétique de la réflexion dans le 'Chevalier au lion' de Chrétien de Troyes* (Amsterdam: Benjamins, 1988), p. 100. Translations are my own.

[53] The lion returns once the duel is over, and accompanies Yvain to Laudine's castle, but seems to disappear from view once Laudine and Yvain are finally reconciled.

[54] Haidu, *The Subject Medieval/Modern*, p. 100.

[55] Jerry Root identifies the fountain as one of two foundational obstacles in the text, upon which the narrative's dynamic of promise/failure turns. The other is the herdsman, who both helps and hinders. See 'Marvelous Crystals, Perilous Mirrors: *Le Roman de la Rose* and the Discontinuity of the Romance Subject', *The Romanic Review*, 102 (2011), 65–89 (p. 70).

agrees that she will undertake to reunite the knight and his lady.[56] It is the more recent critical view that tension, ambiguity, paradox and contradiction are not to be resolved, whether within the narrative or beyond.[57]

This duel in *Yvain* is judicial: the knights fighting to resolve a dispute with which they have no personal involvement. The elder sister tries to deny the younger's rightful claim to half their inheritance, prompting the younger to rush to Arthur's court in the hope of finding justice. Beating her sister there, the eldert enlists Gauvain as her champion and accepts his one condition of secrecy. When Gauvain's niece and nephews come and tell him about the knight (Yvain) who recently saved them from servitude to the giant, Harpin, they pass on Yvain's cryptic message: that Gauvain knows this knight well ('le connissoit'), despite the fact that he doesn't know ('ne savoit') who he is (lines 4751–2). Recalling Lacy's distinction between a knight's identity and his ability to be identified, Yvain's message articulates the possibility of a dissociation between two modes of being that nonetheless coincide in the same single character: Yvain is at once known and unknown.[58]

The elder sister tells the younger that she is not planning to concede, but that if the younger wants to find herself a knight to fight for her, she ought to do it right away. Arthur declares this to be improper; the younger must have much longer. Having heard about the 'chevalier au lion', the younger then sets out to find him within what is now a forty-day window of opportunity. She falls ill on her journey, and so the quest to find Yvain is completed for

[56] Jacques Le Goff and Pierre Vidal-Naquet's structuralist analysis of *Yvain* is an important critical reading of ultimate coherence and reconciliation in the text: 'Lévi-Strauss en Brocéliande: Esquisse pour une analyse d'un roman courtois', in *Textes de et sur Claude Lévi-Strauss*, ed. by Raymond Bellour and Catherine Clément (Paris: Gallimard, 1979), pp. 265–319). Tony Hunt uses the notion of dialectic to make a persuasive case for the genuine coexistence of love and hatred between Yvain and Gauvain during their duel. This kind of opposition is, however, ultimately a method of reaching a 'higher, transcendent truth' and is evidence for the existence of 'a value system which pervades the entire work': 'The Dialectic of "Yvain"', *MLR*, 72 (1977), 285–99 (p. 286). For the classic reading of courtly poetry (in this case of the Troubadours in particular) as an expression and tool of social ideology, including the resolution of class tension, see Erich Köhler, 'Observations historiques et sociologiques sur la poésie des Troudabours', *Cahiers de civilisation médiévale*, 6 (1964), 27–51.

[57] For one, Matilda Tomaryn Bruckner shows that the lion's non-participation in the Gauvain duel is in fact indicative not of Yvain's moral and chivalric rectitude but of a more, rather than less, ambiguous scene, in which right and wrong are not easily determined: 'The Lady and the Dragon in Chrétien's Chevalier au lion', in *From Beasts to Souls: Gender and Embodiment in Medieval Europe*, ed. by E. Jane Burns and Peggy McCracken (Notre Dame: University of Notre Dame Press, 2013), pp. 65–86 (p. 74). See also Barbara Newman, *Medieval Crossover: Reading the Secular against the Sacred* (Notre Dame: University of Notre Dame Press, 2013).

[58] See Lacy, 'On Armor and Identity: Chrétien and Beyond'.

the most part by a different maiden. Nonetheless, eventually he is found and enlisted and the two friends, Yvain and Gauvain, find themselves at Arthur's court, neither being aware of the other's identity. Arthur has already declared that he believes the younger sister to be in the right, and the two heroes have already been set up as virtual equals. The duel is clearly a point at which the very personal – the sisters' family feud – and the absolutely impersonal – the friends fighting each other – collide. To talk in Levinasian terms, we can describe the duel as a face-to-face encounter inasmuch as it is a suspension of the personal, a suspension of the mode by which the face of the other in front of me represents their identity, their history and my relation to them. The knights act as anonymous proxies for an encounter (between the sisters) that is entirely based on unique identities and their unique relation to one another. The knights thus suspend their own individuality and their own relation for the duration of their encounter; their faces in combat are not covered by their helmets; rather, their impersonal, Levinasian faces emerge *as* their helmets.

The central fight scene takes place between line 6104, when Yvain and Gauvain first attack each other, and line 6155, just before the watching crowd discusses the ferocity of the fight. Within this 52-line segment, there are six occasions on which either the face or the helmet is mentioned specifically. This is not unusual in Chrétien, nor is it in his thirteenth-century inheritors. It is, however, significant in the context of the 'fractured symbolic' of the twelfth-century literary knight and his multiple faces. While the face is logically located underneath the helmet, this spatial certainty unravels through the confused textual treatment of the helmet's physical integrity and its revelation/concealment of the face it purports only to cover. The first damage done in the duel is to the knights' armour, specifically to their helmets and their shields:

> S'il s'entr'afolent et mehaignent,
> Les espees riens n'i gaaignent
> Ne li hiame ne li escu,
> Qui sont enbuignié et fendu. (lines 6113–16)

[But now the two friends were striking and injuring one another. Their swords gained no value, nor did their helmets or shields, which were dented and broken][59]

The language evokes cutting and piercing, suggesting that different parts of the knights' armour, including the helmet, have been breached as a protective surface. Since of the sword, shield and helmet the latter is the only one that is

---

[59] *Arthurian Romances*, p. 371.

fixed to the body, we might surmise that, at this stage the face is partly exposed – if not to the eye, at least to the lance or the sword. Shortly afterwards, more damage is evoked by clearly incising blows, but this time the target is a little more ambiguous:

> Car il s'en donnent molt grans flas
> Des trenchans, non mie des plas;
> Et des poins redonnent tes cops
> Sor les naseax et sor les cols
> Et sor les frons et sor les joes,
> Que toutes sont perses et bloes
> La ou li sans chaoit desous. (lines 6119–25)

> [and they dealt such mighty swipes with the sharp edge, and not the flat part, and struck such blows with the pommels on noseguards, necks, foreheads, and cheeks, that they were all black and blue where the blood gathered beneath the skin][60]

The text emphasises that the sword is used here for slicing and cutting ('Des trenchans, non mie des plas'). This formulation is found already when Yvain fights Harpin; in the earlier scene the text tells us that Yvain's slicing sword cuts off a section of the giant's cheek (lines 4207–9). Slicing is associated with flesh, but here, in the duel between two fully armoured knights, the object of the sword's cutting edge is less obviously bodily; the difference between body and armour is a little less distinct. The syntax of the segment leaves open the possibility that what appears to be bruising ('toutes sont perses et bloes') is the result of both the cutting edge and the 'poins'. The 'desous' where the blood 'chaoit' is presumably under the skin, made more visible by the bruising. But again, the distinction between layers is not quite certain: if we take into account the piercing effect of the sharp sword, there is the possibility that the 'desous' is in fact underneath the helmet, where blood now flows on top of the face as the result of flesh wounds. Furthermore, the lexicon of the specific points of contact – 'naseax', 'cols', 'frons' and 'joes' – is associated with both the face and the helmet. The face and helmet don't seem to maintain a fully discrete relation with one another; it is not quite clear, therefore, that the inside/outside dichotomy upon which relies the notion of an inner identity (that can be covered) is fully functional here. The knights are not simply covering their identity, but are, in the moment of combat, identity free.

---

[60] Ibid.

A few lines later, attacks to the helmets are evoked again, and are again used to explain just how brutal the encounter is:

> Car des poins si grans cops se donnent
> Sor les hiames que tuit s'estonnent. (lines 6135–6)

[for they pummelled their helmets so hard that both knights were stunned][61]

In this second set of blows there is no mention of piercing or cutting; there is a direct link between the helmets being hit and the knights suffering. Thus the transference of violence changes its mode: the physiological face is no longer part of the equation, and the helmet itself serves as the direct conduit. What we might read in this, therefore, is that in the second segment the helmet takes on the conceptual role of the face, inasmuch as it is now the primary site of the encounter and the direct object of violence. The evolution of the helmet's protective role leads to a somewhat disturbing paradoxical realisation: if the helmet allows violence not through being breached or punctured but by remaining intact, then the face is always exposed, whether covered or not. To take this a step further, it is possible to derive from this the evolution of what we consider a knight's face: beginning as eyes–nose–mouth, it becomes, in battle, simply his facing surface.

This complex inside/outside, beneath/on top of dynamic is crammed into a very small number of lines, and it is worth requoting some of the above passages in order to get a sense of the density of this spatial play, and to give the context for another intriguing couplet in the knightly face-to-face encounter:

> Car il s'en donnent molt grans flas
> Des trenchans, non mie des plas;
> Et des poins redonnent tes cops
> Sor les naseax et sor les cols
> Et sor les frons et sor les joes,
> Que toutes sont perses et bloes
> La ou li sans chaoit desous.
> Et les haubers ont si derous
> Et les escus si depechiés,
> N'i a celui ne soit blechiés.
> Et tant se painent et travaillent,
> A poi qu'alaines ne lor faillent;

---

[61] Ibid.

Si se combatent une chaude
Que jagonce në esmeraude
N'ont sor les hiames atachie
Ne soit molue et esquachie,
Car des poins si grans cops se donnent
Sor les hiames que tuit s'estonnent
Et par poi qu'il ne s'eschervelent.
Li oeil des chiés lor estinchelent,
Qu'il ont les poins quarrés et gros
Et fors les ners et dur les os,
Si se donnent males grongnies
A ce qu'il tiennent enpoignies
Lors espees qui grant aïe
Lor font quant il fierent a hie. (lines 6119–44, my emphasis)

[they dealt such mighty swipes with the sharp edge, and not the flat part, and struck such blows with the pommels on noseguards, necks, foreheads, and cheeks, that they were all black and blue where the blood gathered beneath the skin. And their hauberks were so torn and their shields so battered that neither knight escaped unharmed; they struggled so hard that both were nearly out of breath. The combat was so heated that all the jacinths and emeralds that decorated their helmets were knocked loose and crushed, for they pummelled their helmets so hard that both knights were stunned and had their brains nearly beaten out. Their eyes gleamed as, with square and mighty fists, strong nerves, and hard bones, they dealt wicked blows to the face as long as they were able to grip their swords, which were most useful in their vicious hammering.][62]

The two italicised lines above (lines 6137–8) offer a further example of the play of inside and outside that is a distinct and persistent undercurrent of the whole battle scene. The text tells us that the blows to the helmets were so fierce that not only were the combatants stunned (as discussed above), but they almost brained each other. The use of this particular verb in the sequence in *Yvain* is marked by its evocation of a violence that threatens not only to reach or reveal what ought to be hidden (the brain), but to bring it out of its proper place and disrupt the difference between the inside and the outside.[63] Once examined, this single line serves to both evoke and destabilise the spatial dynamic with which this entire passage plays so subtly. The inside of the skull having almost

[62] *Arthurian Romances*, pp. 371–2.
[63] We note also that this sense of the improper continues into the modern French adjective, 'écervelé(e)', meaning 'scatterbrained'.

become the improper outside, another inside–out ambiguity is evoked, this time through the image of the knights' eyes: 'Li oeil des chiés lor estinchelent' (line 6138). The logical interpretation is that 'estinchelent' refers to the effect of the stunning blows received to the head, echoing and reinforcing the 'tuit s'estonnent' of line 6136. Hult's modern French translation (as well as Kibler and Carroll's English version) instead suggests that, rather than describing the internal idea of 'seeing stars', the passage is to be read as a description of the eyes' external appearance: 'on ne voit que les yeux qui étincellent' (p. 429 in Hult's edition). The modern reader comes up against two possible interpretations, each at the opposite end of the inside/outside dichotomy: stars are seen (by each knight himself, but also by the narrator and reader) *inside* the knights' heads, or the eyes are perceptible (to each other) *outside* their helmets. What is important for us as modern critics is the coexistence of multiple modes of perceiving a knight: a figure with a discernible inner world, but also a figure of palpable exteriority. Shortly after this couplet, the text recalls the same kind of inside/outside coincidence we noted in lines 6135–6 and again logically invokes either the convergence of the face and the helmet or the acquisition of one's features by the other. We learn that the knights 'se donnent males grongnies' (line 6141); Godefroy defines 'gronger' as 'frapper du poing sur le visage', hinting again either that the helmets are so damaged as to render the face perfectly exposed or that the face is exposed *despite* the protection of the helmet.[64] Throughout the duel, then, the face and the helmet enact an unstable distinction: in this, I argue, we can read a kind of facial 'doubling', whereby the physiological face exists concurrently with a face – in this case the helmet – that is produced in the encounter, and which is related but not identical to the eyes–nose–mouth.

If the helmet invites facial reading because it is so intimately connected to the face as both a protective covering and a kind of facial double, a knight's shield performs many of the same functions without this explicit link to any part of his body. The Arthurian shield is a surface upon which identity is written, rather than a barrier behind which it is located. Here I consider the shield as a counterpoint to the more explicitly facial helmet. If, as I contend, multiple faces circulate in a duel, is the shield part of this network? And, if so, what might this say about how this particular kind of encounter *produces* faces?

In Chrétien's romances, the knight's shield plays a much more varied role than any other part of his armour, setting it apart both physically and functionally. Although clearly the knight's shield bears some relation to the body it protects, it is not, unlike the helmet, limited to this one function:

---

[64] *Dictionnaire de l'ancienne langue française et de tous ses dialectes du ixe au xve siècle*, ed. by Frédéric-Eugène Godefroy, 10 vols (Paris: Vieweg, 1880–1902), IV (1885), p. 366.

knights sleeping in the open use their shields as headrests (see, for example, *Erec* line 3092); Yvain carries his wounded lion companion in his shield (*Yvain* lines 4645–50).[65] During the process of arming, the shield is attached to the knight's neck by a cord, but remains eminently detachable, mobile and versatile. Much more loosely (in both a literal and figural sense) connected to the body of the knight than the helmet, the shield is a mobile surface. The shield plays an important role in identifying knights, both as individuals and simply as knights. In the *Conte du graal*, one episode has Gauvain carry two shields to Tintagel, where he hangs them up on an oak tree as he rests. At first, onlookers think there must be two knights. Later, realising there is just one man, the ladies ask what kind of man would be carrying two shields; one thinks he must be a knight because he looks like one; another is more sceptical and says that he may look like a knight but that doesn't mean he is one, and suggests that he is a salesman, dressed as a knight in order to avoid paying duty on his wares (*Conte du graal*, lines 4889–908; 4980–5018). The implication is that one shield usually equals one knight; the presence of two shields signifies either two knights or none.[66] Shields, however, work differently from helmets in the mechanics of their identification; whereas removing a helmet is equated with revealing identity, removing the shield logically uncovers and exposes, but never exposes anything in particular. Indeed, the most it would uncover

[65] Helmut Nickel notes that the development of specific knee armour diminished the need for a long shield. The shield, in other words, to some extent must mirror the shape of the body: 'Arthurian Armings for War and for Love', *Arthuriana*, 5 (1995), 3–21 (p. 8). *Erec et Enide* references are to Chrétien de Troyes, *Erec et Enide*, ed. by Jean-Marie Fritz (Paris: Livre de poche, 1992).

[66] Lacy compares this scene with *Le Chevalier as deus espees* and explains that 'no one takes Meriadeuc to be a peddler of swords' because the link between armour and identity that was pre-eminent in Chrétien has in later works been 'at least partially undone', as 'authors are engaging in a continuous reexamination and reconceptualization of the connections among armor, identity, identification, and recognition'. My argument is firmly situated in this context inasmuch as I try to read armour as non-representational. From my point of view, however, the shield's capacity to disconnect from processes of identification is only highlighted by the fact that it bears a greater weight of expectation than other parts of the knight's equipment; Perceval, for instance, also famously carries two swords in *Le Conte du graal* but is not mistaken for a salesman. The potential for severance between identity and armour is both examined and re-examined in Chrétien. Furthermore, the scene in *Le Chevalier as deus espees* that plays most pertinently with the connection between identity and armour might be that in which Meriadeuc learns his name from an inscription on a sword (lines 10830–71 in Rockwell's edition): Lacy, 'On Armor and Identity', pp. 369, 373. For a prose rendering of the story of a 'Knight with Two Swords', see *Le Roman de Balain: A Prose Romance of the Thirteenth Century*, ed. by M. Dominica Legge (Manchester: Manchester University Press, 1942). For a discussion of the genealogy of the motif, see Helmut Nickel, 'About the Knight with Two Swords and the Maiden under a Tree', *Arthuriana*, 17 (2007), 29–48.

is a fully armed knight. The shield's capacity to reveal identity works in the opposite direction from its ability to uncover or expose the knight. This is illustrated in a passage in *Erec et Enide* in which Kay fails to recognise Erec explicitly because his shield has been so badly damaged in battle:

> [Erec] conut bien le seneschal
> Et les armes et le cheval,
> Mais Kex pas lui ne reconut,
> Car a ses armes ne parut
> Nule veraie conoissance,
> {Que} tant cop{x} d'espee et de lance
> Avoit sor son escu eüz
> Que li toinz en estoit cheüz. (lines 3965–72)

> [Erec recognized the seneschal and the arms and the horse, but Kay did not recognize him, for on his armour appeared no identifiable markings: he had taken so many blows on it from sword and lance that all the paint had fallen off.][67]

The markings that would have indicated Erec's identity have been erased, and the bare, battered shield is rendered useless in this respect; peeling back the layers here reveals *nothing*. In the same encounter, by contrast, Enide deliberately hides her own identity by covering her face:

> Et la dame par grant voidie,
> Por ce qu'ele ne voloit mie
> Qu'il la coneüst ne veïst,
> Ausi con s'ele le feïst
> Por le halle et por la poudriere,
> Mist sa guimple devant sa chiere. (lines 3973–8)

> [And the lady very cleverly put her wimple over her face, just as she would have done to protect herself from heat or dust, because she did not want Kay to see or recognize her.][68]

While we assume that Erec's face is already covered by his helmet, the text nonetheless makes explicit the contrast between the two modes of forestalling identification: erasing identifying marks and covering them up. Marking *on* the shield occurs in a slightly different mode in Chrétien's *Conte du graal*,

---

[67] *Arthurian Romances*, p. 86.
[68] Ibid.

when Gauvain points to the lion claws embedded in his shield as proof that he did indeed spend the night in the *Lit de la Merveille*:

> Et s'i sont les ongles remeses
> D'un lïon molt fier et cresté
> Qui longuemant avoit esté
> En une chanbre enchaaignez.
> Li lïons me fu amenez
> Et feri si en mon escu
> Qu'as ongles retenuz i fu
> Si que il nes an pot retraire. (lines 8610–17)

[and you can still see the claws of a huge, ferocious, crested lion, which had long been kept chained in its room, caught in my shield. The lion was released and set upon me [...]; it sprang at me and struck my shield with such force that became stuck to it by its claws and couldn't withdraw them][69]

In contrast with this is the face, which is not marked upon but covered up. Indeed, when marks do appear on the face they usually come from *within*: recall the bruising on the knights' faces in *Yvain*, and also consider common facial markers such as blushing. Even the facial scar that famously allows Yvain to be recognised during his period of madness is not simply a surface mark but one that indicates an improper intrusion of the outside on the inside, and vice versa. Is it, therefore, too great a leap to consider the shield a facial surface when not only does it have no proximal relation to the embodied face but it also appears to signify 'in the opposite direction'? While the shield works differently from the face and the helmet in Chrétien's texts, it is indeed part of the circulation of faces that occurs in the moment of the duel and it would be disingenuous to separate it. In the knightly face-to-face there is not, I contend, a group of disparate faces, but a mobile network of faces that come in and out of focus, that are covered and uncovered, and that move in and out of contact with each other. The embodied face of the knight and the exposed and exposing surface of the helmet form part of this network, as does the shield. Logically more separate than the helmet, textually the shield is in close contact with the knight and his facing surface and forms a crucial part of it. Often paired with the helmet in descriptions of suits of armour, the shield is also the other part of the knight that is first to be attacked, first to be damaged and thus first to come into contact with the other:

---

[69] Ibid., p. 487.

> S'il s'entr'afolent et mehaignent,
> Les espees riens n'i gaaignent
> Ne li hiame ne li escu,
> Qui sont enbuignié et fendu. (*Yvain, lines* 6113–16)

[But now the two friends were striking and injuring one another. Their swords gained no value, nor did their helmets or shields, which were dented and broken][70]

Along with the helmet, therefore, the shield constitutes the face of the knight in battle, constituted as such at the moment of facing the other.

The duel between Yvain and Gauvain works, in the manner of an exploded diagram, to pull apart and thus reveal to the observer the mechanics of the Levinasian face-to-face. In this scheme, the 'empirical event' described by Davis is the feud between the sisters, and the ethical face-to-face that takes place within, or at the same time as, that event is the combat between the two knights.[71] While the sisters' fight is deeply personal, the duel is explicitly impersonal; the anonymity of the knights is carefully set up, and the ensuing paradox of two friends wanting both to kill each other and to preserve each other's life is directly expressed by the narrator:

> Li uns ne voldroit avoir fait
> A l'autre ne honte ne lait
> Por quanques Diex a fait por homme
> Ne pour tout l'empire de Roume.
> Or ai je menti laidement
> Que l'en voit bien apertement
> Que li uns velt envaïr l'autre
> Lanche levee sor le fautre;
> Et li uns l'autre velt blecier
> Et lui laidir et empirier,
> Que ja de rien ne s'en faindra. (lines 6073–83)

[Neither would want to shame or hurt the other for all that God has done for man, nor for the wealth of all the Roman Empire. But I've told a terrible lie, for it is perfectly obvious that the one with his lance fewtered is ready to attack his adversary, who in turn wants to wound the knight and bring him shame, and both are absolutely intent on this][72]

---

[70] Ibid., p. 371.
[71] Davis, p. 48.
[72] *Arthurian Romances*, p. 371.

Yvain's identity and identification have been at issue throughout the text, and are again evoked in the context of the duel; arriving at Arthur's court, he opts to spend the night at a nearby 'hostel' in order that he not be recognised (lines 5858–63). The following day he leaves the lion behind; although not explicitly for the purpose of disguise, it is clear that this removes the possibility of even being recognised as the 'chevalier au lion'. When Yvain does present himself at court, it is simply his prowess that is discernible to the elder sister, as she 'devint plus noire que terre' upon seeing him (line 5934). Gauvain's anonymity is also discussed, although he lacks Yvain's complex backstory. Gauvain requests that the sister who enlists him as her champion tell no one of their agreement (lines 4727–9), and we learn as he approaches the court that, although there is no mention of this being his intention, he is rendered unrecognisable by all the new armour he has procured in the meantime (lines 5874–9). The effect of the emphasis on their being unrecognisable is to underline the fact that, without these alterations, Yvain and Gauvain would be known to each other. The conditional aspect of the set-up is highlighted when the narrator tells us that

> A l'asambler les lances froissent
> Qui grosses ierent et de fraisne.
> Li uns l'autre de riens n'arraisne,
> Car s'il entr'arrainié se fuissent
> Autre assamblee fait eüssent.
> Ja n'eüst a lor assamblee
> Feru ne lanche ni espee. (lines 6104–10)

[When they met, their lances shattered, though they were stout and made of ash. Neither knight spoke to the other, yet had they spoken their meeting would have been quite different! There would have been no lance or sword blows struck at that encounter][73]

In other words, their anonymity depends on a series of conditions, some accidental and some deliberate; it is built up for the duration of the encounter, and its shattering is what ends this particular face-off (although nightfall is what initially pauses it). Ironically, perhaps, Yvain's voice is so altered by the effects of battle that it is not this that precipitates identification but, rather, Gauvain's characteristic compulsion to name himself (lines 6253–7). Indeed, recognition ultimately plays no role in the big revelation. These two knights, then, suspend not only the possibility of identification but also their own

[73] Ibid.

identities for the duration of the encounter; fighting on behalf of the sisters, in one sense they are faceless proxies, acting out of a virtually arbitrary obligation that not only requires the suspension of their identities but also contributes to it. In another sense, however, they acquire a new kind of face, the role of which is not to identify them but to facilitate the duel; had they identified each other, the text tells us, they would not have fought.

The duel scene is immediately preceded by a narrative excursus in which it is explained how these two knights can both love and hate each other at the same time (lines 5997–6103). The conclusion offered is that both *Amors* and *Haïne* can coexist in the same body since neither is aware of the other: both are blind, and neither occupies the same place at the same time in the many-chambered individual. This scene is the second in a diptych, the first of which occurs much earlier on when Yvain, having killed Esclados, having been trapped in his castle and fallen in love with his widow, Laudine, asks himself how it is that he can love his enemy (how his 'ami' can also be his 'anemi'). There is a case for a Levinasian reading of the first scene: it is asymmetrical, since Yvain is not only invisible (thanks to a magic ring) but also, when watching the funeral procession, hiding. In addition, as Sarah Kay points out, Laudine is painted as 'an otherworldly, quasispiritual presence. She appears to Yvain to have been made by God himself (1502–10) and thereby endowed with a perfection which is not only aesthetic, but moral and spiritual'.[74] For Levinas, the other is indeed a spiritual being; the relation to the other is the relation to God (although, importantly, the other is not God). Equally, transcendence is the lived experience of facing the other, an experience which interrupts us and which calls our attention, much as Laudine erupts into Yvain's vision and makes new and unanticipated requirements of him *before* he has been able to understand or to articulate this. Indeed, one might argue that this is closer to the kind of ethical encounter that Levinas envisages than the duel scene: not only is the encounter asymmetrical but, despite his initial characterisation of Laudine as his 'anemi', the 'ami' part wins out and the love relation is arguably closer to Levinas's crucial injunction to *not* kill the other; Yvain and Gauvain are, of course, under the opposite injunction. This reading, however, elides the crux of the Levinasian stance, which is the non-representational aspect of the other's face. Yvain falls for Laudine when he sees her beautiful face through a window; the encounter is based on the assignation of value to an other above all others, and this, here, is precisely through Yvain's *reading* Laudine's face, and not simply his apprehension of it (lines 1269–510). Slavoj Žižek draws out the same implication from Levinas's

---

[74] Sarah Kay, *Courtly Contradictions: The Emergence of the Literary Object in the Twelfth Century* (Stanford, CA: Stanford University Press, 2001), p. 268.

work itself, and suggests that to posit universal love is necessarily to imply hatred of an exception, and that love is always 'a violent gesture of cutting into [the] multitude and privileging a One'.[75] For Žižek, the more radically ethical position is one of indifference. Žižek goes further than I would in considering the true object of an ethical relation to be 'NOT here in the face to face relationship'; he nonetheless highlights the fragility of the status of the Levinasian face as a non-symbolic, non-appropriative surface that is, nonetheless, attached to an individual.[76] Yvain's love for Laudine singles her out and it is this that drives his subsequent behaviour, whereas Yvain's fight with Gauvain takes place as a result of the suspension of the individual. In this later scene, the coexistence of love and hate is the condition for the encounter, inasmuch as neither is privileged over the other; in the duel this approximates Žižek's notion of universal indifference, since the encounter is clearly shifted onto a plane where right and wrong, as well as love and hate, are present but have no bearing on behaviour; they fight because they are obliged to fight. For Yvain and Laudine, however, Yvain chooses her face among others and thus 'anemi' resolves into 'ami'.

Importantly, Levinas's thinking not only allows us to talk about different kinds of face but also necessarily requires a new lexicon: the non-representational face is not in fact a lack or a failure or a disguise or a barrier. It is not the space where something used to be, nor is it a concealing layer but, rather, it is a face that *emerges*. It is affirmative inasmuch as it is also, in Levinasian terms, the condition for a truly ethical relation. This kind of face prevents the relentless acquisition of knowledge about the other that ultimately leads to their violent subordination. Contrary to the prevailing modern idea that a person becomes more and more distinct the more is known about them, Levinas asserts that their essential difference is upheld only by their absolute unknowability; the distance from the self to the other is infinite.

Le Chevalier as deus espees

Following the figure of Gauvain into one of his thirteenth-century incarnations, I will now examine an episode in the anonymous *Chevalier as deus espees* in light of the above findings.[77] Thought to have been composed in England, and dated to the first half of the thirteenth century, the text is found only

---

[75] Slavoj Žižek, 'Smashing the Neighbor's Face' <http://www.lacan.com/zizsmash.htm> [accessed 23 February 2016].

[76] Ibid.

[77] All references, including English translations, are to *Le Chevalier as deus espees*, ed. and trans. by Paul Vincent Rockwell, Arthurian Archives, 13 (Cambridge: Brewer, 2006), unless otherwise stated.

in one late thirteenth-century manuscript (Paris, Bibliothèque nationale de France, MS fonds français (BnF fr.) 12603) which contains several other verse romances and *fabliaux*. Among the other texts in this manuscript is Chrétien's *Yvain*, and while the *Chevalier as deus espees* most directly reworks a series of motifs from *Le Conte du graal* (as noted by Rockwell in the introduction to his edition), it is with implicit reference to Chrétien's earlier text that it forms part of a network of commentaries on representation and identity via the figure of the face.

The narrative tells the story of Meriadeuc, an unknown knight who presents himself at Arthur's court and succeeds in ungirding a sword from a beautiful maiden. He disappears before anyone can ask who he is, goes out into the world and makes a name for himself as a questing knight. Meanwhile, Arthur and the court await the return of Gauvain, whom they plan to send out to find the unknown knight. Gauvain eventually does return, and sets out again, precipitating a series of quests and adventures, loosely based on the efforts of Briens de la Gastine to punish Gauvain for being the object of his *amie*'s affections as well as the search for the *chevalier as deus espees* (named in lines 6824–5 as "'Sire de Vaus de Blanquemore" | [...] et "du Lac de Jumeles"' and then in line 10869 as "'Meriadues"'). Meriadeuc eventually learns his own identity and backstory, is crowned and marries, living happily ever after. This relatively long text (12360 lines) is full of moments of misrecognition, anonymity and what Donald Maddox would call 'specular encounter'.[78] In this relatively little-studied text, this density of identity and recognition tropes makes it ripe for a study of faces and faciality.

The particular episode I focus on occurs just over half way through the narrative and is, as I discuss below, immediately preceded by a curious moment of non-recognition followed by recognition. In the main sequence, Meriadeuc's mother tells him the story of the death of his father at the hands of Gauvain. Prompted by Meriadeuc's understanding that Gauvain was the murderer, his mother explains that while he was indeed the killer, the murderer was in fact Briens, who had changed places with Gauvain at the last minute before their combat, ensuring the death of the deceived and therefore underprepared Bleheris. The episode revolves around a fatal deception, the outcome of which relies entirely on the fact that Bleheris misreads the external signs presented to him. It is suggested that the deception's success is ensured by Briens presenting himself to Bleheris before the duel with his armour but without his helmet:

---

[78] Maddox, *Fictions of Identity*. Curiously, however, in this book Maddox makes no mention of this particular text.

Et Brïens vient de l'autre part
Armés, fors de hiaume et si mande
Mon seigneur ki il li demande
Sa bataille et li fait savoir
Quels convenans il doit avoir
Entr'els. [...] (lines 6964–9)

[Brien arrived from the other side of the field/With armor on, except for a helmet, and made known/To my lord that he had come to ask for/His battle and remind him/What agreement had been struck/Between them ...]

While we are told that the purpose of this show is to remind – 'faire savoir' – Bleheris of the agreement between the two, the fact that Bleheris is already present is a clear indicator that, in terms of catalysing events, Briens's demonstration is entirely superfluous. Its primary purpose must therefore be to cause Bleheris to make the link between Briens's face – identifying him as Briens – and the armour that will be worn in combat. Briens then declares that he will return to his tent to complete his preparations and will reappear fully armed and ready for combat. When Gauvain appears wearing Briens's armour, Bleheris has no reason to assume it is not Briens and is fatally wounded by Gauvain, the far superior knight. In reading this sequence with the aid of Levinas, I identify two distinct 'encounters' that take place according to his notion of non-reciprocal, asymmetric relations between what he most broadly defines as an 'être' and an 'être séparé'. The logical surplus created in a non-reciprocal relation is, according to Levinas, precisely the infinite distance between beings; the fact of non-reciprocity therefore is what allows for a relation to occur across an absolute distance. A comparison, with Levinas in mind, of these two encounters adds a new dimension to the notion of a literary 'face'. To take at face value Levinas's crucial assertion that an encounter between a *moi* and an *autre*, or between an 'être' and an 'être séparé', is non-reciprocal and asymmetrical, is to allow a conception of the archetypal Arthurian encounter – the duel – that takes into account the differences in both perception and motivation of the two protagonists. Nowhere is this separation more critical than in an episode in which one protagonist acts according to an erroneous understanding of the other's identity and the other acts independently of his own knowledge.

In the first encounter, let us posit Bleheris as the subject and Briens as the object.[79] In order to make his deception watertight, Briens appears to

---

[79] We must qualify this distinction: a critical aspect of Levinas's work is his conception of a non-objectifiable object. The Levinasian Other is precisely an object that cannot be objectified, assumed, appropriated, known or otherwise interfered with.

Bleheris before the duel wearing his armour but explicitly not wearing his helmet, implicitly revealing his face and, therefore, his identity, ensuring that Bleheris will make the association between his armour and *him* (see lines 6964–9, quoted above). The text tells us that Briens does this in order to remind Bleheris of the duel. Several lines later we learn that the deception is complete: Bleheris, not questioning the identity of the figure beneath the armour, has no reason to fear Briens's skills in combat and makes no effort to arm himself effectively. However, the text in fact draws attention to the superfluity of Briens's performance by explaining that Bleheris begins to arm himself immediately *before* Briens appears:

> Mesire, ki de joie ert plains
> Et la bataille mout couvoite,
> Vient en la plaice et tant esploite
> D'armer, k'il li est mout tart. (lines 6960–3)

> [My lord, who was full of joy/And eagerly awaited the battle,/Came to the designated spot and hurried/To arm himself, for he was anxious to get at it]

Not only does Bleheris clearly not need reminding of the battle since he is, in full sight of Briens, already there, but he has already made the decision to arm himself according to his knowledge of Briens's ineptitude. The broader implication of this is that Bleheris making the association between Briens's armour and Briens's identity is a *fait accompli*; it is essentially impossible for Bleheris to conceive of a disjunction between the inside and the outside of the figure he is about to fight. By choosing to reveal his identity through his face, Briens's performance draws upon the idea of the infallibility of the face as a marker of identity and thus makes it part of a stable interior.[80] At the same time, of course, Briens enacts precisely the fallibility of the face as marker; each knight's perception of the role of the face is critically different, but these perceptions are in fact two sides of the same coin, inasmuch as they are both comments on the representational capacity of the face. Reading this encounter alongside Levinas suggests that Bleheris's fatal error is to read a surface as meaningful, inasmuch as it is associated with something behind. This reveals at the same time the artificiality and the ubiquity of the mechanics behind associating an interior with an exterior; the armour that Gauvain, as it turns out, wears is meaningful only because its signifying associations have

---

[80] It is worth noting here that Gauvain, not much later on, reveals his identity through his voice – both in how it sounds and in what he says with it – and specifically not through his face: Gauvain's taking Bleheris's helmet off as he lies dying makes conspicuous the fact that he must still be wearing his own.

already been set up. Rockwell offers another compelling interpretation that transposes what I read as the expectation of a continuity between appearance and 'essence' onto a temporal plane: he explains Bleheris's fatal error as the inability to account for the possibility that past knowledge might not translate into a present situation.[81] The implications are disturbing, inasmuch as Rockwell's formulation suggests that, to the extent that past knowledge is *sometimes* unreliable in judging present appearance, and that it is not known when it is reliable or not, it is essentially *always* unreliable. When the texts under consideration here play with disguise and misrecognition, therefore, they reveal at once the power and the fragility of representation. To consider the second encounter in the scene between Briens and Bleheris, then, is to consider an encounter that stands alongside, but without, this semiotic.

In Gauvain's encounter with Bleheris, we come across a much more 'Levinasian' encounter insofar as the subject acts not according to an interior via an exterior but according to that exterior itself. Here the kind of knowledge that failed Bleheris is not deficient; it is simply irrelevant. As the result of a *don contraignant*, Gauvain is obliged to do whatever Briens requires of him. In this case, it is to fight Bleheris in the duel that Briens would otherwise almost certainly lose. Gauvain's encounter with Bleheris is, then, not the result of a long-standing and personal feud but of an arbitrary and impersonal obligation that happens because Gauvain is a knight and bound by certain laws; the knight's aimless purposiveness makes him the ideal Levinasian subject. Gauvain truly encounters Bleheris's Levinasian face: he is not motivated by *who* is in front of him, but by the simple fact that *someone* is. The text makes no mention of Gauvain objecting to his task, nor is there the slightest reference to Bleheris's identity, an omission that reinforces the idea that it is, from Gauvain's point of view, for the duration of the encounter, entirely incidental. Gauvain's conduct is markedly impersonal, to the extent that he is not even the grammatical subject of the first of a brief series of verbs that describe the single, fatal blow that he inflicts upon Bleheris:

> Et en ce ke mesire [Bleheris] assamble,
> En astieles a envoie
> Sa lance, mais n'est pas brisie
> La lance mon seigneur Gauvain. (lines 7000–3)

> [And as my lord attacked,/His lance burst into splinters,/But the lance of my lord Gawain/Did not break]

---

[81] Rockwell (ed.), *Le Chevalier as deus espees*, p. 9. For a more detailed discussion of the theme of disjunction and the misreading of signs, see Rockwell, '*Appellation Contrôlée*' and 'The Promise of Laughter'.

What I have been calling the 'encounter' clearly ends with Bleheris's death, which, of course, coincides with the end of Gauvain's period of obligation. After fatally wounding Bleheris, it is as if the spell is broken; no longer governed by the conditions of the *don contraignant*, Gauvain ceases to be an ethical figure in the Levinasian sense of obligation to a facing Other. Bleheris's face, as encountered by Gauvain, is nothing to do with *him*; it coincides only with his being there and not with him being Bleheris. Indeed, if we consider Gauvain to be operating under a Levinasian obligation we can venture that Bleheris's face is less an anatomical feature than 'la manière dont se présente l'Autre' [the way in which the other presents himself].[82] Until, that is, the moment at which Bleheris is fatally wounded and his 'other' – non-Levinasian – face is revealed by the unlacing of his helmet; suddenly Gauvain doesn't know what to do:

> Et mesires se pasme lors,
> Ki l'angoisse de la mort sent.
> Et mesire Gauvains descent
> Sor lui. Le hiaume li deslaice.
> Puis se tint et ne set k'il faice. (lines 7016–20)

> [My lord fell unconscious,/Feeling the pain of death./And my lord Gawain knelt/Over him. He unlaced his helmet for him./Then he held back and did not know what to do]

The use of the present subjunctive in line 7020 evokes not only the uncertainty that Gauvain is suddenly struck with, but also the immediacy of the change. Indeed, the line is a single, sudden sentence, stopping the reader in their tracks as Gauvain himself pauses, finding himself in a brief quagmire before he regains his composure and disappears. The face of an Arthurian combatant, therefore, cannot be hidden by his armour since it is, by definition, exterior. As Gauvain unfastens Bleheris's helmet, he does not reveal anything that he – or we – did not know; the gesture does, however, mark the shift in narrative priority from one of Bleheris's faces to the other: the face of the object of Gauvain's obligation gives way to the face of the unfairly deceived Bleheris, father of Meriadeuc. The time-frame within which priority is given to the face of the Arthurian combatant – known to Gauvain but to all intents and purposes anonymous – is finite, and is a period of time that coincides with the narrative time of the encounter motivated by chivalric, impersonal duty.

---

[82] Levinas, *Totalité et infini*, p. 43; *Totality and Infinity*, p. 50.

It is equally productive to consider how this episode functions within the context of the narrative as a whole. The faces that circulate in the duel between Gauvain and Yvain in *Le Chevalier au lion* are produced in an encounter that is as explicitly reciprocal and egalitarian as possible, not only in terms of the equal prowess displayed by the knights, but also inasmuch as neither one of them knows the other's identity until more or less the same moment. In the combat between Gauvain and Bleheris, however, the terms are entirely unequal in both these senses: not only is Gauvain the superior knight, he is also the only one who knows the identity of each protagonist. This episode is recounted almost at the precise midpoint of the narrative, but is said to have taken place four days earlier (lines 6586–7). While this raises various questions of temporal coherence (which, in turn, make some of the non-recognition scenes seem somewhat unlikely), narrative structure places the episode right at the very beginning of the text, if not a little before. In the first few hundred lines, before the appearance of the eponymous knight, the Lady of Caradigan makes her way to the *gaste capele* on behalf of King Ris, and it is here that she witnesses what later turns out to be Bleheris's burial. The Lady having taken his sword and returned to the court, Meriadeuc turns up and fulfils the prophecy the Lady of Caradigan overheard in the chapel by ungirding the sword and successfully putting it on himself. In other words, we later learn that the narrative motivation that underpins the entire text is the outcome of the duel between Gauvain and Bleheris; the fact that we learn this only half way through creates a loop back to the mysterious beginnings of the text, and heightens the sense of causality. Norris Lacy uses the Hitchcockian concept of the narrative McGuffin to suggest that the otherwise unexplained delivery of the shackles to the *gaste capele*, in which the *dame* finds Bleheris's body, 'serves to launch the central intrigue of the romance'.[83] Of course, the intrigue could not be launched if Bleheris's body had not been in the chapel in the first place. Donald Maddox points out that the Gauvain/Yvain duel in Chrétien's *roman* is, by contrast, almost inconsequential in the narrative movement of *Le Chevalier au lion*, and that its primary function is as a critique of 'the maladroit functioning of the Arthurian court'.[84] The moment of the entirely anonymous and egalitarian duel is absolutely temporary and without consequence; neither party can conceivably win, and the motivation for the combat has nothing to do with the two knights, beyond their (equally) impressive prowess. What is also temporary, therefore, as I have shown, is the faciality of this emphatically discrete encounter; it flares up and dies down

---

[83] Norris J. Lacy, 'Medieval McGuffins: The Arthurian Model', *Arthuriana*, 15 (2005), 53–64 (p. 56).

[84] Donald Maddox, *The Arthurian Romances of Chrétien de Troyes: Once and Future Fictions*, Cambridge Studies in Medieval Literature, 12 (Cambridge: Cambridge University Press, 1991), p. 71.

again, and nothing much has changed. By contrast, the duel between Gauvain and Bleheris is open ended, as its implications underpin the whole narrative; the fact that the duel ends so decisively, as a direct consequence of its non-reciprocal nature, is, paradoxically, precisely what allows the facial encounter to continue.

Might we then suggest that this encounter leaves a kind of residual faciality throughout the rest of the text? If we take into account the observation of simultaneous encounters, along with the notion of the episode as an open-ended narrative catalyst, how differently could we think about faces outside of the sequence? As I suggest above, the face in Arthurian combat is not only the embodied face underneath the armour, but also the facing surface of an adversary. To be more precise: as soon as the deception leads Bleheris to believe that he is fighting Briens, the figure in front of him *is* Briens, at the same time as it *is* Gauvain. Gauvain's real embodied face occupies precisely the same space and time as Briens's imagined (by Bleheris) face, and both are covered by a helmet, the role of which is to both cover up and facilitate the deceit. When Gauvain does reveal his identity to Bleheris, it is too late; although pleased to hear of his mistake, Bleheris is already mortally wounded:

> Quant mesire Gauvains oï
> K'il si humlement se contint,
> De grant courtoisie li vint
> K'il li dist: 'Tous soiés certains
> Que je sui apielés Gauvains,
> Li aisnés des fiex le roi Loth
> D'Orchanie.' Quant oï ot
> Mesire, si fu plus a aise. (lines 7054–61)

[When my lord Gawain heard/Him conduct himself so humbly,/Out of great courtliness it came to him/That he said: 'You may be absolutely certain/That I am called Gawain,/The eldest of the sons of King Loth/Of Orcanie.' Once my lord had heard this,/He was more at ease]

Knowing the identity of his adversary is important to Bleheris, but has no narrative import. What is important in this regard is the gap that is opened up between representational and non-representational faces. Before the battle, we are told that Bleheris believed that he was fighting Briens:

> il cuidoit trestout por voir
> Que ce fust Brïens. (lines 6994–5)

[Since he truly believed/That this was Brien]

After the combat, as he has become aware that the man he faces is not Briens, but before he learns that this man is Gauvain, Bleheris himself explains that he

> cuidai sans faille
> Que Brïens eüst la bataille. (lines 7045–6)
>
> [I believed without question/That Brien had won the battle]

The difference between truth and belief is not simply calqued on the difference between right and wrong; in this case belief, whether right *or* wrong, precipitates one encounter, and truth another, each encounter mediated through a different facial aspect. It is as if the multiple faces have been let loose, as the results of their existence radiate out from this middle section.

Just before the episode in question, Meriadeuc enters his mother's castle; neither one is aware of the identity of the other. Previously, Meriadeuc had encountered a messenger who had been sent by his mother to search for him, and the messenger had given his shield to Meriadeuc, the same shield that is now hanging on the castle wall. Eventually this is pointed out and mother and son are reunited. A rather complex interplay is at work here between different modes of identification, within which I suggest we see the same kind of multiple facial surfaces that we have noted above, albeit outside the context of the duel. We may, of course, claim that the face, even if divorced from the body, as in the case of the shield, does nothing here but identify, but I once again turn to Levinas for an alternative: up until this point he has helped us to recognise how a certain kind of encounter might produce faces – whether embodied or not – that aren't simply markers of identity; now he will help us consider how we might sever the link between resemblance and identity, not through disembodied signs and symbols, but through rethinking how we perceive an embodied, human face. Meriadeuc and his mother identify each other explicitly through the association made by the messenger between the knight and his shield; this is a well-established link and has led me to suggest that we perceive the shield as a kind of face, inasmuch as it signifies, identifies and covers – or, rather, has at a given point covered – the knight's body. At the beginning of *Le Chevalier as deus espees* Gauvain's shield is so battered that it proves useless in identifying him – the implication, as I have discussed, being that it *can*. The most enigmatic part of the episode with Meriadeuc and his mother is, however, an almost throwaway piece of dialogue, in which the mother exclaims:

> Diex, por quoi ai cuer ki me consent
> Que chevalier puisse veoir,
> Ne vous qui samblés por voir

Celui meïsme que je di?
Mal de l'eure que je vous vi
Onques nul jor chaiens venir.
Ce fu por moi plus parhonnir. (lines 6632–8)

[God, why do I have a heart that permits/Me to see a knight,/You who truly resemble/The same knight that I am describing?/Cursed be the hour that I ever/Saw you come here./This was to humiliate me in the utmost]

She expresses anger at the fact that the stranger in front of her reminds her of the son that she fears is dead. Of course, the stranger *is* her son, and so she finds herself in the strange position of claiming that her son resembles himself.[85] In his essay, 'La Réalité et son ombre', Levinas refers to precisely this when discussing 'la simultanéité de la vérité et de l'image':

La ressemblance n'est pas la participation de l'être à une idée [...] elle est la structure même du sensible comme tel. Le sensible – c'est l'être dans la mesure où il se ressemble, où, en dehors de son œuvre triomphale d'être, il jette une ombre, dégage cette essence obscure et insaisissable, cette essence fantomatique que rien ne permet d'identifier avec l'essence révélée dans la vérité. Il n'y a pas d'abord image – vision neutralisée de l'objet – qui, ensuite, diffère du signe et du symbole par sa ressemblance avec l'original: la neutralisation de la position dans l'image est précisément cette ressemblance.

[Resemblance is not a participation of a being in an idea [...] it is the very structure of the sensible as such. The sensible is being insofar as it resembles itself, insofar as, outside of its triumphal work of being, it casts a shadow, emits that obscure and elusive essence, that phantom essence which cannot be identified with the essence revealed in truth. There is not first an image – a neutralized vision of the object – which then differs from a sign or symbol because of its resemblance with the original; the neutralization of position in an image is precisely this resemblance.][86]

---

[85] This motif also crops up in the contemporaneous *Roman de Gliglois*: Gauvain describes a new knight to Arthur by saying that he looks a bit like Gliglois; of course, it *is* Gliglois, a joke that the reader shares with Biautés, who also knows the unknown's identity. See *Le Roman de Gliglois*, ed. by Marie-Luce Chênerie, Classiques français du Moyen Âge, 143 (Paris: Champion, 2003), lines 2262–5.

[86] Emmanuel Levinas, 'La Réalité et son ombre', *Les Temps modernes*, 4 (1948), 771–89 (pp. 780–81); 'Reality and its Shadow', in *The Continental Aesthetics Reader*, ed. by Clive Cazeaux (London: Routledge, 2000), pp. 117–28 (p. 122).

Levinas makes a very subtle point: if truth and image are simultaneously apprehended, and if this sensible apprehension takes place through contact with 'cette essence fantomatique que rien ne permet d'identifier avec l'essence révélée dans la vérité', then image is absolutely not a *means* by which to access truth or reality. Consequently, the link between resemblance and being is severed or, rather, the kind of link that makes resemblance a means of accessing whatever is resembled is severed. Furthermore, Levinas claims that '[l]a réalité tout entière porte sur sa face sa propre allégorie en dehors de sa révélation et de sa vérité' [The whole of reality bears on its face its own allegory, outside of its revelation and its truth].[87] The resemblance and the resembled exist in the same place and time; one does not lead to or make way for the other. Meriadeuc's mother inadvertently claims that he resembles himself; she fails to make the connection between the resemblance and the resembled perhaps precisely because they both occupy the same space and time. In the text, Meriadeuc looks like Meriadeuc because he is Meriadeuc. Levinas's formulation, like the text, admits this. However, in the text as in Levinas, this formula does not work backwards: the acknowledgement and recognition of an image does not guarantee acknowledgement and recognition of the reality with which it exists simultaneously. It is, therefore, up to the disembodied face – the shield – to perform dutifully the work of sign and symbol when the fully exposed, fully recognised, embodied face does not.

La Vengeance Raguidel

Finally, I turn to another thirteenth-century romance, the *Vengeance Raguidel*, in which Gauvain finds himself embroiled in a series of bizarre encounters, mediated by the face, and which exhibit a slightly different configuration of the multiple faces I have been examining thus far. In this text, the facial episodes I look at are less combative than those we have examined up to this point, but can nonetheless be considered life threatening.

Gilles Roussineau dates the text to a period after the composition of Chrétien's *Conte du graal* and before the middle of the thirteenth century, at which point, he argues, the *Vengeance Raguidel* was well known, as witnessed by references in the mid-thirteenth century work of the Dominican monk Etienne de Bourbon, and in the contemporary Arthurian *roman*, *Hunbaut*.[88] It is found in its entirety in two manuscripts, dating from the mid- and late thirteenth century respectively, and two fragments are also extant. Fairly certainly attributed to Raoul de Houdenc, at least for lack of any reasonable

---

[87] 'La Réalité et son ombre', p. 780; 'Reality and its Shadow', p. 122.
[88] Raoul de Houdenc, *La Vengeance Raguidel*, ed. by Gilles Roussineau (Geneva: Droz, 2004), pp. 7–9. All subsequent references are to this edition unless otherwise stated.

alternatives, the *roman* begins with a disconsolate King Arthur noticing the arrival of a mysterious unmanned boat, in which is found the body of a knight, still embedded with a portion of the lance that killed him, and wearing five golden rings on his fingers. It transpires that the knight's death will be avenged by whoever is able to remove the lance, and that this person will be aided by whoever manages to take the rings. Gauvain removes the lance and, a little while later, only seen by Kay, Yder turns up and removes the rings. The rest of the text tells of Gauvain's adventures as he slowly makes his way towards the eventual vengeance of Raguidel's death. We might divide Gauvain's quest into two parts, the first of which occurs before he realises that he has in fact, to his great embarrassment, forgotten the piece of the lance with which the vengeance must be wrought; the second part is therefore the rest of the text, in which, since he has now realised he has forgotten the crucial vengeance tool, Gauvain's questing is much more purposeful. Indeed, we are able to make this distinction because, while Gauvain realises his error only much later (lines 3124–7), the reader learns of his mistake at the moment he makes it (lines 542–7). In the pre-remembrance section of the text, Gauvain has two critical encounters during which each of his adversaries expresses an overpowering desire to kill him in revenge for the various ways in which he has thwarted their amorous projects. In the first of these, Gauvain seeks shelter in a castle surrounded by heads on spikes and, after having fought the castle's owner over the somewhat inconsequential fact that he helped himself to food without permission, discovers that the heads are those of all the knights that have been killed in the Noir Chevalier's search for Gauvain himself, who, he explains, he would not recognise. Hence the terribly inefficient method of killing everyone, in the hope that one of his victims will be his intended target. For my purposes, I consider the 'encounter' to be Gauvain's apprehension of these heads; I hesitate to call it a 'moment' because I suggest that, while the initial encounter is brief and inconsequential, it retrospectively accumulates layers and perspectives which invite us to reconsider its complexity. In the second encounter, Gauvain enters the castle of the Dame de Gaudestroit and is advised by a helpful servant who recognises him that he must assume Kay's identity if he doesn't want to die. Gauvain obliges, just in time, and soon learns that the Dame de Gaudestroit is also waiting for Gauvain to turn up (and, in fact, has imprisoned Gahieret, his brother, in an effort to lure Gauvain to her) so that she can wreak her own revenge for being spurned by him. She shows Gauvain the elaborate trap that awaits him in her chapel: behind a small window lies a double tomb; when Gauvain looks through the window, a blade will decapitate him, the Dame de Gaudestroit will then kill herself and the two will be united in death as they never could have been in life:

Issi me feroit compagnie
mors qant nel puis avoir en vie! (lines 2299–300)

[Thus he will keep me company in death, since I cannot have him alive][89]

The crucial thing is, however, that neither the Noir Chevalier nor the Dame de Gaudestroit knows that they are in fact in the presence of the object of their murderous desires, since neither of them has ever seen his face. What I will examine in this final section of the chapter, therefore, is how this text proliferates faces in a different kind of highly charged encounter, in each example of which the fact that Gauvain's explicitly uncovered face is not recognised is all that lies between him and a particularly gruesome death. At the same time, in each of these episodes the play among embodied faces, facial recognition and face-to-face encounters (in the general sense of interacting with somebody through facing them) is slippery; the text plays specifically with the simultaneous presence of the face as identifier and the face as a non-identifying, facing surface. The coexistence of the 'real' (the Noir Chevalier and the Dame de Gaudestroit are facing Gauvain) and the hypothetical (they explain, to him, what they would do *if* they were facing Gauvain) happens through the multiple functionality of one phenomenon: Gauvain's face.

In the first of these encounters, Gauvain, seeking shelter, has been advised not to go to the castle of the Noir Chevalier, since no one who has sought shelter there has been known to return. In spite of this, he turns up and is entirely unperturbed by the 'mainte teste' [many heads] (line 711) impaled on a series of spikes outside the castle. When we later learn that these heads are the result of the Noir Chevalier's indiscriminate search for Gauvain, we can read back into this initial, apparently insignificant encounter and suggest a slightly more complex scenario. In looking at the heads, Gauvain is in fact, albeit unknowingly, looking not only at the heads of those who were killed in his stead but also at a group of disembodied heads of which one, in the eyes of the Noir Chevalier, might just be Gauvain himself. Since the Noir Chevalier has no idea what Gauvain looks like, he can't know whether he has killed him or not. In this sense his rampage has no logical end, and Gauvain is therefore in a permanent state of suspension between life and death whereby, in a manner not dissimilar to Schrödinger's cat, whether he is dead or not is entirely unverifiable within the parameters set up by the Noir Chevalier when he later says:

---

[89] Translations of the *Vengenace Raguidel* are my own.

Por ce que ne conois sa ciere
ocis tos çaus que puis trover. (lines 1414–15)

[Since I don't know his face, I kill everyone I find]

The motif of severed heads generally symbolises the prowess of a knight by warning others of their fate if they are to challenge him, and, as R. S. Loomis acknowledged, is found in a large variety of medieval tales.[90] Loomis quotes Archer Taylor as noting that the reference to one empty spike, awaiting the head of the next challenger, is particular to Arthurian tales with Celtic connections.[91] In a more recent study of decapitation as an Arthurian motif, Sandy Feinstein makes explicit the link between the head and identification in order to claim that, in Chrétien's *Le Chevalier de la charrette*, decapitation symbolises the silencing of 'self-identifying speech'.[92] To reinforce this, she quotes a passage from Regina Janes's work on the significance of the guillotine, in which Janes takes up the Freudian notion that decapitation is tantamount to castration in order to explain that what therefore distinguishes the head from the genitals in terms of symbolic function is that '"[t]he head tells all. It identifies itself"'.[93] Sartre makes a curious reference to heads on spikes in his essay on the face. He explains that a strict hierarchy exists between the face, the locus of human meaning and the body, which is merely 'un mulet' [a mule] that carries this 'relique cireuse' [waxy relic].[94] He goes on to emphasise the relative unimportance of the *porteur* of this artefact, saying that it is only context that differentiates it from the spikes that carry heads 'par les temps de colère' [in times of anger].[95] Here the fact that a face is on a spike and not on a body makes no difference to its status as the locus of meaning. In Arthurian romance, heads on spikes are almost always anonymous, and serve only to give the impression of quantity of enemies slain and to warn a potential challenger, whoever they may be.[96] The decapitated heads in the *Vengeance Raguidel*

---

[90] Roger Sherman Loomis, 'Arthurian Tradition and Folklore', *Folklore*, 69 (1958), 1–25 (pp. 3–4).

[91] Ibid., p. 4.

[92] Sandy Feinstein, 'Losing Your Head in Chrétien's *Knight of the Cart*', *Arthuriana*, 9 (1999), 45–62 (p. 57).

[93] Ibid.

[94] *Les Écrits de Sartre*, p. 561. Translations of this text are my own.

[95] Ibid. It is worth noting that Sartre, in this essay, implicitly upholds the distinction between face and head that we frequently encounter; that is, that the head is part of the body, and the face is the meaningful overlay: 'des statues sont des corps sans visage [...] la tête c'est le chapiteau' [statues are bodies without faces [...] the head is the capital].

[96] The earliest example in verse romance is in Chrétien's *Erec et Enide*: the enchanted garden in which Erec is to perform the *joie de la cour* contains a series of heads on spikes along with a single spike, on top of which is not a head but a horn (lines 5766–800).

depart from this convention and serve an altogether different purpose, one which chimes more closely with Janes's notion of the head as identifier but which is nonetheless deeply troubled by the failure of both the sender and the recipient of the message of identity. Furthermore, to take Sartre's comparison further, these particular faces seem to have more significatory clout on spikes than they would have had on a human body; not, importantly, because of the quantity of assassinations, but because of the possibility that any one of those heads indicates one particular death. When he later explains the reason behind the heads on spikes, the Noir Chevalier tells Gauvain that he hopes the lady who spurned him will see Gauvain's head, realise that he has been killed by a better knight, and make the victor the renewed object of her affection:

> Por ce fas a tos çaus voler
> les testes que je puis tenir,
> savoir se poroie avenir
> que peüsse la siue avoir.
> Car lors sage bien de fin voir
> que la pucele m'ameroit,
> [...]
> se j'avoie Gavain ocis. (lines 1420–8)

[This is why I take the heads of all those I find, in the hope that I will have his. Because I know well that the damsel will love me [...] if I have killed Gauvain]

A strategy of indiscriminate murder that results from the Noir Chevalier's lack of knowledge of Gauvain's face is, as we learn later, thwarted by the rather comic fact that the *dame* in question doesn't know Gauvain's face either. The 'moment' at which Gauvain apprehends the heads on spikes is thus in fact extended well beyond the four lines it occupies in the narrative as we learn that the cause of the heads' existence is identical to the problem that thwarts their intended effect: the lack of knowledge of Gauvain's face. We also witness here an interplay between the importance of quantity that is usally associated with the heads-on-spikes motif and the importance of quality that is more frequently associated – in both the texts and the theories under discussion – with faces. Swirling around the severed heads, therefore, are several incomplete and imperfect facial functions, not all of which become apparent until we gradually learn more about the discrepancy between the message being conveyed and the inability of the Dame de Gaudestroit (as it turns out) to receive this message. In terms of narrative, the severed heads evoke, on the one hand, a clear distinction between those knights who have no future and the one, Gauvain, who does and, on the other hand, a strange suspension of resolution. The play of recognition and identity among the heads, Gauvain, the Noir Chevalier and the Dame de Gaudestroit defers what, on one level, appears to be a firm conclusion.

It is important to note that I have been talking about these heads without considering the distinction between a head and a face. This has been quite deliberate, since these heads are faces inasmuch as, while they inevitably fail to convey the message of identity, they are tasked with this responsibility; a responsibility that, as we have established earlier in this chapter, is particularly facial. Similarly, as a modified version of the convention of severed heads as a challenge or a warning, the episode recalls the communicative function of the face, a function which, again, the heads conspicuously fail to achieve; Gauvain barely notices them. The heads refer to two conventions that they also deny: they aren't a warning, and they can't signify identity. We have established how, as with the other faces we have come across, they are embedded in this representational system that they also refute. Moreover, the further forwards we go in the narrative (and backwards in terms of the timeframe of the events), the less possible the identification of Gauvain becomes. As the Noir Chevalier explains the moment at which he was defeated in both battle and love by Gauvain, it remains unclear as to how precisely he knows it was Gauvain in the first place:

> Je vos sai bien celui nomer,
> com il ot non et qui il fu.
> Ce fu Gavains, li niés Artu,
> fils le roi Lot de Loenois,
> qui fu sor un ceval norois
> [...]
> Et je feri le chevalier
> desus son escu a l'ion
> de ma lance (lines 1330–44)

> [I know his name well, and who he was. It was Gauvain, Arthur's nephew, son of King Lot of Loonois, who was on a Norse horse [...] I struck the knight with my lance underneath his shield which had a lion emblem]

While the shield is mentioned, there is no textual suggestion that this formed part of the Noir Chevalier's identification of Gauvain. Indeed, this moment is abstracted from the empirical situation, as if the identification happened *ex nihilo*. The knight can't identify Gauvain because he has never seen his face, but his telling of the tournament reveals that he has previously managed to do just this. The face seems, once again, to straddle two realms, one of plausible – whether successful or not – representation, and one of illogical a-representation.

So far I have considered how what is a brief textual encounter expands through the telling and retelling of other kinds of encounter, and suggested that this gradually accumulating network of facial moments reveals once again a kind of face that simultaneously exists in more than one mode. Let us now turn to one more encounter in this text in which a facial play seems to be at work. After his meeting with the Noir Chevalier, Gauvain leaves without revealing his name; he then arrives at the castle of the Dame de Gaudestroit (the very object of the Noir Chevalier's murderous affection). As soon as he arrives, he is recognised by a 'camberiere' who warns him to disguise his identity by pretending that he is Kay. The text labours the point that this recognition happens because the servant, named Mahot, knows Gauvain from an earlier time:

> Si tenoit une camberiere
> la damoisele en sa maison
> qui fu norie a Carlïon
> en la maison le roi Artu. (lines 1740–3)

[The lady had a chambermaid in her house, who had been brought up at King Arthur's house in Caerleon]

> Et la dame de Gaudestroit
> i ot sa mescine envoïe,
> qui bien conisoit la maisnie
> de la Table le roi Artu. (lines 1902–5)

[And the lady of Gaudestroit sent her girl, who well knew the household of King Arthur's table]

We are then told that Gauvain reveals his face, and that it is this that prompts Mahot's recognition:

> et messire Gavains son vis
> devant le porte a desarmé.
> La pucele l'a encontré
> qui ert a la porte venue.
> Messire Gavains le salue
> et ele lui delivrement.
> Bien le conoist, certainnement
> set que c'est messire Gavains. (lines 1908–15)

[and my lord Gauvain revealed his face in front of the door. The damsel met him as he came to the door. My lord Gauvain greeted her and she him. She certainly knew him well, and knew that this was my lord Gauvain]

Once she has convinced, without much difficulty, Gauvain to assume a different persona, he is introduced to the Dame de Gaudestroit, who needs a little more convincing before she accepts what she sees as a mismatch between the reputation of Kay and the prowess of the knight as told by the hunters who have accompanied him to her court. It is precisely Mahot's knowledge that ultimately convinces her, as she twice asks her servant 'conois le tu?' [do you know him?] (lines 1962, 1984). Mahot having established Gauvain's false identity and verified it to a satisfactory degree, a series of curious things occurs. Firstly, Gauvain is asked about Gauvain's health and appears to answer with a ruse that would avoid further deception: 'il est ausi sains com je sui' [he is as well as I am] (line 2057). We are reminded of Iseult's solemn promise that she had never had any man between her legs apart from King Mark and the man who has just carried her across the mud. Gauvain, however, is not under oath, and immediately tells the *dame* that he saw Gauvain only three days ago and that he is in rude health. With relative ease, therefore, the representational function of the face can be manipulated according to the unequal distribution of the initial knowledge required for the semiotic system to work properly. Mahot is able to convince her *dame* that her knowledge of Kay means that the man facing her is Kay, when of course this is exactly the same knowledge that caused the deceit in the first place. When the face is revealed, Mahot knows it and the *dame* doesn't. What happens in the encounter, however, is that Mahot deceives the lady to the point that, to all intents and purposes, the knight facing her *is* Kay. The face has taken on an additional meaning.

After accepting the new identity of the knight in front of her, the Dame de Gaudestroit shows him the elaborate trap she has laid for Gauvain, whereby he is to be decapitated. The lady explains that the ultimate goal of her endeavour is to possess Gauvain in death as she could not in life, and, for her, the ultimate achievement of this is symbolised in the image of the two bodies lying together, 'boce a boce, vis contre vis' [mouth to mouth, face against face] (line 2298). It is with this intriguing image that I will make my final points about multiple and polysemous faces in the *Vengeance Raguidel*. Not an unusual image by any means, what makes this particular face-to-face so interesting here is not only that it must necessarily happen after the head has been severed from the body, but also the fundamental deceit that causes Gauvain to be witness to his own possible death. Earlier in the text, when he has the Noir Chevalier begging for mercy, Gauvain asks him what he would do if the tables were turned. The knight tells him that he would certainly 'trencasse la teste' [cut off his head], and Gauvain responds with the comment,

'Bien adenonciés vostre feste' [you have clearly revealed your feelings] (lines 1203, 1204). In the episode with the Dame de Gaudestroit, Gauvain is also present at the announcement of his own death, except he understands it as such. What Gauvain witnesses is, of course, not only the possible manner of his death but also the kind of afterlife envisioned by the lady. While, given her apparently disturbed state of mind, it is not too great a leap to imagine the Dame de Gaudestroit having the decapitated head of Gauvain somehow reattached to his body in order to enact her grisly face-to-face, it is nonetheless remarkable that she sees the removal of Gauvain's head from his body not only as no barrier to this final reconciliation but also, in fact, as the only way to achieve it. Chopping Gauvain up in order to achieve unity seems to suggest the coexistence of two different kinds of face: on the one hand, the face (as part of the head) is part of the physical act that will kill Gauvain, and on the other hand, it is the explicit site of the symbolic unity that this severance will enable. It symbolises a unity that is at once not dependent on bodily integrity (quite the opposite, in fact) and yet is condensed into the simple and evocative formulation of one face touching another. In this sense, we can once again open up a gap between different kinds of face and claim it as a fundamentally unstable and yet hugely symbolic site. Gauvain – as Gauvain – escapes death because his face works as part of a semiotic system in which prior knowledge of both the signifier and the signified is required; Gauvain – as Kay – embodies what is understood to be Kay's place in an encounter with the Dame de Gaudestroit, and thus is privy to information precisely because this prior knowledge can be manipulated and passed on in a modified form; finally, Gauvain's physical face takes part – hypothetically – in a bizarre and incomplete melding of the embodied and the symbolic.

Conclusion

In this chapter I have used the Levinasian non-representational face as a springboard for thinking about the simultaneous coexistence of different, and sometimes contradictory, faces in a variety of textual encounters. I have tried to tease out the differences among these faces as they are presented to us in dense and complex moments, and have attempted to show how the face can straddle several modes of operation at once. Two phenomena emerge: on the one hand, distinct faces present at the same site. For instance, in the encounters I have focused on in the *Vengeance Raguidel*, a single embodied face becomes imbued with multiple meanings and functions as the narrative unfolds. On the other hand, as witnessed in *Yvain*, the moment of the face-to-face encounter appears to produce faces on sites other than the embodied face; a knight's shield, in particular, not only takes on certain facial features, such as identification, but also enacts the very same movement between functions. The shield is at once a kind of symbolic badge, but is also, in a duel, the facing, exposed face of the knight who carries it. Furthermore, I have shown how it is specifically the moment of the encounter, the moment (which might be, in fact, a series of moments or a sort of telescopic moment, as with encounter with the severed heads in the *Vengenace Raguidel*) in which a face is apprehended, that produces this multiplicity of faces.

The thinking of Emmanuel Levinas has, in my reading of it, opened up a crucial conceptual gap between two different facial modes, a gap which has allowed me to make some sense of the variety of roles that faces appear to play in these texts and to suggest that a close reading witnesses a phenomenon that works across several different planes. On the one hand, I have looked at how the face is deeply embedded in a semiotic system, whereby, with greater or lesser degrees of success, it is understood to reveal certain things about a particular person, whether that be their identity, their character, their state of mind or even their feelings. On the other hand, the face departs quite radically from this semiotic, as it takes on decidedly non-representative roles, communicating nothing but its own existence, or, indeed, forming part of a porous and highly unstable surface. Levinas's deep mistrust of the unrelentingly totalising mode of Western thought led him to propose the face as the facing surface of the Other that expresses precisely its absolute resistance to assimilation, to knowledge or to unity. For Levinas, the face is – or, rather, can be – not a key for unlocking the mysteries of the other in front of us, but the expression of its absolute inscrutability. At the same time, Levinas's thought does not pretend to do away entirely with the signifying mode he is so suspicious of. Rather, he allows for the face to operate in both non-representational and representational modes at the same time and, crucially, in the same place. In other words, the Levinasian face is but one aspect of faciality that is, and always will be, linked to the embodied, physical face.

In this chapter I make particular reference to the chivalric code of ethics that governs the moral comportment of an Arthurian knight, and I suggest that the knight's being ethically constrained makes him the ideal figure with which to examine the possibility of a second kind of facial encounter in which the identifying, representational aspect of the face plays no part. The relative exemplarity of literary knights, and of Gauvain in particular, is the topic of much discussion on the romance genre. Schmolke-Hasselmann offers a pleasingly nuanced assessment of Gauvain when she observes the persistence of his reputation as an exemplary knight despite the fact that he frequently fails to live up to it. She tells us that:

anyone who expects Gawain to bask in unqualified admiration in the works wholly devoted to him will be disappointed. His function as a model of chivalry is often very much relegated to the background.[97]

And yet, she explains, his reputation remains intact. She refers to *Le Chevalier as deus espees* (lines 3310–13) to illustrate how Arthur still considers Gauvain's *raison d'être* to be rescuing and helping maidens.[98] She goes on to note that both *Le Chevalier as deus espees* and *La Vengenace Raguidel* portray the discrepancy between Gauvain's reputation and his actions, especially in terms of the apparently limitless attraction he holds for women and the often traumatic results of the non-coincidence of belief and reality:

> they adore Gawain not as an individual but as an idealized and de-personalized stereotype, the archetypal chivalrous lover.[99]

This splitting of ideal and reality is often seen as part of the generic development of Arthurian romance beyond Chrétien. Schmolke-Hasselmann understands it as a reaction on the part of post-Chrétien authors and their public to an 'excessive and therefore rather tedious idealization of Gawain'.[100] It is, however, a phenomenon found within Chrétien's oeuvre; Yvain's fall from grace in the *Chevalier au lion* is due, of course, to what Joseph Duggan describes as 'good' characters doing 'evil' things, a narrative technique that, he claims, makes Chrétien's characterisation 'interesting'.[101] Indeed, it is this very notion of an individual grappling with expectation that forms the backbone for the entire genre of Arthurian verse romance. What my facial analysis suggests, however, is that what has otherwise been attributed to either an increasing tendency towards psychological realism, an aesthetic concern with more 'interesting' characterisation or a frustration with hyperbolic adoration might also be considered in terms of the possibility of face-to-face encounters that admit several different layers of intersubjective interaction. In other words, the multiplication both of the roles played by the embodied face and of the surfaces we can consider 'facial' allows for the coexistence of different ethical catalysts; on one hand, an Arthurian knight is constrained by chivalric obligation, while on the other he acts according to the specifics of a given situation and the particularities of the figure he faces. These two motivational forces do not,

---

[97] Schmolke-Hasselmann, p. 108. See also Busby, *Gauvain in Old French Literature*.
[98] Schmolke-Hasselmann, p. 111.
[99] Ibid., p. 112.
[100] Ibid., p. 105.
[101] Joseph J. Duggan, *The Romances of Chrétien de Troyes* (London: Yale University Press, 2001), p. 100.

therefore, necessarily belong to different ideological, aesthetic or, indeed, moral realms, but are in fact two radically different orders of perception. It is, as I hope to have demonstrated, precisely this radical difference in terms of semiotic/non-semiotic faciality that allows for the diegetic coincidence of two – or more – motivational systems without the need either to reconcile them or to consider theirs an antithetical relationship.

Finally, I would like to turn to an essay by Jean-Luc Nancy by way of concluding and drawing together the various theoretical strands of thought in this chapter. In *Noli me tangere*, Nancy examines the power of the parable and considers the mechanics behind its particular way of conveying meaning. He explains that the parable is a kind of text that signifies without being part of a semiotic system:

> Dans les noms ou dans les expressions de l'*'ivraie'*, du 'bon Samaritain', du 'fils prodigue' ou des 'ouvriers de la onzième heure', scintille un éclat singulier, résonne un supplément de signifiance absolument irréductible.[102]
>
> [In the names or expressions of the 'rye grass', the 'Good Samaritan,' the 'prodigal son,' or the 'workers of the eleventh hour,' a singular brilliant shines, a supplement of utterly irreducible significance resonates][103]

Nancy is talking specifically about a text, and he likens it to the kind of signifying power of Jesus's injunction to Mary Magdalene not to touch her. He explains that the Greek verb 'haptein', from the original Greek, 'Mè mou haptou', means not only to touch but also to hold back.[104] Nancy's point is that Jesus's prohibition rests on the fact that he is only present-in-absence, that he is already leaving and that he cannot be stopped. To further develop his point, Nancy turns to Rembrandt's rendering of what has become known as the *noli me tangere* scene, and he sees in the play of light in the painting precisely the same evocation of an irreducible, non-appropriative meaning: the artist's rendering of the spaces of light and darkness reveals 'leur tangence sans contact, leur mitoyenneté sans mélange, leur proximité sans intimité' [their tangency without contact, their commonality without mixing, their proximity without intimacy].[105] He goes on, describing this interface as:

---

[102] Jean-Luc Nancy, *Noli me tangere: essai sur la levée du corps* (Paris: Bayard, 2003), pp. 15–16.

[103] Jean-Luc Nancy, *Noli me tangere: On the Raising of the Body*, trans. by Sarah Clift, Pascale-Anne Brault, and Michael Naas (New York: Fordham University Press, 2008), pp. 7–8. All translations are from this edition.

[104] *Essai sur la levée du corps*, p. 29.

[105] *Essai sur la levée du corps* , p. 44; *On the Raising of the Body*, pp. 24–5.

> là où lumière et ombre s'échangent sans se toucher, se partagent en se repoussant – là où l'une est la vérité de l'autre sans médiation ni conversion de l'une en l'autre.
>
> [where light and shadow interact without touching each other, where they are shared out and divided, each pushing the other away – where the one is the truth of the other without mediation or without conversion of the one into the other][106]

It seems to me that Nancy here evokes and condenses so much of what I have found to be happening in the encounters I have examined in this chapter and manages effectively to broaden the scope of this kind of non-significative signification so that it is to be found both at a linguistic level and a wider textual level. Nancy evokes a kind of pointing elsewhere that is, at the same time, that which is always *right there*; a touch that cannot, and must not, make contact or impede movement, but which is also part of a certain understanding, a certain relation with the untouched that communicates some meaning. When Mary Magdalene sees Jesus's face but, unexpectedly, fails to recognise him, his face suddenly becomes precisely the essence of this double posture. In other words, Nancy draws together the text and the face, explaining how they are both endowed with the capacity to straddle conventional semiotics and non-signifying expression and thus to enact what appear on the surface to be contradictory roles:

> Le même qui n'est plus le même, la dissociation de l'aspect et de l'apparence, l'absentement du visage à même la face […]. La partance inscrite sur la présence.
>
> [The same is no longer the same; the aspect is dissociated from the appearance; the visage is made absent right in the face […] The departing is inscribed onto presence][107]

A face in a medieval text does, on the one hand, tell us something 'else' about what is supposed to be behind it. On the other hand, it, like the parable, is a singularity which is both entirely self-contained and through this, paradoxically, able to evoke an intangible otherness within itself that cannot be apprehended through any system of representation or signification. The twelfth-century Arthurian knight's face dramatises his status in between exemplar and individual and, at the same time, highlights the pre-eminence of the radically ethical nature of the face over its signifying, symbolic function.

---

[106] *Essai sur la levée du corps*, p. 45; *On the Raising of the Body*, p. 26.
[107] *Essai sur la levée du corps*, pp. 48–9; *On the Raising of the Body*, p. 28.

2

Marginal Faces

This chapter is about graphic images of faces on the manuscript page and the questions they pose, via the reader's encounter with them, for the processes of meaning formation, signification, representation and reading.[1] The faces I examined in the previous chapter were, first and foremost, verbal constructions. As such, before their diegetic or narrative functions, they played a successful role in verbal signification; to read 'vis', etc. is to refer to and recall in the mind of the reader a universally understood referent. I acknowledged this in

---

[1] From here on in I use the term 'graphic face' or Wittgenstein's 'picture-face' to refer to images of faces drawn on a surface. As the chapter develops, the specificity of the faces drawn on manuscript pages is highlighted. I also refer to these faces as 'doodles', albeit with some hesitancy. Erik Kwakkel is well-known for publicising, notably via his blog, Tumblr and Twitter account, 'doodles' in medieval manuscripts ostensibly produced by bored or mischievous scribes. See <https://medievalbooks.nl/> [accessed 15 May 2015]; <http://erikkwakkel.tumblr.com/> [accessed 15 May 2015]; and for an example of broader interest in these doodles, see Simon Usborne, 'Medieval Doodles Prove that it's Goode to Scribble in ye Margins', *The Independent*, 9 December 2014 <http://www.independent.co.uk/arts-entertainment/books/news/medieval-doodles-prove-that-its-goode-to-scribble-in-ye-margins-9774982.html> [accessed 2 May 2015]. My slight hesitancy in using the term 'doodle' comes from its inflection of frivolity and superfluity. Writing about doodles in a very different context (notarial doodles from colonial Cuzco), Carolyn Dean suggests avoiding the inference of meaninglessness by discarding the term 'doodle' in favour of 'non-prescribed marking' (Carolyn Dean, 'Beyond Prescription: Notarial Doodles and Other Marks', *Word & Image*, 25 (2009), 293–316 (pp. 293–4)). Although its descriptive neutrality is attractive, the term is nonetheless invested in a hierarchy of the page that does not fit the context of my work, and so I will continue to use the usefully brief 'doodle'. Recent scholarship across a number of disciplines has reclaimed the value of the doodle, but seems to see it exclusively as a tool for accessing certain facets of the psychology of the doodler, whereas this chapter looks at the effect of the doodles on the reader. For examples of the variety of work on the importance of the doodle, see the *Beckett and the Phenomenology of Doodles* project at the University of Reading (2006–9) <https://www.reading.ac.uk/ftt/research/ftt-beckettdoodles.aspx> [accessed 5 May 2015]; the *Meaningful Scribbles: Children's Drawings as Psychological Instruments 1880–1950* project at the Max Planck Institute for the History of Science <https://www.mpiwg-berlin.mpg.de/en/research/projects/deptiii_wittmann_meaningful_scribbles> [accessed 5 May 2015]; Jessica Stevenson Stewart, 'Toward a Hermeneutics of Doodling in the Era of Folly', *Word & Image*, 29 (2013), 409–27.

my previous chapter, although it was not the primary object of investigation. In this chapter, however, I want to look at the concept and image of the face under a higher degree of magnification, and delve further into its particular role within signification. The faces I look at here are considered against the backdrop of their perceived function as an image of an image, insofar as the assumption being interrogated in this book is that the primary, conventional role of the face both in literature and in society is to act as an external image or representation of internal and, in this model, pre-existing features.

The argument put forward in this chapter is that the face images found in the margins of a selection of manuscripts are not just images of faces but are faces themselves. In making this point, I argue for a collapse of the hierarchy of faciality that puts the physiological face in prime position, and which thus subordinates all other kinds of face as mimetic reproductions. In the previous chapter, I used a close reading of Arthurian duel scenes to argue, with the aid of Emmanuel Levinas, that 'face' need not only be used in reference to a surface–depth system, whereby the visible exterior (the face) works to reveal something about the qualities of a hitherto invisible interior. With Levinas's understanding that the face is not exclusively concerned with accessing interior meaning, it became possible instead to see emerge in the texts in question a series of surfaces that expressed the presence of a subjectivity (in this case, a knight) without being invested in gathering knowledge about that subjectivity. Consequently, 'face' came to mean something that not only refused to reproduce the priority of the interior over the exterior, but also something that could be divorced from the physiological face. If that which indicates the presence of a knight, and which brings forth the ethical obligations that surround that presence, is his helmet or, indeed, his shield, then those are the surfaces that become the face of that knight.

In this chapter, the question of interiority and faciality is again addressed, this time in terms of graphic marks. Where in the previous chapter the focus was the role of the face in the surface–depth dynamic of the individual in medieval narrative, here I look specifically at narrative's material support and foreground the act of coming into contact with disembodied faces both on the surface of the manuscript page and, in the cases under investigation here, intertwined with, or at the very least attached to, the shape of the letters on that page. The contention that these faces are, indeed, faces in their own right and not just representations of other faces is based primarily on the observation that they explicitly foreclose all avenues down which a reader might travel in order to reach the implied subjectivity or presence. Furthermore, this combines with the peculiar power of the graphic face to evoke in the viewer many of the same sensations as if apprehending the physiological face of a human being. To put this into the context of the argument of the whole book, the graphic face exhibits a kind of primary faciality, inasmuch as it is a face with no human referent; a face with no interior. Again, we find that the medieval textual face troubles the connection between faciality and interiority, and poses fundamental questions for the modern viewer/reader concerning the priority of interiority in the Middle Ages. The argument of this book is that the medieval textual face did not promulgate this priority of interiority as much as it did its illusion; the modern viewer/reader thus comes up against faces that enact complex and dynamic relationships between interior and exterior, and that ultimately prioritise neither. In the case of the graphic faces, then, this relationship takes the form of a powerfully implied interiority that is consistently and explicitly shown to be impossible. In the first instance, I shall outline the material situation of the faces in question. I shall then go on to consider, before moving beyond, the major medieval tradition of the *sainte face* in order to evoke some of the ways in which the face on the manuscript page could be employed at once in the service of both pictorial representation and direct communion between the reader and an absent, and in these cases divine, presence. Next I shall move on to think about the particular relation between the picture-faces, to borrow Wittgenstein's term, and the letters to which they are attached. This section will discuss the distinction between pictorial representation and alphabetic letters, and suggest that the phenomenon of the letter-face works again to challenge an implicit hierarchy between the two. Engaging with the notion that the graphic face does not draw all its affective and communicative power from representing something else, I claim that the letter-face is not most productively considered in terms of an attempt to bring forth an antecedent *animus*. Instead, it is posited that the letters in question have always had a face; a chronological detail that nonetheless allows us to think of the faces independently from a living subject – whether divine or human. Finally, I investigate the faces in terms of the encounter with the reader/viewer.[2] I begin from Silvan Tomkins's affect theory, the premise of which is that the human face is not a secondary manifestation of primary inner feelings of a given subject, but that it is the first site of reaction.[3] Radically reversing the received wisdom that the appearance of the face is the effect of emotional causes, Tomkins's formulation offers a way of conceiving of the face before thinking about a subjectivity behind or before it. Ultimately, the failure of Tomkins's formulation to account entirely for the face doodles serves to highlight some of the irreducible paradoxes of their situation. Lacan then provides a way of thinking about the faces not as subjectivities themselves but as objects that have a disturbing potential when apprehended by the reader. Drawing on the Lacanian notions of the

[2] For brevity's sake, from now on I shall use these terms interchangeably unless otherwise indicated.
[3] Tomkins, 'The Phantasy Behind the Face'.

letter and, to a lesser extent, the gaze, I discuss how the doodles operate as hinges between the symbolic and real orders.[4] Lacanian thinking thus permits the move from observations about the material and representational status of the faces to a discussion of the implications of their unique position. Bruce Fink's description of the Lacanian letter may well be applied to the faciality of the face doodle: it 'seems to lie somewhere between the signifier and its microstructure (which is materialized or represented by type or printed characters without being equated with them)'.[5] I also make use of Žižek's discussion of the Lacanian letter in *Enjoy Your Symptom!* in order to consider how the face doodle works with reference both to the 'materialized agency of the *signifier*' and 'an *object* in the strict sense of materialized enjoyment – the stain, the uncanny excess'.[6]

The face doodle is, like the Lacanian letter, heavily engaged in symbolism (and the symbolic order), but explicitly refuses to be fully subordinated into it. The argument of this chapter can be crudely summarised by the following statement: the face images disrupt the reading experience by forcing the reader to acknowledge the limitations of pictorial and, by extension, graphic representation. Indeed, these faces are situated at the delicate intersection between representation (they resemble other faces we have seen) and primary expression (they are explicitly isolated from any causal subjectivity).

Sources

This chapter arose from the experience of accidentally discovering a series of tiny drawings of faces in the margins of two fourteenth-century manuscripts that each contain different versions of the Life and Miracles of Saint Louis.[7] No 'reason' for their existence was found that seemed to match the strangeness of the encounter with these faces. The most probable explanation – that they are *nota bene* marks[8] – is inadequate in the face of the profundity of the questions

---

[4] As outlined in Lacan, 'Le séminaire sur "La Lettre volée"', in *Écrits*, pp. 11–61 and *Les Quatre concepts*. See also the entries for 'Gaze' and 'Letter' in Evans's *Introductory Dictionary*, pp. 73–4, 102–3.

[5] Bruce Fink, *Lacan to the Letter: Reading 'Écrits' Closely* (Minneapolis: University of Minnesota Press, 2004), p. 79.

[6] Slavoj Žižek, *Enjoy Your Symptom: Jacques Lacan in Hollywood and Out*, 2nd edn (Abingdon: Routledge, 2008), p. 27 (original emphasis).

[7] Paris, Bibliothèque nationale de France (BnF), MS fonds français 5716 (hereafter BnF fr. 5716) and Paris, Bibliothèque nationale de France (BnF), MS fonds français 13568 (hereafter BnF fr. 13568).

[8] The User Guide in the second volume of the *Index of Images* series specifically explains that 'profile heads and other such representations along the edge of a text probably serve a nota bene function': *An Index of Images in English Manuscripts: From the Time*

provoked by these images, and, importantly, the dearth of answers. Firstly, none of the faces presents any certain expression of a readable emotion: while one appears to be on the verge of a frown (see Fig. 1's emphatically arched eyebrows and narrowed eyes), all are at the very least inscrutable. Secondly, they bear little to no relation to the text in an illustrative capacity. The only exception is that the face in Fig. 1 is attached to the text of Miracle XXIX (in BnF fr. 5716), which tells of a priest suddenly afflicted by a facial growth. It may well be that this face is used to highlight the text to which it is attached: 'il eust illec eu aucune chose de mal ou denfleure de quoy il furent adoncques forment merueillez' [there was no sign of disease or swelling, at which they all marvelled], and that the strange, protruding chin is a way of making a connection with the miracle in question. These will, however, remain hypotheses: the question of the faces' purpose and relation to the text is nonetheless open. The final key question raised in the mind of the modern reader is this: whom do these faces represent or portray? A question that may well be answerable in a different context remains out of reach in the case of the images under investigation here.[9] Having established that any historical, fictional or otherwise locatable individual represented by these faces is at most permanently out of reach, and in all likelihood never existed, a series of secondary questions arises. Since each of the faces is in profile, we ask ourselves: what are they looking at? Indeed, the faces are all looking away from the text to which they are attached, making the question even more pertinent; there is no clear object for their gaze. In Jennifer Thompson's doctoral thesis on English animated initials, she describes one face that

---

of Chaucer to Henry VII, c.1380–c.1509, ed. by Kathleen Scott (Turnhout: Harvey Miller, 2000–), II: Lynda Dennison and others, *The Bodleian Library, Oxford: MSS Dodsworth-Marshall* (2001), p. 20 (original emphasis).

[9] Aside from the possibility that the faces illustrate the content of the text, marginal faces are sometimes scribal self-portraits. Lilian M. C. Randall, for instance, has written on the emerging possibilities for scribal self-portraiture in frontal heads in later (fifteenth-century) manuscripts from Paris and the Netherlands. Although she calls 'unlikely' the possibility of reference to an individual, she nonetheless points out an increasing 'interest in artistic identity' and 'elements of realism'. Lilian M. C. Randall, 'Frontal Heads in the Borders of Parisian and South Netherlandish Books of Hours, ca. 1415–60', in *Tributes to Jonathan J. G. Alexander: The Making and Meaning of Illuminated Medieval and Renaissance Manuscripts, Art and Architecture*, ed. by Susan L'Engle and Gerald B. Guest (London: Harvey Miller, 2006), pp. 249–68 (pp. 255–6). Michael Camille, on the other hand, contends that this kind of self-representation in fact occurred from the twelfth century and became less and less frequent with the increasing professionalisation of the manuscript trade. Michael Camille, *Image on the Edge: The Margins of Medieval Art* (Cambridge, MA: Harvard University Press 1992), p. 149. Whether or not it is historically plausible that the manuscripts in question in this chapter might contain scribal self-portraits, the marginal faces therein are, at the very least, too numerous to maintain this as a possibility.

Fig. 1. Bibliothèque nationale de France
(BnF fr. 5716 p. 461 (detail)

resembles those under consideration here. The face in question is found inside a decorated initial, larger and more prominent than mine, but is of a similar level of detail and also apparently anonymous. But Thompson's figure is, by contrast, looking at the text, prompting her to posit a kind of identification between reader and image, and therefore to observe: 'the human profile inside the minor letter invites the reader to look at the text'.[10] However, the striking aspect of this in the context of this book is that the question of what the faces are looking at is asked despite the knowledge that there is no subject behind them. To take this to its logical conclusion, we might say that it is the drawings themselves who are looking.

Having come across the faces in the Louis manuscripts by accident, it was then necessary to undertake to seek more out. Once again, the significance of questions of production and intention paled in comparison with the questions raised by the experience of finding these images. Since these faces are so sporadically catalogued, a more or less random search of digitised French-language manuscripts from a given period was no more time-consuming and no less systematic than searching image databases or catalogues.[11] Paris, BnF fr.

---

[10] Jennifer A. Thompson, 'Reading in the Painted Letter: Human Heads in Twelfth-Century English Initials' (unpublished doctoral thesis, University of St Andrews, 2000), p. 111.

[11] The most extensive and detailed catalogue of the kind of faces examined in this chapter is to be found in the *Index of Images* series (see note 8, above). François Avril and Marie-Thérèse Gousset also catalogue the faces found in BnF fr. 343: François Avril, Marie-Thérèse Gousset with Jean-Pierre Aniel, *Manuscrits enluminés d'origine italienne: xive siècle, Lombardie-Ligurie* (Paris: Bibliothèque nationale de France, 2005), p. 71.

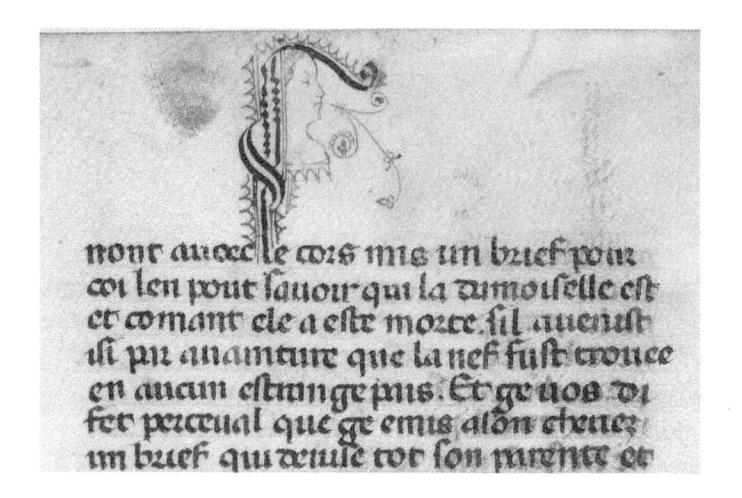

Fig. 2. BnF fr. 343 fol. 60r (detail)

343 yielded an even more extensive series of marginal faces, again all attached to letters, but showing a variety of both profile and frontal presentation. The same questions arose in relation to the faces in this manuscript, all answered with the same lack of certainty. Again, however, the reader is confronted with what appears to be a series of faces either gazing at an unknown object or, perhaps more alarmingly, gazing directly out of the page (see Figs 2 through 5 for examples of both). It is from the attempt to square the circle of faces with no subjects that the argument of this chapter arose. Being looked at by an image that we know not to be a person is an experience that raises profound questions about the nature of that image. Indeed, the specific question that is raised in the case of the manuscript drawings is: what is a face? Consequently, we must also ask: can a face exist without a subject behind it? If so, what is the status of the face if it is not a surface through which we might access a greater depth?

The Louis manuscripts are both dated to the early fourteenth century and contain different versions of the story of Louis's life. Both are generally accepted to be the work of the same scribe and the same illuminator.[12] Both

---

This manuscript was also included as part of the *Medieval Francophone Literary Culture Outside France* project (2011–15) and, as such, a description can be found in the project's online database: <http://www.medievalfrancophone.ac.uk/browse/mss/222/manuscript.html> [accessed 20 September 2016]. The marginal faces are not mentioned here.

[12] Jean de Joinville, *Vie de saint Louis*, ed. by Jacques Monfrin, 2nd ed (Paris: Classiques Garnier, 1998), p. xciv; Guillaume de Saint-Pathus, *Les Miracles de saint Louis*, ed. by

Fig. 3. BnF fr. 343 fol. 60v (detail)   Fig. 4. BnF fr. 343 fol. 60v (detail)

Fig. 5. BnF fr. 343 fol. 78v (detail)

are dated to c. 1330–40, neither manuscript contains any other text and each is a complete version of the one it reproduces.[13] BnF fr. 5716 contains what is thought to be a French translation of an original Latin *Vie et miracles de Saint Louis* by the Franciscan cleric, Guillaume de Saint-Pathus; scenes from both sections are illustrated, and the manuscript contains some marginal decoration, mainly in the form of foliage, with occasional figures and heads, mostly but not exclusively human, and several decorated initials. BnF fr.

Percival B. Fay (Paris: Champion, 1931), p. v; Guillaume de Saint-Pathus, *Vie de saint Louis*, ed. by Henri-François Delaborde (Paris: Picard, 1899), p. xix; Richard H. Rouse and Mary A. Rouse, *Manuscripts and Their Makers: Commercial Book Producers in Medieval Paris, 1200–1500*, 2 vols (Turnhout: Harvey Miller, 2000), II, p. 94; Bibliothèque nationale de France catalogue, Gallicalabs <http://gallicalabs.bnf.fr/ark:/12148/btv1b8447303m/f2.item> [accessed 5 March 2015].

[13] Joinville, *Vie de saint Louis*, ed. by Monfrin, p. xciv.

13568 contains a very different, and much more widely circulated in modern times (due to its perceived historical importance), version of Louis's life as recorded by his contemporary, the knight Jean de Joinville. This *vie* takes the form of a highly personal memoir, but is nonetheless not devoid of the obvious intention to valorise and disseminate the king's saintly nature and good works. Joinville's work focuses heavily on the crusade of 1248, in which the king and the knight-chronicler both participated and during which they shared many critical experiences. Joinville weaves together a broadly chronological narrative of events with a more clearly subjective and propagandist account of King Louis's deeds and judgements in the midst of those events. This manuscript is much more sparsely illustrated and decorated than BnF fr. 5716, containing only two illustrations, and marginal decoration on the same two pages. Both manuscripts have throughout swirling penwork originating from letter forms and splaying out into the margins (Fig. 6). We also find in each manuscript elongated ascenders and descenders, again pushing out from the text into the margins. Incorporated into some of these elongated and distorted letter shapes, in both manuscripts, are what appear to be human faces. In the 665 pages of BnF 5716, three such faces occur: see Figs 1, 7 and 8. BnF 13568 has 391 pages, in which we find two clearly human heads (Figs 9 and 10) and one of more ambiguous species (Fig. 11). I will be concentrating my analysis on the human faces. These faces operate in a space that seems to disrupt the distinction between the margins and the centre of a manuscript page; they are integrated into the text, stretch out beyond the space of the column, perform no discernible illustrative function and yet clearly are not part of the decorative scheme, which comprises mainly foliage and inked patterns.[14]

BnF fr. 343 is a later fourteenth-century (Avril and Gousset date it to c. 1380–85)[15] Italian manuscript that contains a set of post-Vulgate texts: the *Queste del Saint Graal*, the *Mort Artu* and a section of the prose *Tristan*. The manuscript contains frequent, and often unfinished, large out-of-frame illustrations (a typical feature of Italian manuscripts of this period). A small number of decorated and flourished initials (as well as blank spaces) comprise the main decorative scheme. The faces in this manuscript are also, as in the Louis manuscripts, all attached to letters in the main body of the text, but their relation is more tangential; they appear as part of larger, more elaborate extensions to the letter forms, often appearing at the end of a scrolled ascender or descender, and therefore exhibit a different relation to the text than the

---

[14] Camille's work on manuscript margins explored the important point that the margins are not just for the 'other' and that attention must be paid as much to the edge as to the centre. The basis for my chapter, however, is that these faces present a profound challenge to any distinction between margin and centre. See in particular Camille, *Image on the Edge*.
[15] Avril and Gousset, p. 66.

Figure 6. BnF fr. 5716, p. 348 (detail)

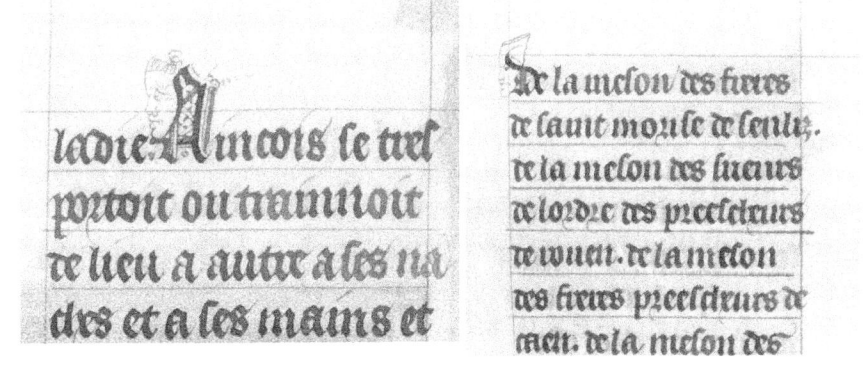

Figure 7. BnF fr. 5716 p. 350 (detail)   Figure 8. BnF fr. 5716 p. 157 (detail)

more closely integrated faces in the Louis manuscripts. The faces in the *Queste* manuscript are also not only more numerous but more concentrated: seventeen such images appear within the manuscript's comparatively few 112 folios.[16] There are eleven frontal faces and six in profile, and each of these

---

[16] A possible eighteenth face is found on fol. 86v; attached to the top of a face in profile is a decorated roundel containing a small circle within which is a smaller, pupil-like black dot. The shape contains no other facial features, but is just facial enough to provoke the question: is this a face? The proximity to what is undeniably a face provokes a subsequent enquiry: if not, why not? I will comment more on this semi-face below. See fig. 15. I have counted among the total two frontal heads situated at the very top of their pages and which

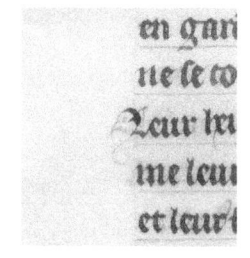

Figure 9. BnF fr. 13568 p. 354 (detail)

Figure 10. BnF fr. 13568 p. 361 (detail)

Figure 11. BnF fr. 13568, p. 359 (detail)

faces is reproduced in detail in Figs 2 through 5 and 12 through 23 (Fig. 21 contains two faces).

As noted above, the faces that are the subject of this chapter occupy ill-defined space, in terms of both the physical space on the manuscript page and their figural space within the manuscripts' communicative and decorative scheme. These faces are marginal but are attached to, and in one instance enclosed by, letters of the text (see Fig. 9).[17] They are not part of initials (although the face in Fig. 8 is attached to a highlighted letter) and cannot properly be considered to illustrate the text in any conventional sense of the term. Equally, they do not appear to fulfil the function of commentary or gloss that is often assigned to marginalia. At the same time, however, they do not appear to belong to the kind of manuscript image the purpose of which is less to illustrate meaning than to provoke an emotional response from the reader, and in certain cases, as Laura Thompson put it in her doctoral thesis on animated initials, to 'provide the audience with a means of apprehending the Godhead'.[18] It is, nonetheless, the tradition of the *sainte face* to which I now turn, in order to consider an important way in which the image of a face on a manuscript has the potential to operate in two modes: as a pictorial

---

have been cropped at some point in the binding process. I have not, however, included in my discussion a series of doodles of faces that appear on the final three blank pages; not only is determining their provenance beyond my expertise, but their complete abstraction from the text places them outside the remit of a discussion of the face as a graphic mark in the context of a populated manuscript page.

[17] On the last but one and last but two folios of BnF fr. 343 (fols. 113r and 113v; the text having ended on fol. 112v) we find a series of scribblings and doodles, among which are several profile faces. Whether these are contemporaneous or not with the faces in the main body of the text, I have chosen to exclude them from my analysis on the grounds that they bear no visual relation to the text. The productive gap between physical proximity and signifying difference or distance is thus not at issue here.

[18] Thompson, p. 20.

representation of a particular aspect of a transcendent divine, on the one hand, and as a facilitator of direct communion between the reader and that transcendence, on the other.

The Picture-face and the *sainte face*

In trying to articulate the particular force of these doodles it is helpful to consider a tradition which is built upon the – sometimes conflicted – purpose of materially depicting and engaging with the transcendent; it is precisely the image of the face that is most often chosen to perform this task. The face is famously the image used in St Paul's first letter to the Corinthians to evoke direct and enlightened communion with God: 'For now we see through a glass, darkly; but then face to face: now I know in part; but then shall I know even as also I am known.'[19] Indeed, the face is singled out as an index of health and, by extension, Louis's sanctity in the prologue to Guillaume's *vie et miracles*: 'Et a ceus qui estoient si courbes que il touchoient a bien pou la terre de leur visages il [Louis] a secouru et les a restablis a pleinne santé, leur faces en haut esdreciees' [And those who were so hunched that their faces practically touched the ground, Louis saved them and restored them to full health, raising their faces up once again].[20] To what extent, however, are these faces metaphorical? The tradition of the *sainte face* draws precisely on the possibility that the face can both represent and *be*; the image of Christ's face both represents him and *is* him. While certainly this is a phenomenon rooted in the metaphysical possibilities of Christianity, it is also, I argue, in part based on the particular attributes of the face as a visual phenomenon.

As discussed in the Introduction to this book, human perception is especially attuned to recognising visual patterns that resemble that of the human face. An important consequence of this is the narrowing of the gap, in terms of both effect and affect, between the human face and its graphic representations. As Wittgenstein explains,

> In some respects I stand towards [the picture-face] as I do towards a human face. I can study its expression, can react to it as to the expression of the human face. A child can talk to picture-men or picture-animals, can treat them as it treats dolls.[21]

---

[19] 1 Corinthians 13. 12.
[20] Guillaume de Saint-Pathus, *Les Miracles de Saint Louis*, ed. by Fay, p. 1. Translations are my own.
[21] Ludwig Wittgenstein, *Philosophical Investigations*, trans. by G. E. M. Anscombe, 2nd edn (Oxford: Blackwell, 1958; repr. 2000), p. 194ᵉ.

The picture-face, then, need not resemble a physiological face as much as, for instance, a picture-sword need resemble a sword, in order to produce an analogous reaction in the viewer. Paradoxically, it is this rapprochement between the image and its referent, in the case of the face, which allows for their radical separation: the picture-face can do everything a face does. Wittgenstein echoes scientific observations that humans' sensitivity to facial patterns is not limited to visual phenomena that closely resemble the detail of a particular face, but is also triggered by patterns that only loosely resemble faces.[22] He goes on to articulate the difference between seeing and knowing, both of which occur in the moment of perception. Wittgenstein explains, in particular, that our knowledge that our perception at a given moment might not be the same as that in a different moment (he gives the example of the famous illusion of the duck-rabbit; at one moment it appears to be a duck, at another a rabbit) does not alter that perception.[23] To transpose this onto the picture-face, our knowledge that it is not a physiological face exists alongside and does not temper our perception of it as a face nonetheless.[24]

The face image, then, is inherently capable of effects on the viewer that would otherwise require a degree of illusion; illusion that is conventionally associated with a high degree of visual resemblance. The *sainte face* is a useful case study. Georges Didi-Huberman noted in 1996 that when modern art historians talk about the *sainte face*, they do so in terms of what it represents rather than what it is.[25] He suggests that we are better able to

---

[22] See in particular Perrett, pp. 50–5. In discussing the relationship between art and illusion, Gombrich makes the same point about the peculiarity of the face image: 'whenever anything remotely facelike enters our field of vision, we are alerted and respond'. E. H. Gombrich, *Art and Illusion: A Study in the Psychology of Pictorial Representation* (New York: Pantheon, 1960), p. 103.

[23] Wittgenstein, p. 195^e.

[24] A curious parallel to this phenomenon is exhibited in the context of face recognition. While not directly pertinent to my argument, inasmuch as it is specifically to do with the affective response to known faces, it is nonetheless useful to note this slightly different iteration of the gap between cognitive response and affective response, specifically in face perception: in cases of the Capgras delusion, patients believe a loved one to be an almost identical imposter. While the cognitive aspect of the face-recognition mechanism functions perfectly well, and the patient recognises that the 'imposter' looks identical to the person in question, the patient nonetheless does not experience the *feeling* that usually accompanies recognition of that person. See Perrett, pp. 40–1. Conversely, patients suffering from prosopagnosia are unable to recognise familiar faces cognitively, but may exhibit the affective response that is missing in the former syndrome. See Graham Hole and Victoria Bourne, *Face Processing: Psychological, Neuropsychological, and Applied Perspectives* (Oxford: Oxford University Press, 2010), pp. 176–7.

[25] Georges Didi-Huberman, 'Face, proche, lointain: l'empreinte du visage et le lieu pour apparaître', in *The Holy Face and the Paradox of Representation*, ed. by Herbert L. Kessler and Gerhard Wolf, Villa Spelman Colloquia, 6 (Bologna: Nuova Alfa, 1998), pp. 95–108 (p. 95). Translations are my own.

approach the truth of the image of Christ's face if we try to do so in terms of its being '*plus qu'une image*' [more than an image]; in other words, if we acknowledge its affective force alongside its representative capacities.[26] The peculiar power of these holy images resides in the productive tension between what they bring towards the viewer and what they keep at a distance: the divine presence-in-absence. For Didi-Huberman, 'le pouvoir facial, frontal et presque tactile de l'objet, s'identifie avec son retrait dans un lointain visuellement agencé' [the facial, frontal and almost tactile power of the object is coupled with its retreat into a distance that is visually constructed].[27] In a sense this recalls Levinasian faciality, inasmuch as the *sainte face* expresses a presence of which it nonetheless refuses to grant knowledge. In this specifically religious context, however, the face image does offer the viewer communion with the divine; access, that is, to something beyond the face. The *sainte face* thus offers a model for a facial image that, thanks to its divine origin, allows the apprehension of something beyond itself via a non-semiotic route.[28]

In a discussion of religious idols, Jean-Luc Marion evokes a similar kind of power, but, in discussing explicitly human-made images, locates a compelling tension between the image and its divine referent.[29] He explains that humans first experience the divine and then, through idols, fashion a face for it.[30] Marion thus characterises the idol as a mirror, inasmuch as it is both restrictive and revelatory: it reveals the divine, but also fixes it within the limits of human experience, which is necessarily mundane.[31] In these two schemes, then, the power of the facial image is located in the divine, whether or not it is mediated by human hands. The Holy Face gives the human viewer access to the divine within the constraints of the senses; it is a 'quasi-sujet', inasmuch as it is an image fixed in the mundane world that has its origins in the divine.[32] For Marion, the idol comes from the divine but is channelled, distorted and restricted through the human senses.

The face doodles that are the subject of this chapter are not divine images, but they do occupy a similar position in between the human viewer and a

---

[26] Ibid., p. 99 (original emphasis).

[27] Ibid., p. 106.

[28] The *sainte face* belongs to the *acheiropoieta*, a class of images understood to have been created without human hands. That is, while they point the human viewer in the direction of the divine, they are also directly *from* the divine and have come to our attention without human intervention.

[29] Jean-Luc Marion, *L'Idole et la distance: cinq études* (Paris: Grasset & Fasquelle, 1977), pp. 21–38.

[30] Ibid., p. 23.

[31] Ibid., pp. 23–5.

[32] Didi-Huberman, p. 100.

'beyond' that is evoked but which cannot quite be reached, and, as such, it is useful to consider them in relation to divine images. Kristeva suggests that images of faces have always been unique in the visual register, since they straddle the modes of icon and mimesis.[33] In Western representation, she argues, two functions are distilled and concentrated in the image of the face: on the one hand, it is an icon, offering communion with the otherwise invisible; on the other hand, it is a figure, and works by evoking resemblance across history. In its capacity as icon, the face image offers a passage between the visible and the invisible modes: 'On comprend qu'elle ne donne pas à voir un référent extérieur, mais se destine à accommoder un regard.' [It is understood that it does not offer a view of an exterior referent, but is meant to accommodate viewing.][34] In its figural capacity, however, while there is still a gap between the image and its 'au-delà', 'cet au-delà prend un aspect substantiel et historique' [that beyond takes on a historical, material aspect].[35] Where the divine is situated behind the kind of facial images discussed by Didi-Huberman, Marion and Kristeva, a different, and differently, ineffable quality seems to sit behind the face doodles. Deleuze's distinction between the figurative and the Figure is useful here: writing on the faces painted by Francis Bacon, Deleuze sees Bacon's faces as departing from the figurative (which he equates with representation) and, instead, as Figures that work through sensation rather than cognition.[36] For Deleuze, the implications are significant: Bacon's faces offer a desirable escape from the restrictions of representation. At the same time, Deleuze acknowledges that the religious element of these images also works towards liberating them from figuration.[37] Here, then, is a formulation of the graphic face that incorporates the non-representational possibilities of imagery that is imbued with the religious but which does not point to, or come from, the divine.

These ways of thinking about the face as a unique visual mark bear a useful relation to the way the face doodles work in the Louis and *Queste* manuscripts and thus go some way towards building up a picture of the power of an encounter with these symbolically inscrutable and yet highly evocative pictures. The contention is not that any of them are religious images; rather, it is that the unknowability of either their purpose or their referents works alongside the fact that they are also mimetic and representative images. The face doodles, to cite Kristeva's formulation, are both mimetic and iconic,

---

[33] Julia Kristeva, *Visions capitales* (Paris: Réunion des musées nationaux, 1998).
[34] Ibid., p. 61; *The Severed Head: Capital Visions*, trans. by Jody Gladding (New York: Columbia University Press, 2012), p. 53.
[35] *Visions capitales*, p. 65; *The Severed Head*, p.59.
[36] Gilles Deleuze, *Francis Bacon: logique de la sensation* (Paris: Seuil, 2002), p. 12.
[37] Ibid., p. 19.

both bodily and spiritual. The corporeal aspect of the face image is linked to the materiality of the manuscript page by Kathryn Rudy, who observes physical evidence that suggests that, in certain cases, a manuscript can be, and has been, used as 'a proxy for the body of Christ'.[38] Priests' missals and personal prayer books sometimes show physical traces of kissing and rubbing, and Rudy observes that the images that bear witness to the greatest amount of devotion, measured via physical touching, are those of the face and body of Christ; the manuscript image thus, for Rudy, approaches the holy relic in its function.[39] My point is that the face image in a religious context has a particular power that straddles that of the bodily relic and the representational, two-dimensional image. Stephen Jaeger makes a distinction between the icon and the relic on the grounds that the former works through representation and the latter as a memento.[40] It is the icon, and not the relic, which possesses charisma: what Jaeger defines as a 'human presence' in a work of art, which can sometimes be so great 'that it often presents itself as godlike'.[41] Jaeger aligns the face with this charismatic power, explaining that a face image has the ability to communicate 'emotionality' once it is 'freed from semiotic function'.[42] Face doodles in manuscripts possess precisely this kind of charisma: they communicate the presence of the human, as if they 'had absorbed a living human being'.[43] Where Jaeger aligns the face specifically with the icon, however, Rudy's observations show that there is also something of the power of the relic in the face image on a manuscript page. Indeed, it is the physical presence of precisely an absent body that constitutes the power of the face image; a presence-in-absence that is evoked, albeit in different ways, by both the icon and the relic. Where, in a religious context, the absent presence is divine, or, in Jaeger's formulation, an 'individual emotionality', the face images we encounter in the three manuscripts under investigation evoke an absent presence that might be termed an 'abstract emotionality'. Linked neither to the divine nor to an individual or even an individuality, the face doodles are as inscrutable as they are arresting; this leads to the possible conclusion that they are not images of faces but, rather, faces in the first degree, exhibiting an empty and yet powerful referentiality.

[38] Kathryn M. Rudy, 'Kissing Images, Unfurling Rolls, Measuring Wounds, Sewing Badges and Carrying Talismans: Considering Some Harley Manuscripts through the Physical Rituals They Reveal', *Electronic British Library Journal*, 2011, article 5 <http://www.bl.uk/eblj/2011articles/article5.html> [accessed 30 January 2015], p. 1.

[39] Ibid., pp. 21, 30.

[40] C. Stephen Jaeger, *Enchantment: On Charisma and the Sublime in the Arts of the West* (Philadelphia: University of Pennsylvania Press, 2012), p. 132.

[41] Ibid., p. 36.

[42] Ibid., p. 110.

[43] Ibid., p. 29.

Letter-faces

In a study of the history of medieval writing and of the communicative and affective potential it possesses (especially in relation to print), Laura Kendrick demonstrates that manuscript evidence shows a keen desire on the part of the culture in which the manuscripts were produced to reinscribe the sense of the living – whether human or divine – into alphabetic writing.[44] Kendrick's point is to show that the opposition between writing and drawing is not as clear cut in the medieval period as it appears in modern print contexts. She offers a timeline whereby pictographic writing gradually became 'denatured' as it evolved into the arbitrary sign system of alphabetic writing.[45] In between this development and the advent of print in the fifteenth century, Kendrick posits a deliberate effort to reinstate into the empty signs the power they had lost:

> The pictorial design of the medieval letter, far from being superfluous decoration, can be an attempt to de-sign it, to reintegrate into alphabetic writing the trace of physical presence – the body – that alphabetic writing has censored and repressed in its replacement both of earlier kinds of pictographic writing and of the speaking, gesturing human body.[46]

Her argument is convincing and compelling: where writing and drawing physically merge into one another, the distinction is indeed both artificial and, as Kendrick points out, anachronistic. Equally, she demonstrates, as I have attempted to above, that the force of religious bodily imagery is not solely derived from the particular circumstances of Christian belief but is also in large part due to the inherent properties of such images; in particular, the picture-face. Indeed, much of what I have tried to show in the case of the Louis and *Queste* face doodles is echoed in Kendrick's framing of her argument with the acknowledgement of animistic, magical, emotional and affective power of imagery: 'all human beings, whether they are willing to admit it or are conscious of it or not, project life upon figures that resemble living forms'.[47] Kendrick also frames her argument in opposition to Derrida's assertion that Western thought and culture has, historically, denigrated alphabetic writing in favour of the pre-eminence of speech.[48] She explains that, in order to reach this conclusion, Derrida has had to wilfully ignore much of the history of writing that, in fact, reveals a

---

[44] Laura Kendrick, *Animating the Letter: The Figurative Embodiment of Writing from Late Antiquity to the Renaissance* (Columbus: Ohio State University Press, 1999).
[45] Ibid., p. 32.
[46] Ibid., p. 35.
[47] Ibid., p. 8.
[48] Ibid., pp. 14, 21.

connection between alphabetic writing and the 'presence-bearing trace' of which Derrida claimed this writing had been stripped.[49]

An important point is raised by this assertion, however: Kendrick's argument for the conscious *re*animation of the alphabetic letter form by medieval scribes is, as she points out, based on the arbitrariness of the letter form as sign. It is only by adding pictographic elements to those letter forms that they become animated. I don't disagree with Kendrick's argument, but I do suggest that it is not as distinct from Derrida's as she suggests: not only historically but also conceptually, she implies that alphabetic writing *in itself* is indeed a series of empty signs; only by filling them with other signs that work mimetically do they take on supplementary meaning. Derrida's target, and the notion that so much of his deconstructionist work tries to move beyond, is not so much the disingenuous positioning of writing at a further remove from an originary self-presence than speech but, rather, the obsession with that origin in the first place.[50] Inscribing presence in writing is still, for Kendrick, achieved through a similar mechanism as that which prioritises speech over writing: positing a living being as its source.

Kendrick is not talking about the kind of letter-faces found in the Louis and *Queste* manuscripts. To read her work alongside these faces is, however, illuminating, and raises an important question: is a letter only 'animated' if we can reasonably posit, firstly, the purpose behind its animation and, secondly, the presence with which it has been animated? Returning to a point made above, the purpose of the faces in the three manuscripts in question here is not simply unknown but unknowable. To draw a dividing line between inhabited initials of the kind Kendrick examines and those the purpose or provenance of which is unknowable on this basis is to deny the face the specificity of its affective power and inadvertently to attribute this force to the body behind it. If the path from the viewer, via the face ('like looking through a window'),[51] to the transcendental presence is blocked, or non-existent, the letter-face is just that: a letter with a face. It is difficult to say whether any given face in the Louis manuscripts was simply an opportunistic addendum, or whether the letter forms were deliberately drawn in such a way as to accommodate the faces. In BnF fr. 343, the scrolled ascenders and descenders are so elaborate that even when, as in Fig. 12, it seems plausible that space for a face was deliberately created, this is by no means the only way to account for the pattern. Indeed, in Fig. 13 we see a similar face that is much less closely determined by the pen marks to which it is attached. While some letters to which faces are attached appear to show a small dot of ink at the point where

[49] Ibid., p. 17.
[50] See, in particular, *De la grammatologie* (Paris: Minuit, 1967).
[51] Kendrick p. 216.

the elongation of the ascender or descender begins, suggesting that the pen was stopped and possibly lifted before the decoration was begun, this is not uniform. Especially in the case of the Louis manuscripts, the proximity of the letter forms and the faces is important in the light of Kendrick's observations: two different kinds of signifier form a single hybrid graphic unit, forcing the reader to question where the dividing line – both literal and figural – should be and, furthermore, what the justification for such a division is in the first place. Like Wittgenstein's duck-rabbit, when confronted with a letter-face such as that in Fig. 7, sometimes we see a face, sometimes we see an 'A' and sometimes, I argue, we see both.[52] Kendrick's formulation of animation – the result of a conscious process of intertwining body forms and letter forms in order to achieve the effect of coming into contact with a living presence – in fact seems partly to restate the distinction between letter and drawing that she sought to overcome, since it relies on the ability of the picture to bring forth a presence that the letter cannot. In terms of animation, then, the face doodles in the Louis manuscripts challenge this implicit hierarchy, since the faces explicitly do not bring forth a presence; these faces look like they are traces of something else, but they explicitly aren't. Who are they? No one. What are they looking at? Nothing. Where is the other side of the face? Nowhere. The combination of these questions and answers is where the power of the doodles lies: they invite questioning, but their answers are always in the negative. In other words, they are faces, but they are nobody's face. They animate the page, but they animate it with faciality.

Affect and the Real: Tomkins and Lacan

I have argued above that Laura Kendrick's compelling notion of the animated letter comes slightly undone when applied to the 'inhabited' letters in the Louis and *Queste* manuscripts, and that this comparison draws out crucial aspects of these images and, by implication, of the medieval face image more generally. Kendrick's exploration of the effect of living presence in bodily images always returns to the notion of an originary life-force, whereas the face doodles at issue in this chapter continuously provoke the reader into acknowledging that they have no such originary life-force; that they are faces without subjects. Having explored the negative aspects of these face images by articulating precisely what is *not* behind or beyond them, I now turn for the rest of this chapter to the question of what they *do*, rather than what they *are* (and are not). Firstly, in order to explore how specifically facial affect can work without, or at the very least, before,

---

[52] Wittgenstein, p. 195^e.

Figure 12. BnF fr. 343 fol. 82r (detail)

Figure 13. BnF fr. 343 fol. 90v (detail)

positing a subjectivity, I look at Silvan Tomkins's affect theory and read the face doodles with reference to his notion of the face as a primary, rather than contingent, site of visual and affective communication. Next, I broach the disturbing possibilities of the encounter with the subject-less face and explore how these apparently innocuous doodles in fact seem to embody some of the most disconcerting of Lacanian ideas concerning the encounter between the real and symbolic orders.[53]

Silvan Tomkins begins a paper entitled 'The Phantasy Behind the Face' with the following statement: 'If, as I believe, the affects are the primary motives of man, and if, as I also believe, the face is the primary site of the affects, then the face *is* the man.'[54] On the one hand, this statement can be read as making an essential connection between the face and the 'man', which works against what I have been saying about the face doodles: that they are faces without 'men'. Indeed, much of Tomkins's work is concerned with 'the decoding of these living hieroglyphics'.[55] His research, however, explores the opposite direction from conventional 'decoding' of facial expressions:

---

[53] For an overview of the 'affective turn' and its recent uses in medievalist scholarship, see Stephanie Trigg's introduction to a 2014 *Exemplaria* special issue on pre-modern emotions: Stephanie Trigg, 'Introduction: Emotional Histories – Beyond the Personalization of the Past and the Abstraction of Affect Theory', *Exemplaria*, 26 (2014), 3–15.

[54] Tomkins, 'The Phantasy Behind the Face' (p. 263).

[55] Ibid.

the implication of Tomkins's assertion is that, far from making the face necessarily contingent upon the presupposition of a person behind it, the face and its affective responses come *first*. In other words, it becomes possible to conceive of the face before conceiving of the subject. Tomkins also articulates a way of thinking about the communicative power of the face that is again not dependent on the presupposition of a causal subject: in a different paper he explains that 'the skills of receiving and sending are intimately interdependent because the face one sees is not so different from the face one lives behind'.[56] To transpose this into the context of graphic images of faces, identification between the face on the page and the face of the reader does not operate via knowledge of a person represented by the graphic face.

In the previous section I proposed that the manuscript face doodles provoke a series of questions with negative responses: coming across the face in Fig. 1, for instance, we ask 'who is this?', only to be confronted with the answer that it is no one. Tomkins helps us to go beyond this apparent impasse and think of the relation with a two-dimensional face in positive terms: rather than confronting the lack of a person who should be there, a projected presence whose actual absence is marked on the page, the encounter with the picture-face can be conceived of as self-contained, inasmuch as it is an encounter between two faces, and not between two subjects (one present, one absent) via their faces.

A closer inspection of the manuscript doodles, however, suggests that, as eloquent as Tomkins's theory is in positing a way of reading subject-less faces, the faces in question refuse even this, and return us to the promise–refusal dynamic evoked earlier in this chapter. Firstly, as explored above, the faces are in fact all, to greater or lesser degrees, letter-faces. The face in Fig. 8, for instance, cannot be perceptually separated from the letter to which it is attached. A wisp of the 'd' form irrupts into the back of the head, curling upwards into a cavity and possibly, although, as always, not certainly, being the reason behind the shape of the head covering.[57] Indeed, in this instance we can also see the margin markings on the page: the question of language is again raised in the choice of whether to situate these lines 'within', 'through' or 'behind' the face. Trying and, to an extent, failing to read this face in line

---

[56] Tomkins, 'What and Where Are the Primary Affects? Some Evidence for a Theory', p. 227.

[57] However, even the distinction between the face and the head covering is problematic and I use the terms only to describe different parts of the same image. Indeed, close inspection of the image reveals that there is no separate line distinguishing these two parts on the left-hand side of the 'd' ascender. What appears at first sight to be such a line is in fact the horizontal margin line; the face image is deeply entwined with both the text and the production markings.

with the precept of Tomkins's affect theory again productively throws into relief crucial questions: if the face is not the foremost trace or imprint of a subjectivity, on what grounds do we then separate it from other lines on the page? I maintain that the face image is peculiar and particular in its effect on the human viewer, but in the case of the self-contained affective-communicative loop between two faces, a serious problem arises when the structural similarity between the two faces breaks down because of the fundamental impossibility of separating the face image from the lines of the text and of the scribal apparatus. Tomkins's theory, however radical its implications in terms of the link between subject and face, nonetheless cannot fully account for an image that is recognisably a face but whose defining boundaries are so indistinct. At the risk of creating a feedback loop in my argument, it is in fact this that is particular about the face image: it is still a face, even if it has lines through it, and letters attached to it. But these features limit even the minimal identification required between the viewer's face and the perceived face for Tomkins's affective communication. The doodles are resolutely facial, even if they consistently refuse to engage in facial signification, as explored above, and communication, as explored here.

The *Queste* faces take different forms but force the same issues on the viewer. We note that a number of the faces have been cropped as the folios have been prepared for binding (see Figs 14 and 15 and, to a lesser degree, 16 and 17). Once again, the material aspects of manuscript production have a constitutive effect on the form of the faces, but not on their being recognisable as such. Indeed, compare Fig. 18: here is a profile head, again attached to an elongated letter form in such a way that the two merge into one another. What is peculiar here is what appears to be a kind of parasitic semi-face attached to the top of the construct. It is nothing like the other faces in the manuscript, but it is also unique in terms of the decorative scheme of the manuscript. Even more liminal and even harder to categorise than the faces, then, this figure comprises an obliquely angled shape within which is found a single, pupil-like dot enclosed in a circle. Not a face in the same sense as the other images, it is nonetheless face-like and its position in relation to another face is provocative: on what grounds is it less of a face than the one beneath it? If it is a matter of less closely resembling a human face, is there any less a sensation that its single 'eye' is looking at us? Here, provoked by the comparison with the lower face, we come more forcefully up against the same kind of paradox as we do in encountering the other faces in the manuscript, a fact which in itself is troubling: if we see the dot-and-circle as an eye, only then to dismiss the possibility on the grounds that it is less eye-like than the one in the lower face, has it not already become an eye? Are we not then constantly repressing its 'eyeness'? In other words, to say that any of these images is not a face is already to have accepted that it is to some extent.

Figure 14. BnF fr. 343 fol. 86v (detail)

Figure 15. BnF fr. 343 fol. 87r (detail)

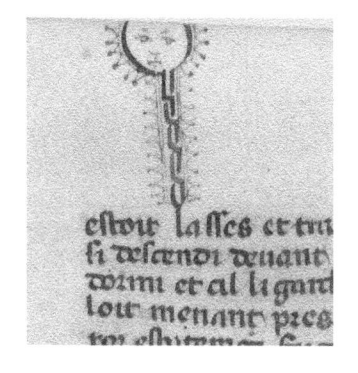

Figure 16. BnF fr. 343 fol. 81v (detail)

Figure 17. BnF fr. 343 fol. 95v (detail)

Figure 18. BnF fr. 343 fol. 86v (detail)

Finally, the question of expression and communication is raised with reference to Tomkins's theory. Adam Frank takes up this aspect of Tomkins's affect to re-examine the mechanics of communication between text and subject in a way that 'does not rely on idealized self-presence and interiority'.[58] Forging a link between Tomkins's affect and Derrida's theory of the sociality of writing and the concomitant multiplicity of subjectivity, Frank develops a mode of literary analysis that focuses on the transferential force of a work.[59] Although his subject is nineteenth- and twentieth-century poetics, Frank's notion of the transferential – of 'the movement of feeling across and between text and reader' – offers some key guidance in thinking about the effect and affect of medieval face doodles.[60] Examining an American comic strip from 1949, Frank notes a character, named Sadly-Sadly, whose perpetually sad face incites powerful responses from those who encounter it: 'Sadly-Sadly's viewers have no idea what the object of his sadness might be; indeed they are prevented from making any judgments at all about the propriety of his feeling. What counts here is expressive intensity rather than emotional authenticity.'[61] The crucial point Frank makes is that the face is a powerful affective communicator and that this function is distinct from any ability to communicate knowledge. Frank traces this back to Tomkins's assertion of the face as the primary site of affect and to the crucial observation that we cannot read back from affect to determine its cause or object. In other words, to see a sad face tells us nothing about what made it sad. Radical as Tomkins's theory is, especially routed through Frank's textual application, in the sense that it allows us to conceive of the face without/before the person, this still relies primarily on facial expression, something which none of the faces in either the Louis or *Queste* manuscripts exhibits. One more time we are confronted with problematic language that reflects the problematic status of the images. The problem is not one of talking about emotion without implying a subject; Frank shows how this is possible. Rather, it lies in describing the lack of expression of emotion. Rather than implying a subject, we instead, in describing a lack of expression, or calling them 'expressionless', imply the possibility that the faces could be otherwise. Even calling them 'neutral' risks placing them on a conceptual scale of possibilities, situating them in between other expressions that they might have shown. The language of faces again fails to describe adequately phenomena that, I argue, are nonetheless faces. It is precisely this, then, that they convey: not simply 'nothing' but, rather, our repetitious encounter with nothing.

[58] Adam Frank, *Transferential Poetics, from Poe to Warhol* (New York: Fordham University Press, 2015), p. 21.
[59] Ibid., p. 15.
[60] Ibid., p. 1.
[61] Ibid., p. 50.

This phenomenon of an object that positively presents nothingness is developed by Lacan, in several different guises, throughout his career. In the first instance, it is the Lacanian object itself which operates as a mediator between subject and other, concealing absence and parrying threat.[62] Žižek refers to the face-recognition disorders mentioned above (note 24) in order to demonstrate the fact that, for Lacan, there is always a psychological stratum to such encounters, which has the potential to disrupt the smooth functioning of biological solutions. He points out that prosopagnosia and the Capgras delusion show 'the gap between the series of positive properties and the mysterious *je ne sais quoi* that accounts for the person's self-identity beyond all positive properties (what Lacan calls *objet petit a*, something "in you more than yourself")'.[63] He goes on to point out that this *je ne sais quoi* reappears outside the frame of the Capgras delusion (in which a person believes a loved one to be an imposter):

> it is not *all* faces that provoke this paranoiac reaction but just *one* close acquaintance, usually a loved one. How, without reference to an inherent psychological dynamics, can we account for this *selective* malfunctioning of the covert system that is not suspended in general but only when it confronts *one* beloved face?[64]

In other words, even the discovery of the covert, affective response to familiar faces does not fully account for an irreducible *je ne sais quoi* present in the encounter with a face. If, however, this is still based on the affective response to a person via their face, what, we must ask ourselves once again, happens when we encounter a face which keeps telling us that there is no subject?

The main thrust of this section is that the encounter with the face doodles in the Louis and *Queste* manuscripts is disturbing, since the faces are situated at a crucial juncture between recognisable, readable, knowable appearance and the threat of the meaningless void. In other words, the faces are constantly poised to tell us something, but in remaining precisely on that verge, they paradoxically only reveal to us the fact that they will never, and indeed, can never, tell, because, ultimately, there is nothing to tell. Recall the notion put forward above, that to call the doodles 'expressionless' is to place them on a continuum between more and less expression; in fact, of course, the

---

[62] Kay, *Courtly Contradictions*, p. 302. Miranda Griffin also demonstrates how the Lacanian object is especially pertinent to the study of medieval texts. See *The Object and the Cause in the Vulgate Cycle* (London: MHRA and Maney, 2005).

[63] Slavoj Žižek, *Organs without Bodies: On Deleuze and Consequences*, 2nd edn (Abingdon: Routledge, 2012), p. 115 (original emphasis).

[64] Ibid. (original emphasis).

faces are static and are timeless, and have never had, nor will they ever have, expression. To put this in more Lacanian terms, the face doodle is an object situated at the juncture between the symbolic and real orders: it is the symbolic overlay that human subjects compulsively apply to an otherwise essentially meaningless signifier. In looking at the face doodles, a constant tension is in play between the knowledge that they mean nothing and what is thus experienced as a compulsive and yet ultimately futile habit of assigning meaning to faces. The face doesn't reveal the real by plunging the subject into its depths, and thereby destroying the subject; rather, it does so by enacting the essentially, and essential, arbitrary representational system which is the symbolic, and within which we, as subjects, constitute ourselves and our relations: 'la détermination majeure que le sujet reçoit du parcours d'un signifiant' [the crucial determination that the subject receives from the path taken by a signifier].[65] For Lacan the fundamental truth of subjectivity is that 'c'est l'ordre symbolique qui est, pour le sujet, constituant' [it is the symbolic order that constitutes the subject].[66]

Lacan uses the notion of the letter, among others, to articulate this phenomenon of the point of contact between the symbolic and the real. Tracing the movements of the letter in Edgar Allen Poe's *The Purloined Letter* (via Baudelaire's translation), Lacan points to its materiality as a way of demonstrating the extent to which the letter assumes a different meaning according to who is in possession of it at any given moment. The material letter – whether a character on a page or, scaled up, a letter of correspondence – is fundamentally the support for something that is not identical to it but which, in assuming its appearance, allows it to enter into a constitutive relationship with the viewing subject. At the same time, the overlay of meaning that is applied to the bare support of the letter is supplied, in part, by the subject themselves. Rather than a neat system in which the material letter can be understood as the middle term, mediating and facilitating a relation between the subject and something that we might, in this set-up, want to call 'truth' or 'reality', the Lacanian letter is in fact much better considered in terms of the relation between the psychic orders. A relation, in other words, that is mutually constitutive, and mutually dependent. According to Lacan, the letter is part of the order of the real, but its function with regard to the subject is to take on a symbolic overlay. Rather than being situated in between these two orders, the letter is part of both. In a similar sleight of hand, Lacan's letter occupies and constructs a position of both presence and absence. These terms converge in the material

---

[65] Jacques Lacan, *Écrits*, p. 12. Translations are my own.
[66] Ibid.

support of the letter, whereby what it comes to mean for the subject is always held in tension with the bare fact of its meaninglessness.

It is the dynamic of the subject's incessant quest to assign meaning to the letter, the oscillation between, and coexistence of, lack of meaning and meaningful overlay, that constitutes the psychic subject, rather than the content of the letter. In his essay on Poe, part of Lacan's project is to demonstrate how much of what was considered radically new in psychoanalysis at that point (the mid-1950s) was in fact to be found, albeit in slightly different guises, in the works of Freud. As an example of this, Lacan points to Freud's observation of a child's game of alternately hiding and revealing an otherwise inconsequential object, and suggests that this game perfectly demonstrates how the psychic subject is constituted not by what this object 'means', but by the present/absent dynamic with which it relates to that subject: '[Ce jeu] manifeste en ses traits radicaux la détermination que l'animal humain reçoit de l'ordre symbolique' [Through its radical features, this game demonstrates the determination that the human animal receives from the symbolic order].[67] Part of the real, but overlaid with symbolic meaning, the letter plays out the present/absent dynamic that Sarah Kay thus characterises: 'the presence of a term in speech takes the place of the thing in reality and banishes it'.[68] Kay explains that the Lacanian real cannot be represented or taken account of in the symbolic, but that the subject can only exist socially within the – punctured – symbolic. The unrepresentable real is thus present in the symbolic as a 'gaping hole,' a 'traumatic residue which infuses speaking subjects with the anxiety that language is "not everything"', alongside the revelation that it is, nonetheless, all that we do have.[69]

This is borne out in the face in Fig. 1, from Guillaume's *vie et miracles*, and its relation to the text to which it is attached: the compulsion to assign meaning is repeatedly invited and then blocked, laying alarmingly bare the normally covert mechanisms by which the subject is constituted. The face in question is found protruding from the left-hand edge of the sixth line of the left column of page 461r in BnF fr. 5716. It emerges from the elongated ascender of a lower case 'd' which forms the top edge and part of the forehead of the figure. In this case, the face is physically further removed from the letter to which it is attached; the strange protrusion of the chin emulates the form of an arrow, pointing and stretching away from the text. As noted above, this particular face bears some relation to the text to which it is attached: the miracle in question is one in which a man is cured of a sudden-onset facial deformity. The possibility that this face is the result of a considered reading

---

[67] Ibid., p. 46.
[68] Kay, *Courtly Contradictions*, p. 29.
[69] Ibid., p. 31.

of the text, and of a desire to illustrate its narrative, invokes in the reader the inverse operation: we read the face back into the text, identifying it, at least partially, with the ostensibly historical subject of the text: 'Garmont, curé de l'eglise de Baailli en la dyocese de Chartres' [Garmont, curate of the church of Baailli in the diocese of Chartres].[70] This face represents in an ambiguous relationship to the text, since it is neither clearly divorced from its content nor unequivocally illustrative of it. The text reads: 'il eust illecques eu aucune chose de mal ou d'enfleure, de quoi il furent adoncques forment merveilliez' [There was no sign of disease or swelling, at which they all marvelled].[71] The miracle tells of a priest who, having ridden his horse in unseasonably cold weather, suddenly succumbed to a facial deformity. The priest prays to Saint Louis and is cured almost immediately. We are told that the speed of his cure is due to his piety and that, once cured, there is no trace left of the ailment on the priest's face. Indeed, the text explains that the canonisation enquiry was presented with the priest's face as evidence that no scar or trace remained. While this is more or less the form of most of the miracle stories, several curiosities mark this particular miracle (twenty-ninth in the series of sixty-five) out from the others, in such a way as to highlight the role of the face doodle. The victim experiences comparatively little ill-effect from the disfigurement, for instance, and is not prevented from carrying out his duties. In a discussion of the representation of disability in Guillaume's *miracles*, Hannah Skoda points to the priest as an example of the humiliation incurred by visible disability.[72] The text does tell us that the priest was *vergondeus* in front of a group of pilgrims, but the emphasis of the narrative is more on the priest's acceptance of God's will and his continued capacity to work.[73] It is twice mentioned that the priest is content to believe that, if the malady is God's will, then it must be so. Finally, unlike in many of the other miracles in the collection, the afflicted person comes across a cure almost by accident: after mass one day, 'il li vint en son memoire le benoiet saint Loÿs' [he remembered the glorious Saint Louis].[74] In this particular case, the letter-face in question bears a direct, although complex, relation to the text it adjoins. In the first instance, it appears also to illustrate a human man with a facial disfigurement. On a slightly smaller scale, the image directly contradicts the sentence to which it is attached: explaining that the victim no longer has any visible trace of the

---

[70] Guillaume de Saint-Pathus, *Les Miracles de Saint Louis*, ed. by Fay, p. 88.
[71] Ibid., p. 90.
[72] Hannah Skoda, 'Representations of Disability in the Thirteenth-Century *Miracles de Saint Louis*', in *Disability in the Middle Ages: Reconsiderations and Reverberations*, ed. by Joshua R. Eyler (Farnham: Ashgate, 2010), pp. 53–66 (p. 63).
[73] Guillaume de Saint-Pathus, *Les Miracles de Saint Louis*, ed. by Fay, p. 89.
[74] Ibid.

affliction (a claim ratified not only at the level of the narrative of the miracle but also at that of the miracle's first telling at the canonisation hearing), the text is nonetheless attached to an image of precisely the opposite: a deformed face. The image plays with the possibility of illustration and affirmation, before engaging with the text apparently through direct contradiction; it overtly toys with its own illustrative potential, ultimately blocking an unequivocal link with the text. In this sense, we return to the brutal discord of unfulfilled meaning and the surplus of signifiers which marks the nothingness of the real; the mortification of the letter and the face as they reinforce each other's primary meaninglessness. Joseph R. Johnson also uses the Lacanian letter in a reading of troubadour lyric and their incarnations in *chansonniers* in which he argues that these manuscripts become a replacement for the lost body and speech of the *joglar*.[75] For Johnson, the Lacanian letter is a useful model for reading Arnaut Daniel's *Autet e bas*, since it occupies a similar juncture between the legibility of the symbolic and 'the Real of the body'.[76] He explains that 'the radical signifying possibilities that [Lacanian letters] enable are inseparable from their fundamental material resistance to stable meaning'.[77] For the letter-faces, we might reformulate this version of the promise–refusal dynamic and say that it is less a question of indicating several possible meanings (and alighting permanently on none) than it is of foreclosing a whole class of possible meanings to which the letter-face nonetheless alludes.

Lacan's letter is, importantly, not simply the recipient of the meaningful overlay with which we desperately shore up the irruption of the real. Rather, the Lacanian letter and, I contend, the face doodles *are* this meaningful overlay. It is the very notion of the face within which the symbolic expectation is contained. As mentioned above in reference to Tomkins, these are faces, but they not *do* the things we expect as part of that designation. They render asunder an apparently indissoluble connection between being a face and performing certain symbolic tasks. The rupture between meaningfulness (the inherent expectation of meaning) and meaninglessness (the actual lack of meaning) is performed by these face doodles and is profoundly disturbing to the viewing subject. Žižek again helps us to take this analysis further in relation to the Lacanian letter by unpacking how 'Lacan's exposition of the way a letter arrives at its destination *lays bare the very mechanism of teleological illusion*'.[78] The signifier – the letter – is always arbitrary, since its significance depends on the subject: signifier and subject are mutually

---

[75] Joseph R. Johnson, 'Flying Letters and Feuilles Volantes: Symptoms of Orality in Two Troubadour Songbooks', *Exemplaria* 28 (2016), 193–211.
[76] Ibid., p. 193.
[77] Ibid., p. 201.
[78] Žižek, *Enjoy Your Symptom*, p. 11 (original emphasis).

constitutive. The letter-face, then, takes on the expectation of meaning, which it ultimately refuses, only in the encounter with the viewing subject: 'one becomes its addressee when one is reached'.[79] The effect of this is the subject's retroactive 'search for a hidden fate that regulates [their] path'.[80] Recalling my suggestion above that to disavow the 'eyeness' of the pattern in Fig. 18 is to constitute it as an eye, we can also say that the picture-face as Lacanian letter always arrives at its destination, since it comes into being at the moment the subject apprehends it. It is the symbolic facial expectation with which I, as subject, burden it that constitutes it as a face. I am, in this sense, the architect of my own downfall: 'the subject/sender receives from the addressee his own message in its true form'.[81] The subject asks for meaning from the picture-face, only to have that request returned to sender, thus provoking the realisation that there is nothing behind the face; nothing behind representation. Lacan makes this point in Seminar XI, using the story of Zeuxis and Parrhasios: the two painters are engaged in a painting contest to see who is the better artist. Zeuxis paints grapes so realistic that birds come to peck at them. When Zeuxis asks Parrhasios to draw back a curtain and reveal his own painting, it is discovered that the curtain is in fact the painting, and so Parrhasios wins the contest. Lacan uses the story to demonstrate that the more fundamental illusion is not that which makes us mistake an image for reality but, rather, that which, like Parrhasios's curtain, makes us ask, 'what is behind the picture?' The answer to which is, of course, 'nothing':

> Si des oiseaux se précipitèrent sur la surface où Zeuxis avait indiqué ses touches, prenant le tableau pour des raisins à becqueter, observons que le succès d'une pareille entreprise n'implique en rien que les raisins fussent admirablement reproduits, tels ceux que nous pouvons voir dans la corbeille que tient le *Bacchus* du Caravage, aux Offices. Si les raisins avaient été ainsi, il est peu probable que les oiseaux s'y soient trompés, car pourquoi les oiseaux verraient-ils des raisins dans ce style de tour de force? Il doit y avoir quelque chose de plus réduit, de plus proche du signe, dans ce qui peut constituer pour des oiseaux la proie raisin. Mais l'exemple opposé de Parrhasios rend clair qu'à vouloir tromper un homme, ce qu'on lui présente c'est la peinture d'un voile, c'est-à-dire de quelque chose au-delà de quoi il demande à voir.
>
> [If the birds rushed to the surface on which Zeuxis had deposited his dabs of colour, taking the picture for edible grapes, let us observe that the success of

---

[79] Ibid., p. 14.
[80] Ibid.
[81] Ibid., p. 16.

such an undertaking does not imply in the least that the grapes were admirably reproduced, like those we can see in the basket held by Caravaggio's *Bacchus* in the Uffizi. If the grapes had been painted in this way, it is not very likely that the birds would have been deceived, for why should the birds see grapes portrayed with such extraordinary verisimilitude? There would have to be something more reduced, something closer to the sign, in something representing grapes for the birds. But the opposite example of Parrhasios makes it clear that if one wishes to deceive a man, what one presents to him is the painting of a veil, that is to say, something that incites him to ask what is behind it.][82]

The illusion presented by the face doodles is similar: we are not fooled into thinking that these are not pictures, but we are compelled to ask what is behind them.

According to Joan Copjec's disentanglement of the Lacanian gaze and its misappropriation at the hands of early film theorists, the gaze, for Lacan, is not the point at which a subject perceives itself on a screen, but is in fact located beyond the screen. It is located at a point which is '*unoccupiable* [...], not, as film theory claims, because it figures an unrealizable ideal but because it indicates an impossible real'.[83] The gaze and the letter thus share the radically destabilising capacity to bring the symbolic subject into contact with the notion that there is nothing beyond representation. The terror of this possibility is evoked by Copjec when she explains that:

> When you encounter the gaze of the Other, you meet not a seeing eye but a blind one. The gaze is not clear or penetrating, not filled with knowledge or recognition; it is clouded over and turned back on itself, absorbed in its own enjoyment.[84]

Telling us that the point of the gaze is the point of the subject's annihilation, Copjec echoes precisely Lacan's exposition of the letter: 'le signifiant [...] matérialise l'instance de la mort' [the signifier [...] materialises the moment of death].[85] What differentiates the gaze and the letter, therefore, is that while both play a role in the subject's (necessarily) delusionary construction

---

[82] Jacques Lacan, *Les Quatre concepts*, p. 102; *The Four Fundamental Concepts of Psycho-Analysis*, trans. by Alan Sheridan (London: Karnca Press, 2004), pp. 111–12. All translations are from this edition.

[83] Joan Copjec, *Read My Desire: Lacan Against the Historicists* (Cambridge, MA: MIT Press, 1994), pp. 34–5 (original emphasis).

[84] Ibid., p. 36.

[85] Lacan, *Écrits*, p. 24.

by shoring it up against the intrusion of the real, at the same time as being themselves the inscription of the real, the letter does this specifically by dint of its involvement in a linguistic semiotic. As an essentially meaningless sign, Lacan's letter '[n'est] par sa nature symbole que d'une absence' [is, by its nature, a symbol only of absence], and is 'ce qui est destiné par nature à signifier l'annulation de ce qu'il signifie' [that which is by nature destined to signify the annulment of what it signifies].[86] The gaze, on the other hand, is not the symbol of absence but is itself absent. Distinct from the Sartrean 'look', Lacan's gaze is fundamentally asymmetrical: the eye and the gaze do not coincide, as we learn from Lacan's famous statement that '*Jamais tu ne me regardes là où je te vois*' [*You never look at me from the place from which I see you*].[87] While we may well apprehend an eye that appears to be trained on us, this is not the point of the gaze and it is this non-coincidence of the eye and the gaze with which the face doodles also confront the reader, compounding their capacity to put the viewer in touch with the otherwise incomprehensible notion of the non-signifying, non-representational and a-subjective face.

Here the faces in BnF fr. 343 (Figs 2–5 and 12–23) come into their own. Their disturbance in the visual field of the manuscript page is, on one level, attributable to Jaeger's notion of the epiphany:

> Epiphany is the sudden appearance of a character who seems to have walked in from another world. Epiphany gives the person who observes it the sensation of the limits of common humanity overcome, of the real existence and sudden embodiment of a spiritual world.[88]

Indeed, as I have argued above, it is against this charismatic background that we do experience the face doodles. There is indeed the sense that a person 'from another world' enters the visual field: unexpected, outside all categories and yet not only physically connected to the text but also recognisable as a highly symbolic image, one which we are, even, biologically set up to read as the revelatory outer surface of an inner subjectivity. To take this initial encounter further – to take a step towards the presumed subject behind the face – is, however, made explicitly and repeatedly impossible. For Jaeger, the epiphany is indeed disruptive, since the figure that appears is not simply 'a sign pointing to a meaning' but is, rather, something that 'wants to get out of

---

[86] Ibid., pp. 24, 33.
[87] Lacan, *Les Quatre concepts*, p. 95; *The Four Fundamental Concepts*, p. 103 (original emphasis). See also Dylan Evans, *An Introductory Dictionary of Lacanian Psychoanalysis* (London: Routledge, 1996), pp. 73–4.
[88] Jaeger, p. 37.

meaning into life'.⁸⁹ Nonetheless, this kind of disruption is one of boundaries being improperly crossed (the 'border between illusion and reality', as well as that between sign and life);⁹⁰ while the effect on the viewer is powerful, it has as its source a 'world' situated behind the image, and a subjectivity situated behind the figure. We can transpose this into the structure of the reciprocal gaze, and Jaeger does when he discusses how it is precisely the 'gaze that knows secrets and shares them with a visitor to a crowded gallery [which] resolves the two realms'.⁹¹ In the case of the face doodles, there are, firstly, no sharing of secrets and, secondly, no secrets to be shared. In the Louis manuscripts we witness (and paradoxically participate in) the non-reciprocal Lacanian gaze in one guise: all the faces are in profile, all look away from the text, and the 'real' effect of the face image means that we instinctually follow the direction of their eyes, while the knowledge that there is no guiding subjectivity behind those eyes tells us that they have no object. They will, to put it bluntly, never turn their gaze on us. The frontal faces in the *Queste* manuscript enact the Lacanian gaze in a more disturbing way still: again the 'real' effect of the face image is such that the immediate impression is of being looked at. It is, however, conversely to Jaeger's epiphany, the sudden appearance of something which looks like a person but isn't; of something that looks like it is looking, but isn't. Crucially, it explicitly isn't, since, as is the argument of this chapter, all avenues down which we might find a subjectivity are cut off. The eye of the face doodle that looks at me in fact reveals that it does not; this divergence between the eye and the gaze is

> this point at which something appears to be missing from representation, some meaning left unrevealed, [which] is the point of the Lacanian gaze. It marks the *absence* of a signified; it is an *unoccupiable* point, not, as film theory claims, because it figures an unrealizable ideal but because it indicates an impossible real.⁹²

For Lacan, 'le tableau ne joue pas dans le champ de la représentation. Sa fin et son effet sont ailleurs' [the picture does not come into play in the field of representation. Its end and effect are elsewhere].⁹³ For us, the same can be said of the face doodles.

---

⁸⁹ Ibid., p. 37.
⁹⁰ Ibid., p. 35.
⁹¹ Ibid.
⁹² Copjec, pp. 34–5 (original emphasis).
⁹³ Lacan, *Les Quatre concepts*, p. 100; *The Four Fundamental Concepts*, p. 108.

Figure 19. BnF fr. 343 fol. 82v (detail)

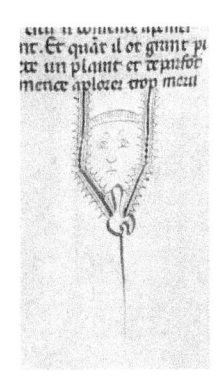

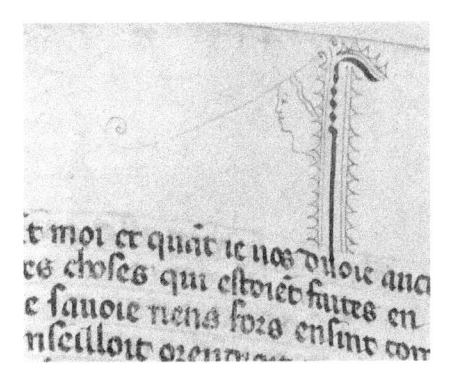

Figure 20. BnF fr. 343 fol. 88v (detail)

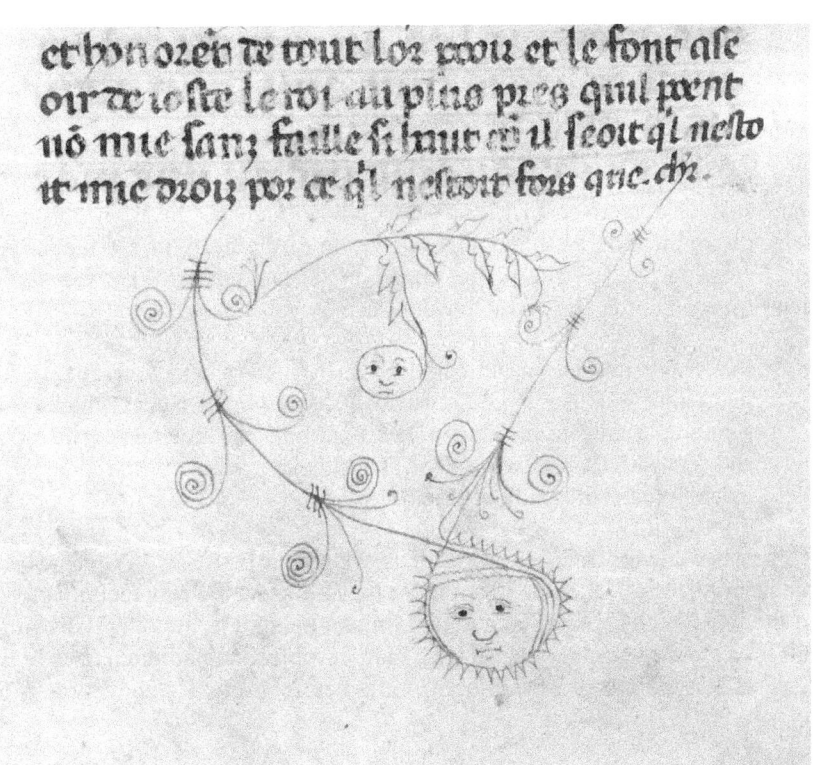

Figure 21. BnF fr. 343 fol. 88v (detail)

Figure 22. BnF fr. 343 fol. 91r
(detail)

Figure 23. BnF fr. 343 fol 97r
(detail)

Conclusion

The confrontation with 'the abyss of the Real' is, in a passage quoted by Žižek, characterised in Lacan's second seminar as 'the flesh one never sees, the foundation of things, the other side of the head, of the face'.[94] On the following page, Žižek points out an important aspect of the real that is demonstrated in the above quote from Lacan:

> the Real is not only death but also life: not only the pale, frozen, lifeless immobility but also 'the flesh from which everything exudes,' the life substance in its mucous palpitation. In other words, the Freudian duality of life and death drives is *not* a symbolic opposition but a tension, and antagonism, inherent to the presymbolic Real.[95]

This interweaving of life and death is what is at issue in the face on the manuscript pages. The doodles, on one hand, *are* faces; we react affectively to them as if they were attached to a human being. On the other hand, they are lifeless; we search in vain for the human subject behind them. It is in this tension that the power of the face doodle lies. This is only enhanced by the

---

[94] Jacques Lacan, *The Seminar of Jacques Lacan, Book ii: The Ego in Freud's Theory and in the Technique of Psychoanalysis* (Cambridge: Cambridge University Press, 1988), pp. 154–5, quoted in Žižek, *Enjoy Your Symptom*, p. 25.
[95] Žižek, *Enjoy Your Symptom*, p. 26.

materiality of the manuscript page: the face, so evocative of life, is drawn on the skin of a dead animal. Kay suggests a kind of affective connection between the manuscript skin and the reader's part-psychic, part-anatomical 'moi-peau', based on the perceived disruption in the reading experience caused by a short-circuit between the skin *of* the parchment and narratives of flaying *on* the parchment.[96] A similar, although not identical, disruption emerges with the face doodles: the symbolic mode by which we expect to understand a page of text, and illustration, is disturbed by the presence of a human face on a surface made of skin. Indeed, the explicit possibility of looking behind the face that I have been evoking throughout this chapter is even more radically foreclosed from this point of view, since what is behind the face is not just skin, but something else's skin. In other words, we again come up against the disjunction between the evocation of a living subject via a bodily trace, and not only the anonymity but primarily the absence of that subject.

Tomkins's affect theory provides the positive foil to Lacan's lack, and the combination of the two is what is at issue in the faciality of the doodles. For Tomkins, the face can be read before and, therefore, without a subject behind it. Through Franks' application of this to literature, we understand that the affective relation between the reader and a face on a page occurs prior to the symbolic reading of the marks – text or image – on that page. In other words, there is a face before there is a subject; the face doodles are faces in their own right. For Lacan, however, this presence paradoxically does reveal a lack, through its provocation of the question 'what is behind this image?'. The mark of the real in the symbolic does not have to be a face, but when it is, the combination of affective response and an absent and yet constantly sought out presence is profoundly powerful. The priority of an interiority behind or beneath these faces is thus both present and frustrated; it is something that we seek despite ourselves. I have argued in this chapter for a reading of these doodles that resists the temptation to solve the mystery of their identity and that, instead, focuses on what this temptation tells us about the nature of the face as a graphic marker and, in turn, what this encounter tells us about our engagement with medieval literary objects. The picture-face and, as I have argued above, the face in a broader sense, is a distillation and a repetition of the power and the enigma of the medieval manuscript: each, perhaps counter-intuitively, forces a confrontation with the lack at the heart of our own subjectivity.

---

[96] Sarah Kay, 'Original Skin: Flaying, Reading, and Thinking in the Legend of Saint Bartholomew and Other Works', *Journal of Medieval and Early Modern Studies*, 36 (2006), 35–73.

3

The *visagéité* of the *Roman de la Rose*

In their chapter on the concept of *visagéité*, Gilles Deleuze and Félix Guattari place an episode from Chrétien's *Perceval* at the centre of their enquiry. In this famous episode, three drops of blood from an injured goose fall on the snow; the formation reminds Perceval of the face of his *amie*, and he promptly falls into a lengthy *reverie*.[1] For Deleuze and Guattari, this episode is illustrative of a wider literary phenomenon whereby protagonists lose their names, their identities and their purposes, and of which chivalric romance is an especially pertinent, although far from unique, example.[2] What Deleuze and Guattari identify in this episode and others is none other than *visagéité* as it is played out in the relationship between a character and their landscape and in the phenomenon of text on a page.[3] For these face theorists, face is a complex concept that describes a variety of interconnected phenomena: the relationship between subjectivity and signification; the way in which particular 'visages concrets' and their human subjects are categorised and organised; a system of representation and meaning assignation by which the world at large is understood; and also a process that produces the conditions of its own escape and dismantling. I argue in this chapter that all these facets of *visagéité* find their productive equivalent in the *Roman de la Rose*; this prophetic dream narrative of the all-consuming pursuit of a highly unstable love object echoes how Deleuze and Guattari describe courtly literature in terms of *visagéité*:

> le chevalier du roman courtois passe son temps à oublier son nom, ce qu'il fait, ce qu'on lui dit, ne sait où il va ni à qui il parle, ne cesse de tracer une ligne de déterritorialization absolue, mais aussi d'y perdre son chemin, de s'arrêter et de tomber dans des trous noirs.

---

[1] Deleuze and Guattari, *Mille plateaux*, p. 213.
[2] Ibid.
[3] Deleuze and Guattari cite examples from across historical periods and literary movements, such as *Don Quixote*, *La Princesse de Clèves* and Beckett's *Molloy*. *Mille plateaux*, p. 213.

[The knight of the novel of courtly love spends his time forgetting his name, what he is doing, what people say to him, he doesn't know where he is going or to whom he is speaking, he is continually drawing a line of absolute deterritorialization, but also losing his way, stopping, and falling into black holes.][4]

By examining the *Rose* in light of this comparison, we are able to shed light on some of the intricate ways in which signification and subjectivity work in the text and to renew our thinking about the deceptively simple work of the face as a literary motif.

The thirteenth-century *Roman de la Rose* is described by Sylvia Huot as a 'lyrico-narrative blend' and by Adrian Armstrong and Sarah Kay as a 'verse montage'.[5] In making these claims, Huot refers to the *Rose*'s mixture of romance narrative authority and lyric 'expression of sentiment' and Armstrong and Kay to the text's incorporation of 'different kinds of discourse, orchestrated by a first-person voice'.[6] The *Rose* is also famously hybrid in terms of its authorship; begun by Guillaume de Lorris around 1225–30, the task of finishing it was then taken on by Jean de Meun sometime between 1268 and 1282.[7] This chapter will focus on Guillaume's poem and will begin with a discussion of how interiority and its exterior representation are problematised in the text's rendering of the wall that surrounds the Garden of Deduit. I argue that the wall is a facial surface, according to the notion of *visagéité* in *Mille plateaux*, the second of two volumes of *Capitalisme et schizophrénie*. Instead of presenting the facial surface as an enemy to be destroyed, Deleuze and Guattari sought rather to provide the stimulus firstly for recognition of the machine of *visagéité* and, secondly, for a different way of articulating it and, therefore, of interacting with it. Described by Brian Massumi as 'less a critique than a sustained, constructive experiment in schizophrenic, or "nomad," thought', *Mille plateaux* comprises a series of responses to 'the representational thinking that has dominated Western metaphysics since Plato'.[8] Deleuze and Guattari take from Deconstruction the radical decentring of textual meaning and move it beyond the limitations

---

4   *Mille plateaux*, p. 213; *A Thousand Plateaus*, p. 174.
5   Sylvia Huot, *From Song to Book: The Poetics of Writing in Old French Lyric and Lyrical Narrative Poetry* (Itahca: Cornell University Press, 1987), p. 83; Adrian Armstrong and Sarah Kay, *Knowing Poetry: Verse in Medieval France from the 'Rose' to the 'Rhétoriqueurs'* (Ithaca: Cornell University Press, 2011), p. 74.
6   Armstrong and Kay, p. 74; Huot, *From Song to Book*, p. 83.
7   Guillaume de Lorris and Jean de Meun, *Le Roman de la rose*, ed. by Félix Lecoy, 3 vols (Paris: Champion, 1965–70), I, pp. vii–viii.
8   Brian Massumi, *A User's Guide to 'Capitalism and Schizophrenia': Deviations from Deleuze and Guattari* (Cambridge, MA: MIT Press, 1992), p. 4.

of critique. Equally, they take up Lacan's decentring of the subject and, instead of situating the subject as a product of the interaction of three psychic orders and as fundamentally constituted by lack, Deleuze and Guattari understand it as constituted by and in the interactions between different phenomena and collections of phenomena: 'les machines désirantes' [desiring-machines].[9] The movement of flux and flow from which the subject arises is also characterised in terms of a continual degradation. In *l'Anti-Œdipe*, the first volume of *Capitalisme et schizophrénie*, Deleuze and Guattari explain: 'Les machines désirantes ne marchent que détraquées, en se détraquant *sans cesse*.' [Desiring-machines work only when they break down, and by *continually* breaking down.][10] In other words, when they later explain that 'Au point que si l'homme a un destin, ce sera plutôt d'échapper au visage, défaire le visage et les visagéifications' [to the point that if human beings have a destiny, it is rather to escape the face, to dismantle the face and facialisations], they advocate not destruction, but *continual* undoing; not ultimate separation from the *visage*, but the act of escap*ing*.[11]

Massumi goes on to describe 'nomad thought' as that which 'does not lodge itself in the edifice of an ordered interiority; it moves freely in an element of exteriority'.[12] In one of the plateaus that make up the *Mille plateaux*, 'Année Zéro – VISAGÉITÉ', Deleuze and Guattari turn to the notion of the face in order to explore how interiority and exteriority have been organised and hierarchised in Western thought in such a way as to embed in our experience the idea that there exists an anterior inner meaning that can be, and is, represented on an exterior surface. According to Deleuze and Guattari, this particular kind of representational thinking is both produced by and results in the face: a surface that is conceptually overlaid with the promise of meaning behind it. Not just limited to the promise that a face reveals, according to a certain set of codes, something about a person, the face is a kind of machine that works on other, inorganic, phenomena. Simon O'Sullivan describes as 'identity thinking' this idea that an object, like a subject, has an inner essence.[13] O'Sullivan goes on to explain that the 'reconceptualisation' offered by Deleuze and Guattari in *Mille plateaux* 'allows us to move from a signifying register to an asignifying

---

[9] For an extremely clear explanation of Lacan's three psychic orders, see the entry for 'Order' in Evans's *Introductory Dictionary*, pp. 134–5.

[10] Gilles Deleuze and Félix Guattari, *Capitalisme et schizophrénie: l'anti-Œdipe* (Paris: Minuit, 1972), p. 14; *Anti-Œdipus: Capitalism and Schizophrenia*, trans. by Robert Hurley, Mark Seem, and Helen R. Lane (Minneapolis: University of Minnesota Press, 1983), p. 8 (my emphasis).

[11] Deleuze and Guattari, *Mille plateaux*, p. 209; *A Thousand Plateaus*, p. 171.

[12] Massumi, p. 5.

[13] Simon O'Sullivan, *Art Encounters Deleuze and Guattari: Thought beyond Representation* (Basingstoke: Palgrave Macmillan, 2006), pp. 20–1.

one' and sums this position up with a pertinent metaphor: 'The world is not, or not only, a book to be read.'[14] It is this aspect of Deleuze and Guattari's non-representational thinking that I use to explore the *Rose*: while understanding the face as a codifying, representational overlay, propping up a strict binary regime of inside and outside, Deleuze and Guattari do not seek to annihilate it but, rather, to throw it into relief and to engage with the conceptual space that is thus opened up among and within perceiving subject, perceived object and meaning. The garden wall in the *Rose* performs a startlingly similar role by explicitly engaging with and disrupting this triad. Situated in between the perceiving subject (Amant and/or the reader) and the garden, the wall, acting as a Deleuzoguattarian face, demarcates the meaning of the garden and regulates access to it. Upon closer examination, however, again like the *visage* of *visagéité*, the wall's relationship with what goes on behind and beyond it, and the distinction between the two spaces, is not straightforward but instead highly ambiguous. Bringing Deleuze and Guattari to bear on the *Rose* allows us to step beyond this ambiguity and to trace how it functions in the broader context of medieval literary conceptions of interiority; how the face is a motif not just of ambiguity but of ambiguity intertwined with legible meaning. To destroy the illusion of a prioritised interiority would reproduce precisely the structure of such an illusion, insofar as the same opposition would be rearticulated in terms of 'illusion' and 'reality'. Rather, with Deleuze and Guattari we can draw our attention away from the overarching hierarchy of inside and outside and see what else there is.

My work is situated within the standard critical view that, whatever the lessons or meaning of the *Rose* are understood to be, they are taught, expressed or demonstrated through irony, juxtaposition, contradiction, deferral and paradox. More specifically, I build on the idea that the text 'acknowledges its own impossibility': it is impossible but it still *is*.[15] The grand claims of the text and its necessary failure revolve around an illusion of interiority: the structuring illusion that there is something more valuable behind the wall is what drives Amant, but it is also what precipitates his failure. The failure is not Amant's – I do not advocate a reading based on his naivety – but is, rather, the structure of illusory interiority with which he interacts, and with which the reader also interacts. Huot proposes that this is the structure of desire in the *Rose*: on the one hand, a quest for knowledge, sought and in some ways attained, but on the other (implicitly Lacanian) hand, an endless quest for an ineffable and impossible object. In this chapter I take the notion

---

[14] Ibid., p. 31.

[15] Sylvia Huot, *Dreams of Lovers and Lies of Poets: Poetry, Knowledge, and Desire in the 'Roman de la Rose'*, Research Monographs in French Studies, 31 (London: MHRA and Maney, 2010), p. 1.

of the impossible consummation and shift it into a Deleuzoguattarian mode, whereby desire – read as the movement of the narrative – is understood as a dynamic of flux and movement among different phenomena. Amant's desire emerges, therefore, as the product of his interaction with the garden wall; as a 'machine abstraite de visagéité' [abstract machine of faciality], the wall is a rigid, codified structure which can nonetheless be circumvented, and it is this movement through, back through and around the wall that constitutes and exemplifies the movement of the text in terms of an illusory, but not deceptive, interiority. The mode of medieval allegory, such as the *Rose*, is to show through concealment: to reveal inner truth via an integument, and therefore to reveal more about that truth than would have been possible with direct exposure. Indeed, in many cases this truth-object can be shown only in this indirect way. Thinking through *visagéité* brings to bear on the allegorical structure of the *Rose*: we can slightly remodel this, and argue that the motif of the face is one that incorporates both an allegorical scheme and the possibility of its undoing. In other words, the face is not a model akin to allegory, or revelation through concealment but, rather, a model of this as one of many possibilities.

Firstly, this chapter will examine Amant's initial encounter with the garden wall and, specifically, with the portraits on its outside edge. Beginning from Huot's assertion that the positions of the lover, narrator and reader move in and out of alignment as Amant approaches the wall and enters the garden, this section will look at how knowledge is transmitted among the wall's surface (the portraits), Amant and the reader. In the text's portrayal of Amant's encounter with and reading of the portraits there is a subtle interplay between intellectual interpretation of the message of the images and an intuitive perception that surpasses the information represented by the portraits. These two modes of interpretation – one based on representation and the other not – work in tandem, rather than antagonism. In line with the critical stance which holds that ambiguity and disruption in the *Rose* are formative elements of the text, I read Amant's encounter with the wall as a textual enactment of precisely the illusion of a prioritised interior, inasmuch as the illusion is not deceptive but something akin to an 'open secret'. The *Rose* is indeed disruptive, but disrupts the modern reader's expectation of spatial coherence and of its correlation with a linear movement from ignorance to knowledge. I do not argue for the opposition between Amant's naive reading of the portraits and the reader's consequent rejection of those readings; rather, I look at how Amant's reading of the portraits is complicated by its mixture of interpretative and intuitive knowledge, and link this with the wall as a facial construct – both highly codified and yet deeply flawed.

In the second section of this chapter, the wall itself is examined as a site of ambiguous spatial organisation which reinforces the specific kind of ambiguity already located in Amant's encounter with the portraits. Close examination of the text reveals a series of moments in which the distinction between the spaces within and without the garden wall breaks down. This is reinforced when the text is read in conjunction with the manuscript tradition and its illuminations. Again, my point is not that the visual presentation of the wall as a permeable barrier is exciting – the communicative gap between text and image is a medieval commonplace, and can be read in a number of different ways. The point is, rather, that this enacts the interplay among different modes of representation in a way that echoes what I have been arguing in relation to the text: *visagéité* is a construct not to be destroyed but to be articulated differently. The illustrations of the garden wall invite us to do precisely this: to look round the wall and to consider it from a different perspective, thus reconsidering the dynamic between inside and outside. For instance, the illustration in Fig. 24 (Oxford, Bodleian Library, MS Douce 371, fol. 4v) allows the viewer to occupy a different perspective – both literal and figural. The dynamic of the open secret in the medieval text again emerges in the guise of the illusion of a prioritised interior; the Deleuzoguattarian *visage* incorporates its own undoing. Moving back and forth across the wall is the dynamic of the text inasmuch as it is the repetitious and continuous undoing of *visagéité*. This dynamic, from the point of view of Deleuze and Guattari, is of primary importance since it is not just how a text works but how the world works *if we let ourselves think like this*. The world of medieval literature works with such a dynamic, if we can take its hints and alter our own perspective.

In the concluding section I will look at some of the key faces within the Garden of Deduit and think about how the dynamics of faciality play out on a smaller scale and how faces and facial surfaces enact the kind of troubled interiority we witness in the wall. Oiseuse's mirror and the fountain of Narcissus play crucial roles in articulating and signposting a certain surface–depth dynamic and place it firmly in the context of subjectivity as depth.

The Vice Portraits

In Guillaume's section of the *Rose* (from the text's beginning to line 4028 in Lecoy's edition; Jean's extends from here to the poem's ending at line 21750) the narrator/poet/protagonist[16] recounts a dream in which, after setting out on a conventionally beautiful May morning, he encounters a wall, behind which lies a beautiful garden:

---

[16] See Huot, *From Song to Book*, pp. 86–90 for a discussion of the shifts between narrative discourse and lyric discourse in Guillaume's poem and the concomitant gap opened up between narrator and protagonist.

Figure 24. Bodleian, MS Douce 371 fol. 4v (detail) Amant and Oiseuse at the garden gate

Quant j'oi un poi avant alé,
si vi un vergier grant et lé,
tot clos de haut mur bataillié,
portret dehors et entaillié
a maintes riches escritures.

[When I had gone a little further, I saw a large and extensive garden, entirely surrounded by a high, crenellated wall, which was decorated on the outside with paintings and carved with many rich inscriptions.][17]

Indeed, following the syntax of the passage it is perhaps more accurate to state that the narrator/protagonist first encounters the garden, and then the wall that surrounds it. This is the first in a dense series of textual hints that the garden wall fails to uphold a coherent binary relationship between its inside and its outside.[18] The wall itself is covered in a series of ten 'ymages', each depicting a vice that is ostensibly absent from the garden: Haïne, Felonie, Vilanie, Covoitise, Avarice, Envie, Tritesce,

---

[17] Lines 129–33 in Lecoy's edition. All subsequent references in parentheses are to this edition unless otherwise noted. *The Romance of the Rose*, trans. by Frances Horgan (Oxford: Oxford University Press, 1999), p. 4. All translations are from this edition.

[18] In a short article, Graham D. Caie notes that the reference to Amant basting his sleeves in lines 91–8 suggests that, rather than accidentally coming across the garden, he deliberately set out to find it. In which case this would in fact be the first indication that Amant knows the contents of the garden before coming across the wall. However, since my analysis is specifically of the wall, I focus on the sequences directly concerning or adjacent to it. See Graham D. Caie, 'An Iconographic Detail in the *Roman de la Rose* and the Middle English *Romaunt*', *Chaucer Review*, 8 (1974), 320–3.

Vielleice, Papelardie and Povreté. The wall is described as a surface upon which something is written (line 133, 'escritures', line 405, 'escrite'), and so clearly is heavily invested in the possibility of being read. Amant (as I will refer to the narrator/protagonist from now on) describes each of the portraits in turn, intertwining in his descriptions their physical features – in terms of both clothing, anatomy and attributes – and the characteristics inherent in their names. In Amant's description of some of the vices, the physical and moral characteristics are listed separately but have clear parallels. Such is the case, for instance, with Haïne:

> Enz en le mileu vi Haïne,
> qui de corroz et d'ataïne
> sembla bien estre meneresse;
> corroceuse et tançoneresse
> et plaine de grant cuvertage
> estoit par semblant cele ymage;
> si n'estoit pas bien atornee,
> ainz sembloit fame forsenee.
> Rechinié avoit et froncié
> le vis, et le nés secorcié;
> hisdeuse estoit et ruïllie,
> et si estoit entorteillie
> hisdeusement d'une toaille. (lines 139–51)

[Right in the middle I saw Hate, who seemed indeed to foment rage and anger; her image was angry and quarrelsome and most vile in appearance, not well attired but looking indeed like a woman wild with fury. Her ill-natured and frowning face had a snub nose, and she was filthy and hideous, hideously wrapped in a towel.][19]

In other descriptions, the distinction between physical and moral characteristics is less clear, and visual language is used to denote ostensibly internal attributes. For instance, the narrator explains that Vilanie

> Bien sembla male criature,
> fole et crueus et outrageuse
> et mesdisant et ramponeuse. (lines 160–2)

[She seemed indeed an evil creature, wild and cruel, an immoderate and insolent scandalmonger.][20]

---

[19] *The Romance of the Rose*, p. 5.
[20] Ibid.

He goes on to laud the absent artist's ability to depict villainy, acknowledging the difficulty but also the possibility of making internal characteristics externally visible:

> Mout bien sot poindre et portroire
> cil qui sot tele image feire,
> qui sembloit chose mout vilaine. (lines 163–5)
>
> [The man who could create such an image knew well how to paint a portrait; it seemed a most villainous thing.][21]

When discussing Tritesce, Amant again explicitly evokes a link between the internal and external features of the figure, recalling the common romance motif of the heart's true aspect being made visible in the colour of the face and implying a causal relationship between the two:

> Tres bien paroit a sa color
> qu'ele avoit au cuer grant dolor. (lines 293–4)
>
> [It was quite apparent from her complexion that she was greatly tormented in her heart][22]

The figure of Vielleice stands out in the series as one of the two vices that are not moral characteristics but, rather, the unfortunate result of circumstances. However, while Povreté is the victim of a condition that she herself embodies, Vielleice is the result of an external cause: the passing of time. The figure is described in almost exclusively physical terms, with a handful of lines telling us that another result of old age is diminished intellectual power (lines 390–7), before the narrator turns to the topic of her clothing. Instead of being presented as an almost purely visual motif, however, Vielleice is unique among the vices inasmuch as she is, as her name requires, positioned squarely within a temporal framework.[23] The victim of the ravages of time, there are explicit references to her past and to how her body has *become*, and not simply how it now *is*; instead, for instance, of simply *having* no teeth, she has explicitly lost them: 'les denz si perdues' (line 356). The passive victim of an external agency (time), Vielleice thus offers yet another configuration of the dynamic

---

[21] Ibid.
[22] Ibid., p. 7.
[23] Other descriptions bear some witness to past events, such as Tritesce having scratched her face and torn her dress (lines 313–18), but Vielleice is the only vice to whom a past existence is attributed.

between visual appearance and meaning that is interrogated in the sequence of 'ymages'. Towards the end of this sequence we come across perhaps the most beguiling couplet in terms of the parallel between inner meaning (or, in the case of Vielleice, also metaphysical cause) and outer features. Papelardie (religious hypocrisy) is described thus:

> Une autre en ot aprés escrite,
> qui sembla bien estre ypocrite. (lines 405–6)

> [The image that was represented next certainly looked like a hypocrite][24]

To appear to be a hypocrite is a deeply problematic position to be in, and is one developed at greater length later on in Jean de Meun's figure of Faus Semblant. This is foreshadowed here by Guillaume, whose Amant subtly evokes the Liar Paradox and thus the possibility of simultaneously perceiving two contradictory statuses. Papelardie is the visual equivalent of the utterance 'this statement is false'; she appears on the outside to be the very thing that makes the concordance between inner character and outer appearance highly suspect. Indeed, in a formulation that finds its trickier counterpart when Jean's Faus Semblant is said to have a traitor's face (lines 11981–4), it is Papelardie's face that plays an important role – which I examine in more depth below – in the inherent deceit of her character:

> C'est cele qui en recelee,
> quant nus ne s'en puet penre garde,
> de nul mal fere n'est coarde;
> et fet dehors le marmiteus,
> s'a ele vis simple et piteus
> et semble seinte criature;
> mes soz ciel n'a male aventure
> qu'ele ne penst en son corage.
> Mout la resemble bien l'ymage,
> qui feite fu a sa semblance,
> qu'el fu de simple contenance. (lines 408–18)

> [She it is who secretly, when no one is paying attention, will fearlessly commit any crime. Her appearance inspires compasssion, for she is simple and gentle of face, and seems a saintly creature, but there is no wickedness under heaven that she does not meditate in her heart. The image made in her likeness resembled her closely, being simple of bearing][25]

---

[24] *The Romance of the Rose*, p. 8.
[25] Ibid.

This kind of representational ambiguity, centred on the portraits, proliferates in the visual schemes of *Rose* manuscript illuminations. Many miniatures reproduce the ambiguity of Amant's own perception and interpretation of the portraits. Huot notes that 'nearly all' the extant manuscripts of the *Rose* depict the vices in a series of individual miniatures, and the variety among them as well as the differences between text and image are especially germane to my project.[26] I don't want to overstate the case, and whether illustrations are commentary, emphasis, a secondary narrative, wilful or accidental contradiction or otherwise is not directly my concern here. However, from a point of view of analysing the surface ambiguities of the wall and its portraits, these images provide a startling array of different Deuleuzoguattarian facial features. The text consistently works within the convention whereby beauty equals good character and ugliness indicates some degree of moral lack or character flaw; the vices are, by definition, ugly. It is difficult to find this consistency in the manuscript illustrations, however; to take but one example, the figure of Tritesce in Paris, BnF fr.12595 (fourteenth century) is illustrated as a beautiful woman (see Fig. 25), while the text explains that she has, in her great distress, torn at her face and garments (lines 313–18). Some scholars, such as Nichols, consider the illustrative scheme of *Rose* manuscripts a kind of 'double narrative'.[27] Similarly, many illuminators circumvent (deliberately or otherwise) the unanswered question of whether the portraits are sculptures or paintings and, like the image of Tritesce in Fig. 25, portray the vices as human figures in the same manner as other characters in the narrative. We might experience the same effect of uncertainty in an encounter with a fifteenth-century manuscript in which all figures throughout the text are minimally coloured, with only details such as hair, weapons or certain garments picked out in colour.[28] The minimal visual differentiation between the vices and the later personifications heightens the effect of ambiguity in terms of the representational system of which the vices are ostensibly a part. Furthermore, in illustrative schemes that appear to make a clearer point of the vices as statues, they often appear to tread a fine line between static manifestations and dynamic figures. In Oxford, Bodleian Library MS Douce 195 (fifteenth century) the vices are each set within a niche in the wall, but strike dynamic poses or have parts of their garments appearing to flow in a breeze (Fig. 26). In illuminated manuscripts of the *Rose* the miniatures contribute to the sense of ambiguity surrounding the vices, their status as representational 'ymages' and

---

[26] Huot, *From Song to Book*, p. 87.
[27] Stephen G. Nichols, 'Ekphrasis, Iconoclasm, and Desire', in *Rethinking the 'Romance of the Rose': Text, Image, Reception*, ed. by Kevin Brownlee and Sylvia Huot (Philadelphia: University of Pennsylvania Press, 1992), pp. 133–66 (p. 151).
[28] Los Angeles, J. Paul Getty Museum, MS Ludwig XV 7.

Figure 25. BnF fr. 12595, fol. 3v (detail), Tritesce

Figure 26. Bodleian, MS Douce 195, fol. 2v (detail) Covoitise and Avarice

their relation to the wall.[29] Indeed, it is noteworthy that in most manuscripts, as in the example above from MS Douce 195, the decision has been taken to depict the vices apart from the wall. Again, although individual artistic decisions were no doubt heavily indebted to convention, the visual separation of the vices from the wall does at the very least raise questions about their status in the text as signposts marking the difference between an inside and an outside.

In a conspicuous example of how illustrations necessarily add to the ambiguity of the episode, Amant's description of the vice Papelardie weaves together clearly visual signs (the appearance of her face, for instance) and a meaning that is, by definition, impossible to garner from visual signs (the deceitful nature of her face). How can an illuminator depict the kind of knowledge that Amant clearly does not gather from a portrait? In the case of Vielleice, too, the necessity to provide a one-dimensional manuscript illustration of a figure whose own past as well as the passing of time in general is part of her very meaning exposes the difference between representational and non-representational modes that is, I argue, a crucial part of the role of the vices in the text. The difference between Amant's intellectual knowledge of the vices (and, as discussed below, the contents of the garden) and his intuitive knowledge is not in itself the focus of my argument. Rather, it is the fact that this difference maps onto a discernible difference between representational and non-representational systems and that these are both woven together in and by Amant's encounter with the wall. This is an eminently facial feature of the text, according to Deleuze and Guattari's scheme: the strictly binary, representational organisation of *visagéité* contains within itself, indeed, relies upon the possibility of, its own undoing:

> chaque trait libéré de visagéité fait rhizome avec un trait libéré de paysagéité, de picturalité, de musicalité : non pas une collection d'objets partiels, mais un bloc vivant, une connexion de tiges où les traits d'un visage entrenet dans une multiplicité réelle [...] S'ouvre un possible rhizomatique, operant une potentialisation du possible, contre le possible arborescent qui marquait une fermeture, une impuissance.

> [Each freed faciality trait forms a rhizome with a freed trait of landscapity, picturality, or musicality. This is not a collection of pat-objects but a liv-

---

[29] In this, my prime reference is Simon Gaunt's discussion of the effect of different artistic decisions on the reader's experience of the gender of Bel Acueil in Jean de Meun's *Rose*. Attempts to resolve ambiguous language, Gaunt contends, inevitably produce their own ambiguities: 'Bel Acueil and the Improper Allegory of the *Romance of the Rose*', *New Medieval Literatures*, 2 (1998), 65–93.

ing block, a connecting of stems by which the traits of a face enter a real multiplicity [...] Thus opens a rhizomatic realm of possibility effecting the potentialization of the possible, as opposed to arborescent possibility, which marks a closure, an impotence.][30]

At this stage in Guillaume's poem, as Amant approaches the wall, the narrator and protagonist are closely unified, and it is in Amant's perception as he relays it to the reader that the deeply problematic notion of interiority and its representation lies. Huot explains that 'the narrator is identified with the protagonist, and the miniatures at this point represent not what the protagonist does but what he sees'.[31] David Hult explains that the allegorical text is explicitly communicative:

> The self-proclaimed allegorical text treats its fiction as a mere pretext for the doctrinal message, which will come about through a collusion between writer and reader. [...] It is no wonder, then, that the author appears so often as a character in the midst of the allegorical fiction, his communicative desire constituting the ultimate justification for the very literary fiction he is recounting.[32]

Hult goes on to couch his observations, like Huot, in terms of what he identifies as the *Rose*'s lyric forebears and intertext. He explains how Guillaume's *Rose* departs from the lyric *chanson* in the status of its spring opening: 'whereas in the lyric it is clear that in most cases the images [of nature] simply *exist* in the broadest metaphysical sense, in the *Roman de la Rose* they are being looked at, contextualized in all of their mortal contingency'.[33] Crucially, then, Guillaume's Amant is a perceptual subject, seeing and interpreting what he encounters in his textual world and communicating it to the reader as part of a broader allegorical scheme. When Amant describes the portraits on the wall, the ekphrastic passages allow the reader intermittently to come even closer to occupying or sharing Amant's perceptual position; sometimes it seems we read him describing, at other times interpreting. Often, and, indeed more often than it seems, the two merge. Nichols has noted that in some of Amant's descriptions of the vice portraits (he gives Envie as a specific example) there is an observable distinction between Amant's description and his judgement.[34]

---

[30] Deleuze and Guattari, *Mille plateaux*, p. 233; *A Thousand Plateaus*, p. 190.
[31] Huot, *From Song to Book*, p. 87.
[32] David F. Hult, *Self-Fulfilling Prophecies: Readership and Authority in the First 'Roman de La Rose'* (Cambridge: Cambridge University Press, 1986), p. 97.
[33] Ibid., p. 210 (original emphasis).
[34] Nichols, p. 153.

Nichols explains that 'Guillaume gazes at the portrait and then analyzes it'.[35] However, I would suggest that the text of the poem very rarely affords this kind of clear differentiation. Instead it seems that gazing and analysing form part of the same action. Indeed, in the section Nichols designates as description and not judgement, we learn that Envie 'ne rist onques en sa vie' (line 236) [never in her life laughed], for instance, and, in a slightly later formulation, the narrator/Amant explains that

> *je cuit* que s'ele conoissoit
> le tres plus prodome qui soit
> par deça mer ne dela mer,
> si le voudroit ele blasmer. (lines 269–72, my emphasis)

[I think that if she knew the best and noblest man alive, whether here or beyond the sea, she would still find fault with him][36]

Amant provides much more than simply a description of the portrait as it stands in front of him. He also tell us explicitly that some of this knowledge comes from him ('je cuit') and is not gleaned exclusively from what he sees. Gazing is not a disinterested activity; rather, it is fraught with interpretation and prior knowledge. The portraits on the wall, and Amant's telling of his perception of them, weave together description and interpretation in such a way as to question the very possibility of their distinction. Hult notes that it is unclear whether Amant identifies the portraits from their appearance or from their labels ('escritures', line 133) and emphasises the variety of referents that the portraits point to: qualities, behaviours and, in the case of Papelardie (who is dressed in a nun's habit), 'a specific social group'.[37] It is in the implications of these ambiguities that my reading departs slightly from Hult's. Where Hult suggests that the static portraits nonetheless offer 'direct insights' into their meaning that, as opposed to walking, talking personifications that appear later in the poem, don't require the reader to 'retranslate the actions as metaphor', it seems to me that these static images and Amant's interpretative interaction with them are in fact riddled with foundational ambiguity.[38]

These portraits on the wall find their productive parallel in Deleuze and Guattari's facial surface in several compelling ways. Firstly, and most obviously, there is a distinct connection between the wall covered in portraits and the aspect of the face that Deleuze and Guattari describe as the 'mur blanc

---

[35] Ibid.
[36] *The Romance of the Rose*, p. 6.
[37] Hult, pp. 226, 225.
[38] Ibid., pp. 224, 223.

sur lequel [la signifiance] inscrit ses signes et ses redondances' [white wall upon which [signifiance] inscribes its signs and redundancies] and the 'mur dont le signifiant a besoin pour rebondir, [...] le mur du signifiant, le cadre ou l'écran' [the wall that the signifier needs in order to bounce off of; [...] the wall of the signifier, the frame or screen].[39] A few lines later, they clarify: 'Ce n'est pas exactement le visage qui constitue le mur du signifiant [...]. Le visage, du moins le visage concret, commencerait à se dessiner vaguement *sur* le mur blanc.' [It is not exactly the face that constitutes the wall of the signifier [...]. The face, at least the concrete face, vaguely begins to take shape on the white wall.][40] The white wall is a screen onto which meaning is projected; it facilitates meaning as a visible, representable, readable and static phenomenon. Displayed on this surface, meaning, and therefore knowledge, are accessible and graspable. The Deleuzoguattarian *visage* is primarily an enabling constraint and a construct, through which phenomena are fixed and codified; to read them is to enter into a particular way of thinking that validates while paying the price of ossification and exclusion, and which, conversely, constrains at the same time as it creates the conditions for its own liberating, exciting undoing.The portraits are similarly apparently static images, placed there according to a certain regime of representation, and read by Amant accordingly. He, and the reader, successfully understand their meaning in terms of both their individual properties and morals as well as their position of exclusion outside the garden; vices to be avoided by the adherent to the virtues of courtly love.[41] The *visage*, however, places less emphasis on exclusion and more on the 'mur blanc' as endlessly inclusive. The portraits are read as vices that are, and which should be, excluded from the garden, but they are included in its representational and value system. For Deleuze and Guattari, this endless, and dangerous, inclusivity (on which more below) is facilitated by not just the 'mur blanc' but also the 'trou noir': 'On ne peut former une trame de subjectivités que si l'on possède un œil central, trou noir qui capture tout ce qui excéderait, tout ce qui transformerait les affects assignés non moins que les significations dominantes.' [One can form a web of subjectivities only if one possesses a central eye, a black hole capturing everything that would exceed or transform either the assigned affects or the dominant significations.][42] Although only Amant appears to

[39] Deleuze and Guattari, *Mille plateaux*, pp. 205, 206; *A Thousand Plateaus*, pp. 167, 168.
[40] Deleuze and Guattari, *Mille plateaux*, p. 206; *A Thousand Plateaus*, p. 168 (original emphasis).
[41] These vice portraits have historically been read as either part of an ironic commentary on the inevitable pitfalls of love and desire (most famously in John V. Fleming, *The 'Roman de La Rose': A Study in Allegory and Iconography* (Princeton: Princeton University Press, 1969)), or as part of a celebration of the same (or, indeed, as something in between; a poetic exploration. But this reading is mostly reserved for Jean's poem). Whichever critical position is adopted, they are still understood as negative exempla.
[42] Deleuze and Guattari, *Mille plateaux*, p. 220; *A Thousand Plateaus*, p. 179.

pass through the door, accepted by this 'trou noir', the presence alone of the structure, as that which facilitates or, in theory, refuses access, is what suggests the possibility, albeit unrealised, of refusal. I discuss in more detail below how the text deals with the inevitability of Amant's entrance, as well as the appearance of the vices inside the garden from which they are supposed to be excluded. The important point here is that the structure of the wall, as an exemplary facial surface consisting of a 'mur blanc' and 'trou noir', does not just allow it to refuse the vices and admit Amant, but is in fact performing the same function when it also admits those vices.

The fact that the vice portraits are, of course, images of faces is not incidental to my reading of the wall, and nor is the physiological face simply a convenient visual metaphor used by Deleuze and Guattari. The faces of the vices are often where meaning is concentrated, and where meaning coincides with the partial subjectivity of the figures. For Deleuze and Guattari, it is the 'visage concret' that is not just a useful template but also the site of so much primary signification. They also refer to the psychology of faces, and relate *visagéité* to the early experience of the mother's body and the infant's ascribing meaning to it.[43] The physiological face, however, is not the origin of faciality, and the relation between the two is not one of resemblance (specifically, not a relation that implies the anteriority of one of the two terms). In the first instance, the face is not a universal template, but a specific one: 'c'est l'Homme blanc lui-même, avec ses larges joues blanches et le trou noir des yeux. Le visage, c'est le Christ. Le visage, c'est l'Européen type' [it is White Man himself, with his broad white cheeks and the black hole of his eyes. The face is Christ. The face is the typical European].[44] Deleuze and Guattari's analysis of the cultural role of the face acknowledges that the apparently neutral, universal face is in fact a white, male, European, Christian face. Indeed, it is worth noting that it is specifically the implicitly racialised 'mur blanc' of the face that is the locus of this tension between the universal and the particular. At the same time, the face of an individual is that which is used to judge that individual's value within the broader facial system: 'c'est un homme *ou* une femme, un riche ou un pauvre, un adulte ou un enfant' [it is a man *or* a woman, a rich person or a poor one, an adult or a child].[45] In the 'gouttes de sang' episode in *Perceval*, what is of crucial import for Deleuze and Guattari is the coincidence of an image that

---

[43] Paul de Man makes a similar point: the first act of recognition is directed towards the mother's face, and is the first of many acts by which we assign meaning to certain visual patterns, universalising and totalising both meaning and pattern as a result. See chapter 5, 'Wordsworth and the Victorians', in *The Rhetoric of Romanticism*, pp. 83–92.

[44] Deleuze and Guattari, *Mille plateaux*, pp. 216–17; *A Thousand Plateaus*, p. 176.

[45] *Mille plateaux*, p. 217; *A Thousand Plateaus*, p. 177 (original emphasis).

represents an individual's face and an image that reduces that face to the key components of *visagéité*: a white wall with black, or dark, holes. The faces of the vice portraits perform a similar function inasmuch as they, too, signify in two different directions: on the one hand they, like the 'gouttes de sang', point *towards* a broader facial signifying system, in this case specifically one in which the beauty of a face and the beauty of character are analogous; on the other hand, the faces of the portraits point towards a particular vice. Recall Tritesce tearing at her face, the colour of which betrays the condition of her character, and Papelardie's 'simple et piteus' [simple and gentle] face belying her true nature (lines 293–4, 313–15, 412); in both instances, the face is the point around which turns a complex network of representation. In each example the text makes it clear that the faces work as part of a broader signifying system: in the case of Tritesce, the rhyme of 'color' with 'dolor' (lines 293–4) emphasises an apparently natural connection between the colour of the face (no specific colour is mentioned) and a range of characteristics that it might reveal. Equally, when she scratches at her face, the syntax tells us that it is the visible sign of scratching her face that tells us that she is 'dolente'. In other words, instead of emphasising the fact that the feeling causes the gesture, the text highlights how the gesture reveals the feeling:

> Mout sembloit bien ester dolente,
> *car* el n'avoit pas esté lente
> d'esgratiner tote sa chiere (lines 313–15, emphasis added)

[She seemed indeed to be very sorrowful, for she had not been slow to scratch her own face][46]

Finally, the text comments on the accuracy of Papelardie's portrait and, in doing so, offers another indication that these portraits and their descriptions are not simply the descriptions of vices but also of the system within which those vices can be successfully represented. We learn that Papelardie's portrait is especially good at representing her:

> Mout la resemble bien l'ymage,
> qui feite fu a sa semblance,
> qu'el fu de simple contenance;
> et si fu chaucie et vestue
> tot ausi com fame rendue. (lines 416–20)

---

[46] *The Romance of the Rose*, p. 7.

[The image made in her likeness resembled her closely, being simple of bearing and shod and clothed like a nun][47]

In other words, we learn that it is possible for a visual image successfully to represent hypocrisy, specifically because it is particularly good at representing the misleading exterior; no mention is made of how, or how well, the image might represent the disjunction between interior and exterior that is at the heart of Papelardie's identity. For Deleuze and Guattari, the face is not a natural or universal phenomenon but, rather, one whose function is contingent upon it assuming the role of something that is natural or universal: 'Le visage est donc une idée tout à fait particulière dans sa nature, ce qui ne l'empêche pas d'avoir acquis et d'excercer la function la plus générale.' [Thus the face is by nature an entirely specific idea, which did not preclude its acquiring and exercising the most general of functions.][48] Not only do the vice portraits perform as if they are universal signifiers, but in the particular way they do this they also tell us that this is a fiction. These 'visages concrets' are, to a certain extent, products of the 'machine abstraite de *visagéité*' that endows them with meaning, but they are also part of its architecture. In the *Rose*, then, the faces on the wall introduce how the faces function in the rest of the text; this is not just a moment at which Amant crosses over into an allegorical space, but also the moment at which the reader crosses into a facial space. In the *Rose*, this facial space is demarcated by a physical barrier that works to keep certain elements (the vices) out, and to let certain others (Amant, courtly virtues) in. Having touched on this notion above, with reference to the vices' position as a constitutive part of the system from which they must be seen to be excluded, I will now explore in more detail the way in which the wall works as a disingenuous prohibitor. Deleuze and Guattari explain that 'Le visage n'est pas un universel' but that it '*facies totius universi*' [The face is not a universal [...] but it *facies totius universi*].[49] It is the second structural element of the face that is primarily concerned here: 'un trou noir où [la subjectivation] loge sa conscience, sa passion, ses redondances' [a black hole in which [subjectification] lodges its consciousness, passion, and redundancies].[50] The 'trou noir' performs a sorting function: 'L'œil vide du trou noir absorbe ou rejette, comme un despote à moitié gâteux fait encore un signe d'acquiescement ou de refus.' [The empty eye absorbs or rejects, like a half-doddering despot who can still give a signal of acquiescence or

---

[47] Ibid., p. 8.
[48] Deleuze and Guattari, *Mille plateaux*, p. 217; *A Thousand Plateaus*, p. 176.
[49] *Mille plateaux*, pp. 216, 217; *A Thousand Plateaus*, p. 176. (original emphasis).
[50] *Mille plateaux*, p. 205; *A Thousand Plateaus*, p. 167.

refusal.]⁵¹ The inevitable and continual movement inwards mentioned above is the domain of the 'trou noir'; whereas the 'mur blanc' is the canvas on which meaning is projected, the 'trou noir' is the part of the face that performs the operation of validation:

> Quel que soit le contenu qu'on lui donne, la machine va procéder à la constitution d'une unité de visage […]. Le déplacement du trou noir sur l'écran, le parcours du troisième œil sur la surface de référence constitue autant de dichotomies.
>
> [Regardless of the content one gives it, the machine constitutes a facial unit […] The movement of the black hole across the screen, the trajectory of the third eye over the surface of reference, constitutes so many dichotomies]⁵²

> la machine abstraite de visagéité prend un rôle de réponse sélective ou de choix: un visage concret étant donné, la machine juge s'il passe ou ne passe pas.
>
> [the abstract machine of faciality assumes a role of selective response, or choice: given a concrete face, the machine judges whether it passes or not]⁵³

Working via a series of successive choices, the 'trou noir' ensures not exclusion but an endless movement of inclusion. If something fails to fit into the grid the first time around, it is simply a question of altering the parameters. Using racism as a startling example of this totalising machine, Deleuze and Guattari explain that 'il n'y a pas d'extérieur, il n'y a pas de gens du dehors […] La coupure ne passe plus entre un dedans et un dehors, mais à l'intérieur des chaînes signifiantes simultanées et des choix subjectifs successifs' [there is no exterior, there are no people on the outside […] The dividing line is not between inside and outside but rather is internal to simultaneous signifying chains and successive subjective choices].⁵⁴ They tell us that racism has historically not been a question of outright exclusion but, rather, one of classification and reclassification, whereby certain groups are categorised according to their degree of difference from the 'homme blanc' and tolerated by society to a corresponding extent. In a sense this inevitable incorporation is what happens at the door through which Amant enters the garden in an

---

51 *Mille plateaux*, p. 217; *A Thousand Plateaus*, p. 177.
52 Ibid.
53 Ibid.
54 *Mille plateaux*, p. 218; *A Thousand Plateaus*, p. 178.

apparently wilful act of self-determination. Having circled the garden and found no entrance, he finds the doorway. In Guillaume's text, the uniqueness of this entrance is emphasised, as is its small size:

> Lors m'en alai grant aleüre,
> acernant la compasseüre
> et la cloison dou mur querré,
> tant c'un huisset mout bien serré
> trovai, petitet et estroit.
> Par autre leu nus n'i entroit.
> A l'uis comançai a ferir,
> qu'autre entree n'i soi querir. (lines 511–18)

[Then I set off in great haste, skirting the enclosure and the wall that surrounded it on all sides until I found a very cramped, small, and narrow little door. No one could enter any other way. I began to knock at the door, for I did not know where to look for any other entrance][55]

Amant himself is initially anguished by the thought that he may not be able to enter, and his frustration is palpable. Beyond his point of view, however, and in the grander scheme of the text, the dream, and the value system of which he is a part, his movement through the doorway and into the garden is entirely inevitable and, indeed, crucial. Hult observes that it is not the meeting with Oiseuse, the guardian of the doorway, that causes the idleness in Amant that leads him to find and enter the garden. Invoking the logical impossibility of placing side by side 'a personification and a total human being', Hult shows that the meeting with the figure of Oiseuse is not transformational, but that it is 'a reduplication of a transformation that has already taken place (or will take place)'.[56] Evelyn Birge Vitz, from a narratological point of view, suggests that Amant is bound to pass through the garden wall since it is a condition of being a desiring subject to be constantly passing from outside to inside.[57] For Vitz, the inside/outside dichotomy is an important narrative structure in Guillaume's *Rose*, but it is a relative structure, inasmuch as the outside is where Amant always is, and the inside is where he always desires to be. The notion that the

---

[55] *The Romance of the Rose*, p. 10.
[56] Hult, p. 223.
[57] Evelyn Birge Vitz, *Medieval Narrative and Modern Narratology: Subjects and Objects of Desire* (New York: New York University Press, 1989), p. 86. For an earlier interpretation in terms of desire of the series of barriers in Guillaume's *Rose*, see Paul Verhuyck, 'Guillaume de Lorris ou la multiplication des cadres', *Neophilologus*, 58 (1974), 283–93.

inside/outside is always relative to Amant's position is compelling, inasmuch as it accounts for the inevitability of Amant crossing the wall as well as the curious ineffectiveness of the wall as an impermeable and absolute barrier between two distinct spaces. For instance, although Oiseuse is what drives Amant to enter the garden, the figure also functions as a kind of gatekeeper: after opening the doorway, but before she lets Amant in, she tells him the story of the garden's creation, deferring his entrance by nearly fifty lines (lines 580–628). Before this, we are given a lengthy description of Oiseuse's physical features (another fifty lines: lines 524–72), which also serves as a kind of barrier, delaying and deferring the inevitable acceptance of Amant into the realm of Deduit. Roughly one hundred lines of Oiseuse pass between the gate's being opened and Amant's passing through it, a delay that playfully hints at the inadmissible prospect of not entering the garden. I argue below that the wall does exhibit certain features that undo the inside/outside binary, but a crucial part of my argument is that it undoes that binary at the same time as maintaining it. This temporality is important: it is not the static coexistence of contradictory features that is at stake in a facial experience of the wall, but constant movement. Movement, that is, that occurs at the same time and in the same place as an illusion of stable meaning (it is this illusion that is properly termed 'face'). One does not contradict or work against the other. In the light of the desiring motif analysed by Birge Vitz, inside and outside are less undone than perpetually redone. Indeed, Birge Vitz's structuralist formulation places the desiring subject at the shifting centre of this mobile configuration; according to this, inside and outside exist in a contingent relation to Amant. Following Deleuze and Guattari, however, we might want to do away with the predicate of a central point altogether. To think in terms of faciality is to acknowledge the illusion of a central and coherent subjectivity, and does not deny its importance in structuring experience. At the same time, however, Deleuze and Guattari propose a way of thinking that goes beyond shifting the centre of meaning, even goes beyond destroying it, and instead attempts to think without this kind of meaning. As they explain in the introductory chapter to *Mille plateaux*, it is not a matter of not saying 'I', but of it not mattering whether I do or not.[58] They explain that a deliberate attempt, such as we might find in deconstructionist critique, to debunk the idea of a central, originary unity, cannot fail, ultimately, to preserve its primacy and to extend its reach:

> Les avorteurs de l'unité sont bien ici des faiseurs d'anges, *doctores angelici*, puisqu'ils affirment une unité proprement angélique et supérieure. […]

---

[58] Deleuze and Guattari, *Mille plateaux*, p. 9.

l'unité ne cesse d'être contrariée et empêchée dans l'objet, tandis qu'un nouveau type d'unité triomphe dans le sujet.

[The abortionists of unity are indeed angel makers, *doctores angelici*, because they affirm a properly angelic and superior unity. [...] unity is consistently thwarted and obstructed in the object, while a new type of unity triumphs in the subject][59]

This is an important element of Deleuze and Guattari's thought and of my own application of it and is central to my point that the ambiguity of the modern reader's encounter with the *Rose* is specifically facial: it is an ambiguity of and on the surface, and not of or in meaning. Sarah Kay makes use of *visagéité* when analysing medieval texts and suggests that it is a productive way of thinking about the signifying system that makes sense of faces without having to posit a body underneath.[60] Kay argues for the particular appropriateness of faciality as a way of reading medieval texts, describing it as 'a machine that generates meanings by facing the reader off against a surface, rather than enclosing him within one'.[61] In my reading of the *Rose*, then, the surface of the wall, including the portraits and the doorway, is specifically not a surface that works only simultaneously to reveal and conceal depth but is, rather, a surface which incorporates, promotes and maintains this illusion. In Guillaume's *Rose*, the surface of the wall sets up the representational system of the narrative (the structuring ambiguities of which will be further addressed below), and the door draws Amant into that disingenuous system of which he was always going to be a part. Together, they encompass the conditions of possibility of everything that happens in Guillaume's text and, indeed, in Jean's.

In a later article exploring surface reading of medieval texts, Kay describes faciality as 'a congealed promise of legibility that can only be misread'.[62] Echoing the deconstructionist assertion that a text is a series of broken promises, the 'congealed' face also works on the basis that misreading and legibility go hand in hand. Nothing, in other words, can be read, since misreading is a condition of legibility. Amant's understanding of the portraits is not erroneous, nor is the wall deceitful. Rather, the encounter fixes the wall's legibility, at the

---

[59] *Mille plateaux*, p. 12; *A Thousand Plateaus*, p. 6.
[60] Sarah Kay 'Legible Skins: Animals and the Ethics of Medieval Reading', *Postmedieval*, 2 (2011), 13–32. The other two articles in Kay's 'surface reading' series are: 'Original Skin' and 'Surface and Symptom on a Bestiary Page: Orifices on Folios 61ᵛ–62ʳ of Cambridge, Fitzwilliam Museum, MS 20', *Exemplaria*, 26 (2014), 127–47.
[61] Kay, 'Legible Skins', p. 28.
[62] Kay, 'Surface and Symptom', p. 128.

same time as Amant's subjectivity. It is the job of the modern reader to see the contingent nature of the combination of subject and facial surface and thus to posit the simultaneous possibility of flight. *Mille plateaux* puts forward the *visage* as a constraining, imperialist overlay of artificial and restrictive codes, and advocates flight from it: 'Au point que si l'homme a un destin, ce sera plutôt d'échapper au visage, défaire le visage et les visagéifications' [To the point that if human beings have a destiny, it is rather to escape the face, to dismantle the face and facialisations].[63] Several other chapters of *Mille plateaux* explore different strategies of flight away from the kind of restrictive machine that *visagéité* is. Various terms are employed in service either to restrictive representation or to escape from it. The former, of which *visagéité* is a part, is broadly defined as 'stratification'. The opposition (I use the term advisedly) is also expressed in terms of Being versus Becoming, or of 'territorialisation' versus 'déterritorialisation'. Importantly, this is not a matter of antithesis but, rather, of mutual dependence. Even while advocating flight from stratification, Deleuze and Guattari recognise that 'Le pire n'est pas de rester stratifié – organisé, signifié, assujetti – mais de précipiter les strates dans un effondrement suicidaire ou dément, qui les fait retomber sur nous, plus lourdes à jamais' [Staying stratified – organized, signified, subjected – is not the worst that can happen; the worst that can happen is if you throw the strata into demented or suicidal collapse, which brings them back down on us heavier than ever].[64] Indeed, to take flight from stratification or from facialisation is not undertaken with the goal of seeking a refuge; deterritorialisation does not have as its end point a new territory. Rather, these all denote a relative and constant movement; an always moving away *from* something. In other words, the movement itself cannot happen without the thing from which it takes its flight: 'Le programme, le slogan de la schizo-analyse devient ici: cherchez vos trous noirs et vos murs blancs, connaissez-les, connaissez vos visages, vous ne les déferez pas autrement, vous ne tracerez pas autrement vos lignes de fuite.' [Here, the program, the slogan, of schizoanalysis is: Find your black holes and white walls, know them, know your faces; it is the only way you will be able to dismantle them and draw your lines of flight].[65] In a similar but more elaborate formulation, they state that

> C'est que le mur blanc du signifiant, le trou noir de la subjectivité, la machine de visage sont bien des impasses, la mesure de nos soumissions, de nos assujettissements; mais nous sommes né là-dedans, et c'est là-dessus qu'il faut nous débattre. Pas au sens d'un moment nécessaire, mais au sens

---

[63] Deleuze and Guattari, *Mille plateaux*, p. 209; *A Thousand Plateaus*, p. 171.
[64] *Mille plateaux*, p. 199; *A Thousand Plateaus*, p. 161.
[65] *Mille plateaux*, p. 230; *A Thousand Plateaus*, p. 188.

d'un instrument pour lequel il faut inventer un nouvel usage. C'est seulement à travers le mur du signifiant qu'on fera passer les lignes d'asignifiance qui annulent tout souvenir, tout renvoi, toute signification possible et toute interprétation donnable. C'est seulement dans le trou noir de la conscience et de la passion subjectives qu'on découvrira les particules capturées, échauffées, transformées qu'il faut relancer pour un amour vivant, non subjectif, où chacun se connecte aux espaces inconnus de l'autre sans y entrer ni les conquérir, où les lignes se composent comme des lignes brisées.

[The white wall of the signifier, the black hole of subjectivity, and the facial machine are impasses, the measure of our submissions and subjections; but we are born into them, and it is there we must stand battle. Not in the sense of a necessary stage, but in the sense of a tool for which a new use must be invented. Only across the wall of the signifier can you run lines of asignifiance that void all memory, all return, all possible signification and interpretation. Only in the black hole of subjective consciousness and passion do you discover the transformed, heated, captured particles you must relaunch for a nonsubjective, living love in which each party connects with unknown tracts in the other without entering or conquering them, in which the lines composed are broken lines.][66]

Referring to another pair of terms used by Deleuze and Guattari, O'Sullivan points out that 'you need the root to produce the rhizome'.[67] To transpose this onto faciality, we might say that one needs the face to produce defacialisation. Guillaume's wall is a face that necessarily contains the possibility of its own undoing. The portraits on the wall, as explored above, have a highly ambiguous relationship with the representational system of which they are undeniably a part. This plays out, for instance, in the seamless transitions back and forth between the different ways in which Amant gathers his knowledge of the portraits and their meanings. Often this happens, as expected, through an interpretation of visual clues. But sometimes it almost imperceptibly switches to a kind of intuitive knowledge that has no direct link to the visual clues. Similarly, as noted above, it is consistently unclear whether Amant identifies the portraits from their labels or from their appearance (or, indeed, from intuition). The portraits both are embedded in the terms of representation and also provide and contain the terms of representation's undoing.

---

[66] *Mille plateaux*, pp. 231–32; *A Thousand Plateaus*, p. 189.
[67] O'Sullivan, p. 33.

The Garden Wall

The wall presents its own function in terms of a fundamental, structuring difference between an inner meaning and an outer representation of that meaning. The garden wall can thus be read as an echo of the signifier–signified relationship, famously characterised by Saussure as a 'feuille de papier', inasmuch as it appears to work according to an overarching structure of legible representation by which inner and outer function symbiotically.[68] To read the outside of the wall is, in other words, to understand something of what is contained inside it. Similarly, to read the portraits on the wall is to learn something about the abstract notions that they represent, and which exist elsewhere. It has been shown above that Amant's perception of the wall works within this paradigm and without; his knowledge of the inner garden is partly based on the readable system of the portraits, and partly on a kind of uncanny intuition. The text, I have argued, does not definitively distinguish between the two, giving the impression to the reader that the representative scheme is present but not absolutely dominant; contingent rather than necessary. A deconstructionist approach to the place of the wall in the text yields certain productive parallels: a key element of deconstructionist reading is that it understands a text as both claiming access to meaning and undoing its own authority to do so. This encompasses much of what has been argued in this chapter thus far: the garden wall in Guillaume's *Rose* promotes stable and accessible meaning at the same time as it enacts its impossibility. The contradiction that Derrida saw as a key condition of language is present in the textual wall, which seems also to undo the idea that meaning necessarily precedes representation.

What a facial reading, after Deleuze and Guattari, offers in addition to this is the possibility of an encounter with the wall that is not a legible encounter; to paraphrase a quotation from the beginning of this chapter, the wall is not *only* a book to be read. This section will now look in greater detail at the structure of the wall and consider how faciality – as both legibility and possible flight – is at play in the wall's strange permeability. On the one hand, in order to fulfil its function with regard to Amant's necessary passage from one zone to another and the shoring up of his identity *as* Amant, the wall is a barrier, excluding undesirable vices, admitting only those who conform to its ethos and delimiting a coherent narrative space. On the other hand, however, the wall serves as a springboard for the kind of escape from stratification that Deleuze and Guattari see as the result of their kind of non-representational thinking. The wall in fact seems to have multiple crossing points and fails fully

---

[68] Ferdinand de Saussure, *Cours de linguistique générale*, ed. by Tullio de Mauro (Paris: Payot, 1972), p. 157.

to uphold the spatial integrity of the garden. Indeed, the wall is necessarily multiple and mutable rather than monolithic.

The wall's barrier function has figured in most *Rose* scholarship to date as a threshold that Amant must cross in order to enter what David Hult calls a different 'allegorical figurative mode'.[69] Indeed, it is a consistent feature of *Rose* scholarship that the garden is described in terms that have the perhaps unintended consequence of closing it off as a discrete area, foreclosing the possibility of interaction between the two sides of the wall. In Stephen Nichols's discussion of the portraits that line the wall, he refers to the garden itself as both a space in which Amant 'will undergo a formative lesson in love' and 'a privileged hunting ground of Amor, the God of Love'.[70] The wall thus takes part in marking out a particular mode of signification by demarcating an area with a particular value system: the wall itself is there to be passed through as a kind of right of passage, and that passing is to be regulated by a single crossing point. Hult's reading of the garden stems from a discussion of how the *Rose* incorporates elements of lyric tradition into romance and how it is the form rather than any didactic intent that dictates the content of the poem. Rejecting moralising readings such as Fleming's, Hult suggested that the very idea of an allegorical personification is 'at bottom the expansion of a figure of speech'.[71] While acknowledging the inherent and insurmountable difficulty at the heart of a poetic mode in which supposedly internal characteristics appear outside the protagonist's head and interact with him (bypassing for the moment the fact that, as a dream narrative, the entire poem 'happens' within the protagonist's head), Hult nonetheless reads the wall as a barrier that is to be passed through in order to enter the realm of these troublesome, active personifications.[72] While one could argue effectively for other central, transformative moments in the *Rose*, the wall plays this role especially clearly, and it is the combination of this codified role and its non-linear characteristics which makes it facial.

Suzanne Conklin Akbari writes, like Birge Vitz and Verhuyck (see above), about the series of barriers encountered by Amant in Guillaume's *Rose* and suggests that we read the wall as the second in a symmetrical series of barriers through which Amant passes in his quest, the first being the entrance into the dream world, and the third and fourth being the rosebush and Jalousie's tower, respectively.[73] Thus positioning (with many others) the mirror of Narcissus

[69] Hult, p. 226.
[70] Nichols, pp. 136, 150.
[71] Hult, p. 222 n. 66.
[72] Ibid., p. 226.
[73] Suzanne Conklin Akbari, *Seeing through the Veil: Optical Theory and Medieval Allegory* (Toronto: University of Toronto Press, 2004), pp. 51–3.

at the centre of the poem, Akbari sees Guillaume's text as an exercise in scepticism directed at the 'early medieval acceptance of vision's seamless mediation between subject and object'.[74] Akbari explains that the poem exhibits a 'pattern of what is closed becoming open', but that the barriers get increasingly difficult to pass through (Jalousie's castle is not breached in Guillaume's poem) as the poet/lover realises the impossibility of his task: 'His account of the dream stops just short of the recognition of the fact that the shifting object of his desire is actually himself.'[75] In this scheme, whereby the gap between visual perception and understanding grows increasingly wider, the wall and its portraits work, in the first instance, according to a straightforward conception of visual perception and legibility. In light of this, I am arguing that the wall, and Amant's encounter with it, is in fact representative or, rather, performative, of both 'basic' perception (based on representation) and a kind of interaction that cannot be reduced to representation. The wall is a barrier to be crossed at a single point (an exemplary 'trou noir') but is also permeable, inasmuch as its inside and outside seep into one another.

I discuss above how the figure of Oiseuse both delays and facilitates Amant's entrance into the garden, and how this works within the facial system described by Deleuze and Guattari. Here I revisit this moment of Amant's crossing, and focus specifically on a detailed analysis of how the language of the encounter enacts a temporal disjunction that is at odds with the apparent order of events. This schism lies at the heart of the text, in its language and in its temporal logic. After enumerating the portraits on the wall of the garden, Amant begins his desperate search for some way of getting through. At first he thinks the structure to be impenetrable, but he then decides that there must be some kind of entrance and sets out systematically circling the wall to find it. As I have noted above, it is clear that Amant knows the contents of the garden before he enters it and, in addition, before he is apparently able to see into it. At first glance, however, the wall is explicitly an interruption: the lines immediately preceding its perception emphasise the continuous meandering of Amant through use of the present participle; he has not reached anywhere in particular when the wall appears:

> Lors m'en alai par mi la pree
> contreval l'eve esbanoiant,
> tot le rivage costoiant.
> Quant j'oi un poi avant alé,
> si vi un vergier grant et lé,
> tot clos de haut mur bataillié. (lines 126–31)

---

[74] Ibid., pp. 47, 19.
[75] Ibid., pp. 48, 51.

> [Then I set off through the meadow, wandering happily downstream, keeping to the river bank. When I had gone a little further, I saw a large and extensive garden, entirely surrounded by a high, crenellated wall][76]

As we, along with Amant, learn more about the wall's structure and apparent impenetrability, the wall's function as a barrier is similarly reinforced. Seduced by the birdsong coming from within the garden, Amant is desperate to enter, and becomes distressed as he fails to find an entrance:

> Quant j'oï les oisiaus chanter,
> forment me pris a dementer
> par quel art ne par quel engin
> je porroie entrer el jardin.
> Mes je ne poi onques trover
> leu par ou je peüse entrer. (lines 495–500)

> [When I heard the birds singing, I strove with great distress to discover by what device or trick I might enter the garden. But I could find no place to get in][77]

His increasing fervour as he approaches the garden wall suggests that his intuition extends beyond the portraits and into the garden itself. When he does find this entrance, and when it is opened for him by Oiseuse, he is overjoyed; the possibility of moving from the outside to the inside marks for him a change in fortune and a change in expectation. For the reader, too, it is clear that this movement across the wall marks a change in modes of reading: Oiseuse carries a mirror, a conventional symbol not only of enhanced perception but also of deception and of unreality. We are thus invited to recalibrate our reading practice in this new realm to allow us to read allegorically and figuratively. Crossing over into this new mode promises much, and, conversely, reinforces the relative paucity of both the pleasure and meaning that Amant intuits from the wall's surface. Something more substantial, more pleasurable and more meaningful lies inside. This demarcation is not sustained in the text, however, and it remains superficial. After having studied the portraits, Amant explains how the wall encloses the garden, and goes on to evoke its contents:

> Hauz fu li murs et toz quarez;
> si en estoit clos et barez,
> en leu de haies, uns vergiers,

---

[76] *The Romance of the Rose*, p. 4.
[77] Ibid., p. 10.

ou onc n'avoit esté bergiers.
Cil vergiers en trop biau leu sist:
qui dedenz mener me vosist,
ou par eschiele ou par degré,
je l'en seüse mout bon gré,
car tel joie ne tel deduit
ne vit mes hom, si com je cuit,
come il avoit en cel vergier. (lines 465–75)

[The wall, which was high and formed a square, served instead of a hedge to enclose and fence off a garden where no shepherd had ever been. This garden was most beautifully situated, and I would have been very grateful to anyone who had been willing to take me inside by way of a ladder or staircase, for it is my opinion that no man ever saw such joy or such delight as were in that garden.][78]

As briefly noted above, Amant's desire to enter the wall is not mediated by ignorant curiosity, a desire to know what is inside, but, rather, by knowledge of what is inside. Once he has found the emphatically unique door he knocks at it repeatedly (lines 519–21) until it is opened. The emphasis on Amant's desire to enter the garden as well as his apparent ability to know the contents disrupt the 'before-and-after' aspect of the wall as boundary between two realms of possibility; the wall loses its power to conceal, and to refuse, and the doorway loses its power to reveal and admit. In line 473 (above), Amant explains that *deduit* is to be found inside the garden. At this stage the word is used as an abstract evocation of the 'pleasure' that lies within the garden and has yet to become its personified proprietor. This happens shortly afterwards (lines 580–616); not only the proprietor of the garden, Deduit is also the maker of (or at least the agency behind the making of) the wall that encloses it. Not only, therefore, does Amant already know the content of the garden, but he also, in some sense, perceives its source and its founding principle. We could even argue that the moment verges on punning: Amant tells us that no man has ever seen such pleasure and joy as is to be found within the garden; in saying this, however, he reveals that he himself does see that pleasure. Huot emphasises the identification at this point of the narrator and protagonist, which accounts for narrative knowledge being put into Amant's mouth.[79] Read in terms of faciality, however, the multiple perspectives afforded a single figure also signal the broader possibility of multiple modes of perception; the wall may be perceived simultaneously in different ways because it is simultaneously a

[78] Ibid., p. 9.
[79] Huot, *From Song to Book*, p. 87.

codified, demarcating structure and a permeable, mutable construct. It is, in other words, a *visage* inasmuch as it incorporates the possibility of multiple modes of being and representation at the same time as appearing to sustain only one.

The faciality of the garden wall comes dramatically into play when we take into account the further opening up of perspective and of perception that takes place when again referring to its illustrations. I have been arguing from the point of view that *Mille plateaux* and, especially, the notion of *visagéité*, can be of particular use in allowing the receptive modern reader to see the multiplicity and ambiguity in Guillaume's *Rose* as the enactment of a medieval engagement with the productive illusion of interiority and, specifically, to see the text's dynamic of surface and depth as contingent rather than necessary. Consequently, this chapter claims that there is conceptual space around and outside of the linear forward movement across barriers. This space is partly opened up by the reader's perspective, but is also echoed in the text itself. Manuscript illustrations by necessity depict both the reader's perspective and the narrative in the same medium and on the same plane, thus enabling a holistic, facial reading that takes into account inside, outside and around.

In the first instance, I turn to illustrations in which the irruption of the reader's perspective is rendered as a cut or an opening in the wall. The illustration in Fig. 27, from a fifteenth-century *Rose* manuscript, shows Amant approaching the door and knocking at it, or on the verge of pushing it open, with Oiseuse waiting on the other side, holding a mirror and a comb.[80] Oiseuse's mirror is held at such an angle that the reader sees her reflection in it. Oiseuse, however, stares straight ahead, as if through the door to Amant, whose gaze is directed slightly upwards. Each has one hand raised, the other not, and the colour of each figure's attire matches the background against which they stand. There is a formal similarity between the two figures which is countered by small irregularities: the two visible faces of Oiseuse and the slight mismatch of their gazes. It is also noteworthy that what features in the narrative as an enclosed space is figured here as the opposite: while a tiny fragment of sky is visible above the dominant wall on the left-hand side, Oiseuse stands against a background of open sky, with the continuation of the wall in the distance. The garden as an open space of possibility enters into dialogue with its iteration as closed-off space in terms of values. Most importantly, however, this illustration is indicative of how the reader's perspective interacts with the distinction between the two spaces. Showing both Amant and Oiseuse before they meet in the narrative necessitates a second opening in the wall (the

---

[80] Avril and Reynaud date the manuscript to c. 1460: François Avril and Nicole Reynaud, *Les Manuscrits à peintures en France: 1440–1520* (Paris: Flammarion, 1993), p. 120.

Figure 27. BnF fr. 19153, fol. 5v (detail), Amant and Oiseuse at the garden gate

first being the hitherto unique doorway). The wall's faciality becomes visible here in the visual rendering, necessitated by the reader's third perspective, of the apparent contradiction of a barrier that is at once highly regulated and codified, which is put in place to facilitate movement across it from ignorance to knowledge, and yet which is also permeable, and which, here, has not only two sides but three. The same thing occurs in the image in Fig. 24, from a much earlier (early fourteenth-century) manuscript. Here, again, both Amant and Oiseuse are shown on their respective sides of the doorway, necessitating the same cut in the wall. In this image, the wall is not simply cut at one end, but apparently at both; we are shown a discrete segment of the wall, which appears rather like a screen, symbolically separating the two sides and the two figures. A notable feature of this illustration is that the doorway is tiny; Amant is bending down just to reach it; he will certainly not fit through it. It is of course the case that the illustrations depict the wall's symbolic role as a dividing line between two different modes. What also emerges, however, in these illustrations, through the weaving of the reader's perspective into the depiction of narrative events and their symbolism, is a new possibility: the wall marks the difference between interior and exterior, and it maintains

Figure 28. Arsénal, MS 5226, fol. 6v (detail), Amant and Oiseuse at the garden gate

the priority of the former, but it leaves space for this to be undone, or, rather, to be seen from a different angle. This is what Deleuze and Guattari urge: to recognise codified facial surfaces for what they are and thus to open up a conceptual space around them. The interior/exterior dynamic in these illustrations is explicitly an illusion. A final example is found in Fig. 28, from a mid-fourteenth-century manuscript from the Paris workshop of Jeanne and Richard de Montbaston. Here again the wall is depicted as a discrete block, but this time Oiseuse is on the left-hand side, and is shown pointing through the doorway into the garden as Amant disappears inside. On the right-hand side, a second Amant is shown walking away from the wall. Movement is at issue in this illustration: Amant's movement is depicted by the two figures, and it is implied that Oiseuse has moved from her domain within the garden outside, and that (since she is seen in the carol) she will move back in. This deliberately naive reading seeks to highlight again that the illustrations necessarily echo what in the text appears secondary to the main symbolic thread: that the wall is a permeable barrier, that its contents can be seen from outside, and that, as I show below, there is an undercurrent of movement in two directions across the wall.

The appearance of some of the vices depicted in the portraits as personifications within the garden turns the wall's surface outside-in; not only this, but the portraits in fact have their origins within the garden:

> Quant li arbre furent creü,
> le mur que vos avez veü
> fist Deduiz lors tot entor fere
> et si fist au dehors portreire
> les ymages qui i sont pointes,
> qui ne sont mignotes ne cointes,
> ainz sont doloreuses et tristes,
> si con vos orendroit veïstes. (lines 593–600)

> [When the trees had grown, Pleasure commanded that the wall you have seen be built all around, and that the images painted on the outside be set there; as you saw just now, they are neither elegant nor charming, but sad and mournful][81]

Thus there is a movement, explicitly mediated by the wall, from the inside outwards, and then from the outside inwards. Certain *Rose* illuminations open up new crossing points in the wall and suggest that the movement is not one of retracing (permitted by a symmetrical structure, whereby the initial movement is 'undone') but, rather, part of a continual, albeit constantly reversing, process. In the lines above, we observe that Deduit, the grammatical subject and narrative agent, is inside the garden, while the 'ymages' – the effect of his agency – are explicitly outside. Syntactically, through the 'si fist' + infinitive construction, Deduit's agency is doubly removed; his sphere of influence is not confined to the garden. Indeed, this doubling occurs again as we learn that Deduit 'fist aporter' the trees that occupy the garden from Alexandria (line 591); the trees that we observe breaking out of the confines of the garden in illustrations such as that in Fig. 28 are not simply escaping the garden but are in fact reversing the movement that brought them into it in the first place (I return to this image below).

I have mentioned several times the fact that the 'excluded' vices in fact reappear later in the text within the garden. Framing this slightly differently, there is clearly a distinction between the 'stationary figures' on the outside of the wall and those within it who are, on the contrary, compelled to act 'out

---

[81] *The Romance of the Rose*, p. 11.

of conformity with their "natures"' when Amant's love quest begins.[82] There is thus a kind of counterpoint between the stationary and consistent figures on the wall and their interactive and therefore inconsistent (in terms of the interplay of their behaviour, speech and ostensible nature) analogues within the garden. For our purposes, it is productive to consider what appears to be a shift in modes in a slightly different light: this re-emergence of the portraits is not simply a 'fleshing out' of otherwise static symbols in an allegorical mode, but is emblematic itself of the wall's insufficient power to keep these different modes distinct. The vices on the wall reappear in the garden in Amor's speech to the newly enamoured Amant, for instance, and Amant's agreement to live by the God of Love's commandments is 'less a narrative advance than a rehearsal, in literal terms, of the allegorical configurations through which the lover has already passed'.[83] Instead of demarcating the surface image from inner meaning, the wall itself participates on both planes and, rather like a Möbius Strip, refuses any attempt to make a coherent distinction between inside and outside, while nonetheless paying very obvious lip-service to this binary structure. As Alexandre Leupin uses the Möbius Strip's unique structure as a way of talking about Guillaume and Jean without reducing their relationship to either 'being opposed or merged into a unity', so I suggest that the wall similarly be considered a surface that distinguishes but does not oppose, and that links but does not unify.[84]

In MS Douce 195 (Fig. 29), a striking image of Amant and Oiseuse helps us to conceptualise a further nuance of the role of the wall in the text's representational scheme. In this illustration, the outside is shown *as* inside, with the patterned floor giving the distinct impression of an interior scene, and Oiseuse is shown in the process of leading Amant from this interior out into a space tantalisingly denoted by two small patches of blue sky beyond the crenellations. What is textually outside is now visually inside, and vice versa, and this apparent, and apparently banal, contradiction between text and image is in fact indicative of another of the features described by Deleuze and Guattari: the *visage*, the facial surface, is a deeply contingent structure. In a facial system it is the interior that appears to be prioritised over the exterior: the ostensible goal is always to access the former via the latter. Amant's entrance into the garden is a pivotal and, as discussed above, inevitable narrative moment. Birge Vitz characterises this in structuralist terms, explaining that

---

[82] Sarah Kay, *The Romance of the Rose*, Critical Guides to French Texts, 110 (London: Grant & Cutler, 1995), p. 26.

[83] Ibid., pp. 56–7.

[84] Alexandre Leupin, 'The *Roman de la Rose* as a Möbius Strip (on Interpretation)', in *The Medieval Author in Medieval French Literature*, ed. by Virginie Greene (New York: Palgrave Macmillan, 2006), pp. 61–75 (p. 62).

Figure 29. Bodleian, MS Douce 195, fol. 5r (detail), Amant and Oiseuse at the garden gate

what is important in Guillaume's narrative is not where Amant is, nor where he ends up, but where he is going. For Birge Vitz, 'The inside is defined with respect to and is centered on, not him [Amant], but the place where he wants to be at any given moment.'[85] Daniel Heller-Roazen sees this binary structure in terms of the *Rose* as a whole, and explains that the text's composite authorship encodes within the fabric of the text the possibility 'of being otherwise than it is'.[86] At the same time, of course, the structures of the *visage* itself are what provide the means for its undoing: 'C'est seulement au sein du visage, du fond de son trou noir et sur son mur blanc, qu'on pourra libérer les traits de *visagéité* [...] Moment incertain où le système mur blanc-trou noir, point

---

[85] Birge Vitz, p. 86.
[86] Daniel Heller-Roazen, *Fortune's Faces: The 'Roman de la Rose' and the Poetics of Contingency* (Baltimore: Johns Hopkins University Press, 2003), p. 7.

noir-plage blanche [...] ne fait plus qu'un avec sa propre sortie, sa proper échappée, sa traversée.' [Only on your face and at the bottom of your black hole and upon your white wall will you be able to set faciality traits free [...] The uncertain moment at which the white wall/black hole, black point/white shore system [...] itself becomes one with the act of leaving it, breaking away from and crossing through it.][87] This dynamic is dramatised in the depiction of Amant and Oiseuse in Fig. 29, whereby the inside and outside, the binary distinction between two different spaces, is clearly the structuring concept of the image at the same time as its integrity is being undone: inside and outside seem to have swapped places in their shift from text to image, and where Amant is going now appears to be where he *is*. In an important sense, then, not only is this a thorn in the side of the binary structures in the text, it also poses a problem for the role of movement, of forward progress. Movement across a binary structure is vital for the text, but it is also, as each of these episodes hints at, full of gaps, inconsistencies and contingencies, all of which hint, in turn, at what Deleuze and Guattari characterise as 'lignes de fuite' from the 'forte organisation' that is *visagéité*.[88]

The undermining of the structural possibility of an inside/outside distinction is also played out in many of the text's formal characteristics, suggesting that what we observe in the consistently problematic barriers with which the text presents us emerges from and reflects the text itself. Kay's study of subjectivity in troubadour poetry examines how the formal development of lyric poetry and the subsequent appearance of narratives such as the *Rose* resulted in the fundamental and irreconcilable division of the literary speaking subject and that this mirrors 'the irremediable confusion of self and other, inside and outside' that is a human experience.[89] Focusing on troubadour poetry, Kay nonetheless refers to the *Rose* as the '*fine fleur* of this poetic revolution' and dedicates a section of the book to examining how the *Rose* has taken on the instabilities that she first identifies in the troubadours' complex appropriation of first-person subjectivity within allegorical modes.[90] The crux of Kay's argument, building on Hult's assertion that the coexistence of the poet-subject and personified abstractions on the same plane is always ultimately untenable, is that the appearance of personified virtues, vices and individual faculties within a first-person lyric or narrative, and therefore within the same linguistic field, blurs the boundaries between self and other and erodes the possibility of

---

[87] Deleuze and Guattari, *Mille plateaux*, p. 232; *A Thousand Plateaus*, p. 189.
[88] *Mille plateaux*, p. 230.
[89] Sarah Kay, *Subjectivity in Troubadour Poetry* (Cambridge: Cambridge University Press, 1990), p. 80.
[90] Ibid., p. 52 (original emphasis); pp. 171–83.

a discrete and coherent self.[91] Crucially for our purposes, Kay makes the link between the eroded coherence of the speaking subject and a broader scheme of instability between notions of inside and outside. Her suggestion that 'for the medieval lover bilocation is just a fact of life' is taken up in a later chapter as she specifically examines this phenomenon in the *Rose* and concludes that not only are the personifications more problematic because they are more developed, but also the inside/outside instability that they pose seeps into the 'spatial metaphors which organize the narrative'.[92] In the context of an elucidation of ways in which the garden wall in Guillaume's *Rose* is problematised in terms of its function as a barrier, Kay suggests that its figural and literal meanings diverge at the point when Amant enters the garden:

> if, by leaving behind the images on the wall, [Amant] marks his freedom from their taint and demonstrates that Oiseuse and all the figures in Deduit's dance inhere in him, then the figurative meaning of the wall is the reverse of its literal meaning, and the 'garden' is *inside* him.[93]

This clearly echoes the points made above in relation to some of the *Rose*'s illuminations: in visual, narrative and figurative terms, the distinction between spaces within and without the wall is consistently problematised. In a similar vein, Huot notes that the garden as a logically coherent space is undermined by the description of Amor and that this once again comes to a head through Amant's interactions; the first-person subject's presence is a crucially destabilising factor. Huot observes that Amor is clothed in birds and flowers, and that he is therefore, to some extent, emblematic of the garden itself. Not only, therefore, is his presence *within* the garden difficult to reconcile with this observation, but Huot goes one step further and explains that

> as the Lover gazes into [the fountain's] crystals, he is simultaneously in the garden; staring at an image of the entire garden and himself in it; and being stared at by a personification of that very garden. [...] it is at this point that [the Lover] is infused with the desire that underwrites the garden's very existence.[94]

The ways in which the *Rose* breaks down subject/object and inside/outside divides are too numerous to elaborate fully here; my point is that a careful reading of the poetic devices at play reveals the fact that the *Rose* is infused

---

[91] Hult, pp. 223, 249–50.
[92] Kay, *Subjectivity in Troubadour Poetry*, pp. 67, 181.
[93] Ibid., p. 181 (original emphasis).
[94] Huot, *Dreams of Lovers*, pp. 17–18.

with a particularly facial instability, and that this is not simply mirrored in the garden wall, but that the very notion of a wall is a crucial part of this system. The surprising porosity of the garden wall, which emerges not only in the text but also in its illuminations, is not that surprising if we consider how the text as a whole expresses the impossibility of upholding any kind of inside/outside dichotomy; it is perhaps only surprising if we approach the poem with moral or theological expectations. Or, indeed, as a blind participant in the imperialist project of totalising *visagéité*.

Another kind of faciality is at work in and among the facial surfaces we have observed, a faciality that is both complemented and facilitated by the recognisable *visagéité* of the surfaces and barriers in the *Roman de la Rose*. We may recall the curious interplay that Deleuze and Guattari elaborate between 'real' faces and the concept of *visagéité*: 'Tantôt des visages apparaîtraient sur le mur, avec leurs trous; tantôt ils apparaîtraient dans le trou, avec leur mur linéarisé, enroulé.' [Sometimes faces appear on the wall, with their holes; sometimes they appear in the hole, with their linearized, rolled-up wall.][95] We may also recall how they place special emphasis on the reciprocal relationship between the machine and its product:

> Le visage construit le mur dont le signifiant a besoin pour rebondir, il constitue le mur du signifiant, le cadre ou l'écran. Le visage creuse le trou dont la subjectivation a besoin pour percer, il constitue le trou noir de la subjectivité comme conscience ou passion, la caméra, le troisième œil.
>
> [The face constructs the wall that the signifier needs in order to bounce off of; it constitutes the wall of the signifier, the frame or screen. The face digs the hole that subjectification needs in order to break through; it constitutes the black hole of subjectivity as consciousness or passion, the camera, the third eye][96]
>
> Les visages concrets naissent d'une *machine abstraite de visagéité*, qui va les produire en même temps qu'elle donne au signifiant son mur blanc, à la subjectivité son trou noir.
>
> [Concrete faces [...] are engendered by an *abstract machine of faciality (visagéité)*, which produces them at the same time as it gives the signifier its white wall and subjectivity its black hole][97]

---

[95] Deleuze and Guattari, *Mille plateaux*, pp. 206–7; *A Thousand Plateaus*, p. 168.
[96] *Mille plateaux*, p. 206; *A Thousand Plateaus*, p. 168.
[97] *Mille plateaux*, p. 207; *A Thousand Plateaus*, p. 168 (original emphasis).

It is with this in mind that I end this chapter with a turn to an evocative image of Jalousie's castle that appears in the late fifteenth-century manuscript London, British Library, MS Harley 4425 (Fig. 30), and in which we observe the face of Dangier staring directly at us from among the battlements. Dangier's identification with the outer wall is emphasised by the fact that he stands at a distance from the door that he is supposed to be guarding, to which he holds the keys, and above which his name is inscribed. Slotting in between the battlements, the presence of Dangier's arresting face draws the reader's attention to what we might call the organic nature of the enclosure: it is born from a situation arising from highly complex allegorical interplay, and it will be destroyed in the same way. Dangier's face also operates as the *trou noir* which effects the crucial sorting mechanism at the heart of *visagéité*, whereby all that is outside is eventually subsumed into the system, logically rendering the notion of 'outside' merely a temporary and ephemeral spatial category. Dangier's face evokes, to the reader caught in his gaze, a subjectivity that, to put it bluntly, is not there.

Deleuze and Guattari's example is startlingly human and reinforces, once again, the foundational role of human faces, and the human gaze, in a facial system:

> Ah, ce n'est ni un homme ni une femme, c'est un travesti: le rapport binaire s'établit entre le 'non' de première catégorie et un 'oui' de catégorie suivante qui peut aussi bien marquer une tolérance sous certaines conditions qu'indiquer un ennemi qu'il faut abattre à tout prix.

> [A ha! It's not a man and it's not a woman, so it must be a transvestite; the binary relation is between the 'no' of the first category and the 'yes' of the following category, which under certain conditions may just as easily mark a tolerance as indicate an enemy to be mowed down at all costs][98]

Supposedly denying access to the rose, Dangier is, as we have seen, of dubiously stable character, despite his name, and so the possibility of upholding the inside/outside dichotomy ostensibly upheld by the apparently impenetrable nature of Jalousie's castle is further undermined, along with the possibility of subjective depth. Indeed, the somewhat startling appearance of his face brings the reader into direct contact with this system; we are apprehended and judged by the ruthless and yet ultimately unreadable face of Dangier, and we become implicated in the sorting mechanism of *visagéité* by which the inside and the outside become one. As the outside is constantly subsumed

---

[98] *Mille plateaux.*, p. 218; *A Thousand Plateaus*, p. 177.

Figure 30. British Library, MS Harley 4425 fol. 39r (detail), Jalousie's castle, with Dangier. © The British Library Board

into inside, the circumstances of the castle's creation – enclosing that which was not enclosed – are recreated, and its destruction in Jean's *Rose* – as that which is enclosed returns to its original state – is anticipated. A constantly porous and shifting membrane, acting out a system of social and psychic organisation, the castle wall is another facial surface. Curiously, Amant is figured in this illustration outside the sorting grid constructed by Dangier's outward gaze. Amant stands outside the outer wall of the edifice, hovering by a corner and looking not at Dangier, but at some indeterminate point on the inner tower. Hands extended as if speaking, he draws specific attention to a space outside the fortress that is not threatened by Dangier's consuming and faux-subjective gaze, nor which takes part in the kind of facial back and forth that I have noted in other illuminations. In this image, *visagéité* is a more localised and more closely targeted system; while the reader is implicated in it, Amant here, like the reader in the illustrations of the garden wall discussed above, seems to embody the possibility of existing alongside and not within a totalising signifying system. It is this space for possibility that is the result of thinking in terms of *visagéité*.

Conclusion

By way of conclusion, I would like to offer some suggestions of moments away from the garden wall that bear witness to the repetition of faces and facial surfaces that is one of the characteristics of *visagéité*:

> La machine de *visagéité* n'est pas une annexe du significant et du sujet, elle en est plutôt connexe, et conditionnaire: les bi-univocités, les binarités de visage doublent les autres, les redondances de visage font redondance avec les redondances signifitantes et subjectives.

> [The faciality machine is not an annex to the signifier and the subject; rather, it is subjacent […] to them and is their condition of possibility. Facial biunivocalities and binarities double the others; facial redundancies are in redundancy with signifying and subjective redundancies][99]

These 'other' faces form part of an undercurrent of faciality that structures the text's engagement with the medieval dynamic of interiority and exteriority. They, individually and collectively, signal the text's engagement with the nature of meaning and its expression and communication. It is worth conducting a brief survey of these signals with explicit reference to the *visage* and thus to reinforce its coherence as a model for thinking the spaces and dynamics of the text.

Perhaps the first indication of the face as an explicitly problematic mediator between surface and depth and interior and exterior comes in the form of the mirror held by Oiseuse as she leads Amant into the garden. Traditionally, along with the comb that Oiseuse also holds, a symbol of *luxuria*, the mirror has been considered to 'expose [the holder's] physical beauty as an illusion which masks rather than adorns her true nature'.[100] The mirror, however, does not simply indicate illusion, but also enacts it. Indeed, what it really enacts is the interplay of illusion and revelation; mirrors distort, but they also

---

[99] Deleuze and Guattari, *Mille plateaux*, p. 220; *A Thousand Plateaus*, p. 180.
[100] Fleming, p. 75.

reveal things that cannot be seen otherwise. Specifically, a mirror reveals the beholder's face to themselves in a way that is impossible without it, and is therefore encoded by Lacan as an instrument that offers the infant an image of a coherent self that is both illusory and essential for psychic development.[101] Where for Lacan the illusion is of a coherent subjectivity, in the *Rose* the mirror can be read as a sign specifically of the contingency of this kind of illusion: mirrors are framed, and reveal their image only when looked at. In other words, the revelation-illusion of the mirror image highlights the facial mode of Guillaume's *Rose*: the illusion of interiority can indeed be revelatory, but it can – and, for Deleuze and Guattari, should – also be circumvented.

The possibility of avoiding the illusion of the *visage* meets resistance in the episode in which Amant faces the fountain of Narcissus within the garden. As discussed in this book's Introduction, Narcissus is perhaps the archetypal literary face, and his presence in any text suggests an engagement, direct or otherwise, with the problems inherent in reading and/or misreading faces. In the *Rose*, the role of Narcissus and his fountain also frames a series of textual characteristics that clearly form part of an overarching structure of *visagéité*. Amant's approach to the fountain is unforced, and it is not until he reaches it that he reads the inscription which explains that there 'estoit morz li biau Narcisus' (line 1436) [fair Narcissus had died there]. As Jane Gilbert points out, the analogy we expect between Amant and Narcissus is 'deferred' in the narrative by various devices, one of which is Amant's own fear at approaching the fountain.[102] However, Gilbert's argument is that it is Amant's repudiation of Narcissus as a model for his own behaviour that ironically connects the two: 'Guillaume renders with particular clarity and pointed irony the connection between refusing and assuming the Narcissan prototype.'[103] Repudiation and identification ultimately amounting to the same thing, the implication is that the encounter with the mirror is akin to the process of endless internalising that is part of Deleuze and Guattari's *visage*: a position outside the grid is only ever an illusion, since the real perimeters of that grid are ceaselessly shifting and accommodating. To be outside is, ultimately, to be inside. In the encounter with the fountain, where is the space of possibility from which one might launch a 'ligne de fuite'? A possible answer lies in the optics of the pool and in its function as a mirror. Claire Nouvet makes two crucial points in this regard: firstly, she notes that while the text emphasises how the miraculous crystals at the bottom of the fountain allow Amant to see the whole garden,

---

[101] See 'Le stade du miroir comme formateur de la fonction du Je', in Lacan, *Écrits*, pp. 93–100.
[102] Gilbert, '"I am Not He"', p. 948.
[103] Ibid., p. 949.

he has in fact already seen it all.[104] There are echoes here of Amant's ability to see and to know what is in the garden while still on the outside of the wall. Secondly, Nouvet points out that the optics of the pool tally with the medieval concept of the mechanics of vision; the eye is not a tool for direct perception but, rather, works in a manner more akin to a mirror's indirect manipulation of an image.[105] Eyes and mirrors are both imperfect tools of perception. This correlation is significant, since it undoes the opposition between reality and illusion which is at the heart of the codified *visage*; the Middle Ages' illusion of a prioritised interiority is based on a profound awareness of the limits of perception, and thus inflects depictions of surfaces, mirrors, walls and faces with the possibility that they might be otherwise, or might work otherwise than in terms of a representational structure of perceiving an inside via an outside. It is this possibility of seeing and thinking otherwise that is the goal of recognising *visagéité*.

This chapter has sought to show how the concept of *visagéité* can be usefully applied to a thirteenth-century narrative poem in order to shed some light on how the text engages with the binary dynamic of interior and exterior. Specifically, the chapter has made an analogy between this dynamic and the broader notion of linguistic and graphic representation, by which an inner core is accessed through an outer visible layer, and sees this analogy reflected in the garden wall's role as both signpost and rite of passage. Delving into the way in which the text presents a key surface – the garden wall – I have argued that its depiction in both the text and its illuminations reveals a concept of interiority that is close to *visagéité*, and that both present a representational structure that, crucially, incorporates the possibility of its own undoing. Through this analysis we can see in the text not quite the subversion of representational thinking – since it is an illusion rather than a deception – but, rather, an articulation of it that also leaves space around it; to paraphrase O'Sullivan again: the garden wall is not only a surface to be read.

---

[104] Claire Nouvet, 'An Allegorical Mirror: The Pool of Narcissus in Guillaume de Lorris' *Roman de la Rose*', *Romanic Review*, 91 (2000), 353–74 (p. 353).
[105] Ibid., p. 357.

4

Faces and Genitals in the *fabliaux*

In this final chapter I turn to the human body and explore the status of the face and faciality with reference to (and challenging the idea of) its bodily origins in a selection of *fabliaux*. Specifically, in this chapter I ask about the limits and definition of faciality in texts that appear to effect a certain kind of distortion on the face through pairing it with its ostensible opposite: the genitals. In *Trubert*, the genitals of an anonymous woman are successfully passed off as the mouth and nostrils of a king; in *Le Chevalier qui fist parler les cons*, vaginas and anuses speak when spoken to, and in both *Du vit et de la coille* and *Do con, do vet et de la soriz*, human genitals walk and talk independently of 'whole' human subjects. The questions raised by these texts and examined in this chapter concern the nature of the relationship between the face and other body parts which play its roles.

The *fabliaux* in which this is at issue engage with oppositional subversion, in terms of their experiments with closing the gap between ostensible opposites: face and genitals. What the texts subvert, I argue, is not the face itself, but the idea of the face as part of a stable binary. Instead of debasing the revered face by blurring the line between it and its conceptual and physiological opposite, the texts introduce and play on the possibility that this oppositional structure doesn't work. Into this I then read the literary enactment of the inherent instability of faciality. In other words, these texts don't invert – although they repeatedly hint at it – and so they posit the idea that there isn't anything to invert.

Throughout the book my goal has been to interrogate the face as a marker of interiority, and to give pause to the notion that it works exclusively to represent or to symbolise. The question of what, if anything, is 'behind' the face has guided much of my investigation, and I have explored various different ways in which the concept of the face moves away from the dynamic by which it is the physical, visible, surface signifier of an inner, less tangible essence. I have tried to open up a space between the face as a structural concept and the face as a physiological phenomenon. The two are linked but are not identical, and it is this difference that I have sought to recognise in a selection of courtly texts as well as in some examples of manuscript pages. In the texts I have looked at so far, the question of interiority has been key to the narrative: in the Arthurian romance of

Chapter 1, the status of the individual knight is at stake; the *Rose* deals with the interaction among different allegorical, linguistic and moral modes.

In this chapter, then, I look at a genre of medieval literature which has a different relationship to interiority, and in which the focus of the narrative is less on the development of an individual, or on value systems and their language, and is more on material matters such as food, sex and physical violence. The material focus of the *fabliaux* has given rise to a strand of criticism vaunting their connection to the 'reality' of daily medieval life.[1] Underpinning this argument is an assumption of the priority of the material over its linguistic signs, and, moreover, of the ability of those linguistic signs to provide faithful and accurate access to that materiality. R. Howard Bloch laments that, despite a shift in the focus of medieval literary scholarship from the historical to the textual, scholars nonetheless still make 'increasingly excessive claims concerning the mimetic accuracy of the fabliaux'.[2] Bloch picks apart how scholars have seen in the *fabliaux* an ally in the quest for '[t]he innocent text [which] permits direct access to the bodies and lives of poets'.[3] He argues vehemently against this reading, explaining that the *fabliaux* in fact operate according to the inherent inability of language to represent faithfully, and that the texts partake in 'a constant questioning of the sufficiency of poetic representation'.[4] Making links between the bodily subject matter of the *fabliaux* and the linguistic games employed in their narratives, Bloch's reading unpicks the foundational position of the human body, and shows how the *fabliaux* '[risk] exposing the inessential – fictive, conventional – status of the difference between inner and outer'.[5] With Bloch, I agree that these texts do indeed radically disrupt the link between outer representation and inner referent. Where in the other chapters of this book the face as outer representation has been interrogated, here I look at the face as the referent; other parts of the body refer to the face, and it is this relationship which is under scrutiny here. Bloch asks: 'Is it possible to conceive of a stable point of reference against which the fabliaux might be considered to be particularly transgressive?'[6] Here I interrogate the status of the face as a stable reference point against which the facial genitals might be considered transgressive.

The first stage of my argument is that in these tales of genital faciality the ostensible structure is one of imitation, whereby genitals look or act like faces, but that closer inspection reveals that this relation fails to be upheld.

---

[1] See Bloch, *The Scandal of the Fabliaux*, p. 132 n. 18.
[2] Ibid., p. 5.
[3] Ibid., p. 9.
[4] Ibid., p. 101.
[5] Ibid., p. 128.
[6] Ibid., p. 60.

In *Trubert*, the genitals are presented as something that effectively stands in for a face. There are several references to the fact that this is based on visual resemblance, and yet these references are incoherent and fail to provide a path from the genitals to their apparent referent: the face. In the texts which feature walking, talking genitals, the question of this relationship is posed in terms of the status of the body as a marker of stable subjectivity. Here, again, the face emerges as a kind of ephemeral point of origin: despite the persistent suggestion that the 'eyes–nose–mouth' face is the 'degree zero of faciality', that it is the model for the facial genitals and that it is a formative part of a unified and recognisable subject, the texts repeatedly deny such a simplistic genealogy. Two interwoven implications thus arise from my analysis: firstly, that the face in its 'proper' physiological place (on the front of the head) is not the 'degree zero of faciality', and secondly, that other parts of the body acting or appearing like this 'proper' face are in fact also faces themselves. In this chapter – and, indeed, throughout this book – I argue that certain literary phenomena engender a reappraisal of how the quality of faciality relates to the physiological face, and I suggest not only that the two must be understood separately, but also that faciality can be bestowed upon or exhibited by a much broader range of body parts, surfaces and objects than simply the 'eyes–nose–mouth' found on the front of a human being's head. The final step in this train of thought is that which denies the physiological face the status of originary or 'model' face. It is, rather, one of many potential faces.

The *fabliaux* world permits this crossing over from imitation to being; its blend of the 'natural' and the fantastic, or of the 'real' and the dream world, is startling in both its nonchalance and its comprehensiveness. This is a literary world in which boundaries are not so much crossed as non-existent. The most pertinent examples of dream and reality blending into one, or failing to observe a boundary between them, are *Le Moigne* (*NRCF*, x, 125, pp. 265–75), *Le Sohait des vez* (*NRCF*, vi, 70, pp. 260–72) and *La Damoisele qui sonjoit* (*NRCF*, iv, 25, pp. 45–55), in each of which the main protagonist has a dream and, after waking, acts according to what was dreamed.[7] We also note a similar kind of cohabitation of reality and fiction in the *fabliaux* in which characters recount fictional narratives for their body parts as they simultaneously enact their 'real' function.[8] These are distinguished from those

---

[7] References in parentheses to the *NRCF* refer to the *Nouveau recueil complet des fabliaux*, ed. by Willem Noomen and Nico van den Boogaard, 10 vols (Assen: Van Gorcum, 1983–1998). References will give the volume number, the classification number of the *fabliau* in question and the page range. When quoting from the *NRCF* I will also give line numbers from the critical edition, unless otherwise noted. Translations of the *fabliaux* in this chapter are my own, unless otherwise attributed.

[8] See in particular *La Damoisele qui ne pooit oïr parler de foutre* (*NRCF*, iv, 26, pp.

fabliaux in which the coexistence of truth and falsity is the result of a mistake, such as *Aloul* and *Les Deux Vilains*.[9] In *Le Vilain de bailleul*[10] a husband is convinced that he is dead and that he therefore isn't really witnessing his wife's adultery, and in *Le Prestre qui abevete*[11] an adulterous priest convinces his *amie*'s husband that an enchanted key-hole is only making him think he's seeing the pair making love. Another kind of dream–reality interference is found in *Le Prestre qui manja mores*,[12] in which a priest, standing on his horse, wonders what would happen if he says 'het' and accidentally says it out loud, causing the horse to bolt. What is at stake in many *fabliaux*, then, is the fragility of the boundary separating fantasy and reality, and the erosion of a hierarchical relationship between the two, specifically explored through the morphology of the human body. While, as Anne Cobby points out, 'the literal interpretation of metaphors is inherently funny', it also raises profound questions concerning the separation of the two.[13]

Alison Moore claims that the engagement of the *fabliaux* with the idea of the dismembered body reflects a particular – although often complex –

57–89), *Cele qui fu foutue et desfoutue* (*NRCF*, IV, 30, pp. 151–87), *L'Esquiriel* (*NRCF*, VI, 58, pp. 33–49), *La Pucele qui voloit voler* (*NRCF*, VI, 65, pp. 155–70), *La Sorisete des Estopes* (*NRCF*, VI, 66, pp. 171–84), *Porcelet* (*NRCF*, VI, 67, pp. 185–92), *Le Maignien qui foti la dame* (*NRCF*, VI, 73, pp. 301–11), *Gauteron et Marion* (*NRCF*, VIII, 84, pp. 127–32), *Le Fol Vilain* (*NRCF*, IX, 106, pp. 149–68), *La Dame qui aviene demandoit pour morel sa provende avoir* (*NRCF*, IX, 108, pp. 183–99) and even *La Dame escoillee* (*NRCF*, VIII, 83, pp. 1–125), in which a women is convinced that she has hidden testicles and undergoes surgery to have them removed.

9 (*NRCF*, III, 14, pp. 1–44); (*NRCF*, IX, 107, pp. 169–81).
10 (*NRCF*, V, 49, pp. 223–49).
11 (*NRCF*, VIII, 98, pp. 299–309).
12 (*NRCF*, VII, 75, pp. 191–202).
13 Anne Elizabeth Cobby, *Ambivalent Conventions: Formula and Parody in Old French*, Faux Titre, 101 (Amsterdam: Rodopi, 1995), p. 26. Cobby also explains her approach to the *fabliaux* in a way that has influenced my own thinking: her work focuses on details in the texts, showing how '[what is found there] enhances the texts in which it occurs, without claiming that it fully explains the fabliaux' (p. 25). I also bear in mind in this chapter the question of the genre of the *fabliaux*. I share the scepticism set out by Norris Lacy in his 1987 essay, 'Fabliaux and the Question of Genre' (in *Reading Medieval Studies*, 13 (1987), 25–34). Lacy points out the risks of subscribing to any one method of defining the *fabliaux* corpus, or of using a too restrictive set of criteria. Along with Cobby, I begin with individual texts and indirectly comment on the genre. At the same time, however, I group these texts together because of the common theme of facial genitals, and I recognise in them a similar nonchalance towards both 'the ubiquitous theme of bodily dismemberment' and the very thin line between fantasy and reality (see Bloch, p. 101). Equally, while I do not assume the *fabliaux* all to have a common cause, what the particular examples under scrutiny here all demonstrate is both clearly and profoundly subversive. Of what, and in what way, is at issue in this chapter.

historical attitude towards the notion of bodily fragmentation.[14] As part of her argument, she refers to the two complementary dream-*fabliaux*, in which a dreamer finds themselves in a market that sells an assortment of genitals; a monk dreams that he is in a vagina market (*Le Moigne*), and a woman has a dream in which the only goods on offer are 'coilles et viz' [balls and pricks] (*Le Sohait des vez*, line 82). Moore observes that, in the *fabliaux* that deal almost exclusively with dismembered body parts, the members themselves are never described as actual dismembered flesh; that, for instance, there is never any mention of blood.[15] Moore does not mention that this is the case across the board in the *fabliaux*, and not a phenomenon unique to dream sequences. A more faithful reading of these mysteriously sanitised body parts is, I contend, to see them as one among several *fabliaux* elements that belong neither to a naturalistic portrait nor to a fictionalised dream-world. It is this position that I take in the following analysis.

Trubert

In the thirteenth-century quasi-*fabliau Trubert*, attributed to an otherwise unknown Douin de Lavesne, one episode stands out among many, and yet has received little dedicated critical comment. There has been some debate over the text's classification. While it calls itself a *fabliau* ('En fabliaus doit fables avoir | s'i a il, ce sachiez de voir: | por ce est fabliaus apelez | que de faubles est aünez', lines 1–4 in de Lage's edition [*Fabliaux* must contain fable; they do, so know this to be true: this is why they are called *fabliaux*, because they are composed of fable]), some have suggested that both its relative length and the fact that there is a single protagonist distance it from this group.[16] Mary Jane Stearns Schenck excludes *Trubert* from her list of 'typical' *fabliaux*, despite it meeting her requirement of self-designation, on the grounds of its length and of its lack of narrative or moral 'closure'.[17] Keith Busby also notes

---

[14] Alison Moore, 'The Medieval Body and the Modern Eye: A Corporeal Reading of the Old French *Fabliaux*', in *Worshipping Women: Misogyny and Mysticism in the Middle Ages*, ed. by John O. Ward and Francesca C. Bussey, Sydney Studies in History, 7 (Sydney: University of Sydney, 1997), pp. 237–82.

[15] Ibid., pp. 264–5.

[16] de Lage includes lacunae and thus puts the total number of lines at 2984, while the *NRCF* does not and thus produces a slighter shorter text of 2978 lines. For a brief summary of attitudes towards the text's generic status, see de Lage's introduction to his edition: Douin de Lavesne, *Trubert: fabliau du XIIIe siècle*, ed. by G. Reynaud de Lage (Geneva: Droz, 1974), pp. xxi–xxvi. All subsequent references to *Trubert* are to this edition unless otherwise noted.

[17] Mary Jane Stearns Schenck, *The Fabliaux: Tales of Wit and Deception*, Purdue University Monographs in Romance Languages, 24 (Amsterdam: John Benjamins, 1987),

the difficulties of classification posed by the text, but ultimately argues that the 'integration of *Trubert* [...] and its source material into the wider corpus of Old French verse narrative' positions it 'at the centre rather than at the periphery of the literary enterprise'.[18] In an earlier article, Busby claimed that *Trubert*'s self-designation as a *fabliau* set up certain expectations on the part of the audience and thus went some way towards tempering 'the unremitting evil of the hero's deeds'.[19] My concern is not with designating either the text or its hero, although the persistent tendencies to categorise serve as a background to my study.[20]

What makes this text particularly useful for my study is the inclusion of one episode within the context of a series of tricks, deceits and disguises. In what is acknowledged as an especially nasty story even by the standards of its fellow *fabliaux*, this particular incident is exceptional both in its gruesomeness and in the dismissive and callous brevity of its textual treatment. Larissa Tracy discusses excessive violence in three other *fabliaux* and decides that, in her examples, the texts emphasise the excess of the violent acts, 'thus directly criticizing this degree of violence'.[21] This violent act of Trubert's is, on the contrary, passed over in almost complicit silence. In this episode, the eponymous hero chops off the vagina and anus of a passing woman in order to give them as a 'present' to the duke of Burgundy, the almost constant object of Trubert's trickery throughout the text. As he gives the body parts to the duke, Trubert explains that they are in fact the mouth and nostrils of the duke's enemy, King Golias, and that they are therefore proof of the latter's death. The duke is delighted, and puts the items in a box for safe-keeping. The question I want to ask is deceptively simple: how can a *con* and a *cul* represent a human face?

In attempting to answer this question, this section will discuss firstly the literary and folkloric precedent of a substantive and symbolic link between the

---

p. 62.

[18] Keith Busby, *Codex and Context: Reading Old French Verse Narrative in Manuscript*, Faux titre, 221, 222, 2 vols (Amsterdam: Rodopi, 2002), I, p. 459.

[19] Keith Busby, 'The Diabolic Hero in Medieval French Narrative: *Trubert* and *Wistasse le Moine*', in *The Court and Cultural Diversity*, ed. by Evelyn Mullally and John Thompson (Cambridge: Brewer, 1997), pp. 415–25 (p. 417).

[20] Kathryn Gravdal observes that Trubert is neither courtly nor *vilain*, and that he moves between these spaces. I share this point of view inasmuch as it allows for Trubert to occupy two apparently opposed positions; this binary itself serves more as an expectation against which Trubert acts out his transgression. See Kathryn Gravdal, *'Vilain' and 'Courtois': Transgressive Parody in French Literature of the Twelfth and Thirteenth Centuries* (Lincoln: University of Nebraska Press, 1989), p. 119.

[21] Larissa Tracy, 'The Uses of Torture and Violence in the Fabliaux: When Comedy Crosses the Line', *Florilegium*, 23 (2006), 143–68 (p. 149).

face and the genitals. I will then think about how *Trubert* deals specifically with the language of anatomy and how it ultimately renders uncertain the physiological details upon which the deception ostensibly relies. What exactly, I ask, is the duke looking at? Finally, I will examine what this bizarre but nonetheless successful substitution says about the face itself. What is needed to represent and reproduce the face? Can we thus work backwards and approach a notion of the basic components of a recognisable face? More broadly, this whole chapter engages with the notion of the face via its medieval textual treatment and asks if, circulating within and around these texts, there is a perceptible concept of what I am calling the 'degree zero of faciality'. That is to say, a minimum set of requirements in order that something be a face, or be like a face. Here, then, I approach this question via one particularly wayward text's engagement with the possibility that faciality can convincingly be exhibited by other body parts.

Trubert is the telling, over roughly 3000 lines, of a series of tricks that the eponymous protagonist plays on a gullible duke. The text is found in a single manuscript (Paris, BnF fr. 2188), dated by de Lage to around 1270 (a date based on its similarity to a manuscript from 1273, and corroborated by the editors of the *NRCF*).[22] The text itself appears, again according to the *NRCF*, whose editors dismiss various attempts to date it more precisely, to have been written in the first half of the thirteenth century.[23] While de Lage suggests a relatively precise provenance for the author, this is dismissed by the *NRCF* on the grounds that Douin's tendency towards poetic imprecision makes it impossible to draw firm conclusions regarding the text's regional characteristics.[24] The story begins with the 'nice', Trubert, who lives in the woods with his mother and sister, deciding to take the family heifer to market in order to raise funds to buy his sister some new clothes. After some farcical and confusing business dealings, Trubert has a newly acquired goat garishly painted. Walking past the window of the local château, Trubert's goat is spotted and admired by the duchess of Burgundy, who sends for him. Trubert convinces the duchess to sleep with him in exchange for the goat (which she never gets), and so begins a series of ever more elaborate disguises and tricks that Trubert plays on the duke and his household, culminating in his dressing up as a woman and being married off to the duke's enemy, King Golias, as a peace offering. The text is usually discussed in terms of a clearly discernible series of five such episodes: Trubert has his goat painted and seduces the duchess; Trubert disguises himself as a carpenter, ties the duke to a tree and beats him; Trubert disguises himself as a doctor and persuades the duke that

---

[22] Douin de Lavesne, *Trubert*, p. vii; *NRCF*, III, p. 146.
[23] *NRCF*, x, p. 146.
[24] Ibid., p. 147.

the dog shit he smears all over his body is really a powerful ointment, before beating the duke once again; Trubert dresses as a knight, answers the duke's call to arms against King Golias and, thanks to his frightening appearance that is the result of his inability to correctly don his armour, manages to scare away the enemy troops and is hailed as a hero at the duke's court; finally, after the duke realises how he has been tricked, Trubert dresses in his own sister's clothes in order to evade capture and manages, once again, to infiltrate the duke's household. Believing the trickster to be a young girl, the duke allows him to share his own daughter's bed, in which Trubert tricks the daughter into repeated sexual encounters (explaining that his penis is a friendly bunny-rabbit) and is eventually sent to Golias as his new bride. On their wedding night, Trubert makes use of a purse to trick the king into thinking he's having sex with his new wife, before he then switches places with a serving girl, at which point the narrative ends.

The episode in question occurs during the fourth disguise, when Trubert is pretending to be a knight. After having spooked the king's scout, who returns to the king and advises him and his troops to disperse, Trubert, the worse for wear after his accidental, though fortunate, escapade, spots a woman on her way to deliver food to her husband. Trubert tricks her into approaching him and then cuts off her genitals and anus, while the narrative voice rather cryptically tells the reader that Trubert wants to give them to the duke:

> Que qu'il estoit en telle error,
> une famë a son seignor
> portoit a mengier en l'essart.
> 'Dame, fet il, se Deus vos gart,
> venez si m'aidiez a monter.'
> Cele ne li ose veer,
> a lui s'en vient, et il la prent,
> a terre la giete et estent;
> le cul et le con li coupa,
> en s'aloiere le bouta;
> au duc en velt feire present. (lines 1919–29)

[While he was deliberating, a woman was in the clearing taking food to her lord. 'Lady', he said, 'may God protect you. Come and help me mount this horse.' She didn't dare refuse him and so she approached him. Trubert grabbed her, threw her to the ground and laid her out. He cut off her arsehole and her cunt and put them in his bag; he wanted to give them to the duke as a gift]

Trubert rides off and, with his armour convincingly battered, enters the duke's castle in triumph. Trubert then presents the genitals to the duke, explaining that they are, in fact, the mouth and nostrils of King Golias and are, as such, proof that the duke's enemy has been slain:

> Trubert a tret de s'aloiere
> le cul et le con qui i ere;
> au duc en a fet un present.
> Li dus entre ses mains le prent,
> puis li demande que ce est.
> 'Sire, dit il, la bouche i est
> de Goulïas et les narilles.
> — Par foi, je croi bien, dit li sires;
> einsi faite bouche avoit il.
> Et qu'est ce ci? est ce sorcil?
> — Ce sont les narilles, par foi;
> onques mes ne vi sifet roi!' (lines 1963–74)

[Trubert drew from his pouch the arsehole and cunt that were in there and gave them to the duke as a gift. The duke took them in his hands, then asked Trubert what they were. 'My Lord', he said, 'this is the mouth and nostrils of Golias.' 'My faith! So it is', said the duke, 'his mouth was just like this. And this, what is this? Is it an eyebrow?'. 'Those are his nostrils, by my faith! I've never seen a king who looks like this.'

Trubert goes on to explain why he has only these parts of the king's face, rather than the more conventional trophy head, through an admission of weakness that goes unnoticed by the credulous and, no doubt, relieved duke:

> Quant la teste li oi coupee,
> volentiers l'eüsse aportee,
> mes onques ne la poi lever.
> N'oi pas loisir de sejorner,
> erraument en tranchai ce jus. (lines 1975–9)

[When I cut his head off, I would gladly have brought it to you, but I could hardly lift it. I didn't want to waste any time, so I quickly cut off these parts]

The duke then puts the body parts into a box, satisfied that they are proof of his enemy's downfall and his own victory. Trubert takes his leave, and shortly afterwards the duke is presented with a message from Golias. The duke claims that this cannot be true, since

la narille et la bouche en ai
ceanz en un cofre enfermé. (lines 2060–1)

[I have his nostrils and mouth locked up in a box]

Meanwhile, Trubert encounters a knight on his way to the duke's court, and the trickster tells him how he duped the duke and asks the knight to relay the awful truth, which he does. Thence follows the final disguise episode, in which Trubert dresses up as his sister in order to fool the duke's men.

In studies that discuss the progressive depravity of Trubert's deeds, the *cul/con* episode (as I will call it from now on) is listed as one of a series of bodily infractions. When it is singled out, it is usually to highlight its superlative nastiness: Jean-Charles Payen refers to it euphemistically as a 'certain épisode dont la cruauté gratuite est, à la limite, insoutenable' [a certain episode, the gratuitous cruelty of which is borderline intolerable] and relegates its summary to the notes.[25] More recently, Daron Burrows cites it among 'signs of the penetrability and permeability of the human body' alongside 'Trubert's penetration into the backside of the duke and the vaginas of the duchess and her daughter, […] his own flatulence, and his emission of seminal *angeloz*'.[26] In a 2008 essay focusing on the motif of disguise in *Trubert*, Corinne Füg-Pierreville notes the violence not of the act but of the words used to describe it: 'Les termes crus employés pour désigner les parties de son [the woman's] anatomie la privent de toute dignité.' [The crude names used for parts of the woman's anatomy deny her any dignity].[27] She then goes on to suggest that Trubert's presentation of the *con* and the *cul* as parts of King Golias's face figures among the myriad disguises Trubert effects not only on his own body but on bodies and objects around him:

> Il fait passer une chèvre peinte pour un animal extraordinaire, une crotte de chien pour un onguent miraculeux, un sexe masculin pour un petit lapin, un sac pour un sexe féminin, un marchand pour un coupable, un chevalier pour un criminel, un chapelain pour un violeur, une suivante pour une reine, le *con* et le *cul* d'une vieille pour la bouche et les narines d'un roi.

---

[25] Jean-Charles Payen, '*Trubert* ou le triomphe de la marginalité', in *Exclus et systèmes d'exclusion dans la littérature et la civilisation médiévales*, Senefiance, 5 (Aix-en-Provence: Cuer, 1978), pp. 119–33 (p. 123). Translation is my own.

[26] Daron Burrows, '*Trubert*: Transgression, Revolution, Abjection', *Reinardus*, 19 (2006), 37–52 (pp. 48–9).

[27] Corinne Füg-Pierreville, 'Le Déguisement dans *Trubert*: l'identité en question', *Moyen Age: revue d'histoire et de philologie*, 114 (2008), 315–34 (p. 324). Translations are my own.

> [He makes people believe that a painted goat is a fantastic animal, that a dog turd is a miraculous ointment, that a penis is a little rabbit, that a bag is a vagina, that an innocent merchant is guilty, that a knight is a criminal, that a chaplain is a rapist, that a servant is a queen, that the cunt and arsehole of an old woman are the mouth and nostrils of a king][28]

Füg-Pierreville touches on the metamorphic promise of the episode in the context of her observation that 'le texte présent effectivement Trubert dans ce rôle de géniteur réel ou symbolique' [the text effectively presents Trubert as a father-creator, whether real or symbolic].[29] Her essay hints, albeit sometimes in paradoxical terms, at the possibility that disguise effects real transformation: '[Trubert] enfreint la différence irréductible entre les sexes quand il se travestit en femme' [Trubert broaches the irreducible difference between the sexes when he dresses up as a woman].[30] She also notes this at a textual level:

> Le succès de ces transformations se montre d'ailleurs entériné dans le texte même, car Trubert est souvent désigné, au sein de la narration, par ses nouvelles fonctions ou son nouveau nom.
>
> [Indeed, the success of these transformations is confirmed in the text itself as, in the course of the narrative, Trubert is often referred to in his new role or by his new name][31]

Nevertheless, the particular significance of the transformation effected on the *cul/con* remains to be addressed. While its brutality has marked it out for contemporary commentators, this has not, as far as I can see, been examined together with the particular importance of the face in the equation.

Mikhail Bakhtin's study of Rabelaisian grotesque provides a useful initial framework for the imaginary within which the face/genitals continuum exists. He explains a dualism whereby the cosmic system of 'upwards'/Heaven versus 'downwards'/Earth is mapped onto the human body, with the head and face belonging to the upper stratum, while the 'the genital organs, the belly, and the buttocks' occupy the lower.[32] He goes on to explain that the grotesque body – clearly at play across the *fabliau* corpus – is an excessive and incomplete body:

---

[28] Ibid., p. 333.
[29] Ibid.
[30] Ibid., p. 317.
[31] Ibid., p. 327.
[32] Mikhail Bakhtin, *Rabelais and His World*, trans. by Hélène Iswolsky (Cambridge, MA: MIT Press, 1968), p. 21.

The stress is laid on those parts of the body that are open to the outside world, that is, the parts through which the world enters the body or emerges from it, or through which the body itself goes out to meet the world [...]: the open mouth, the genital organs, the breasts, the phallus, the pot-belly, the nose.[33]

The mouth, in particular, emblemises the symbiotic relationship between the two cosmic poles. Trubert himself, as noted above, is the agent of a series of severe infractions of the inside/outside dichotomy, either through the violation of existing bodily orifices or by the creation of new and improper apertures. In this sense, for Burrows, Trubert's behaviour also brings his victims into contact with the Kristevan abject.[34]

It is well attested that medieval medicine was relatively ignorant of the particularities of the female body; the hidden – and therefore unknown – nature of female genitalia dovetails with the medieval conception of woman as an essentially mysterious creature.[35] Capricious, volatile, deceitful, the woman resists reading, unless, as E. Jane Burns points out, she is co-opted into a male imaginary in which she is to be 'stripped of the vagina around which her own subjectivity might have been formed'.[36] Burns notes that the mouth and the vagina are 'female orifices that, within the antifeminist discourse of the French Middle Ages, typically make trouble for men'.[37] In other words, the vagina is at once part of a broad scheme of bodily infraction, in which it is paired with the mouth, and also part of the specifically feminine aspect of this infraction. A fear not only of the feminine but specifically of female genitals is noted by Julia Kristeva in a book written to accompany an exhibition at the Louvre. She describes prehistoric artists' attempts at deflecting the power of the vulva either by substituting other images or by exaggerating the size of the genitals depicted.[38] Samantha Riches and Bettina Bildhauer evoke the mythical power of female genitalia in medieval thought, noting that the

---

[33] Ibid., p. 26.

[34] Burrows, '*Trubert*: Transgression, Revolution, Abjection', p. 50.

[35] See, in particular, *A Cultural History of the Human Body in the Medieval Age*, ed. by Linda Kalof (Oxford: Berg, 2010) and Thomas Laqueur, *Making Sex: Body and Gender from the Greeks to Freud* (Cambridge, MA: Harvard University Press, 1992).

[36] E. Jane Burns, *Bodytalk: When Women Speak in Old French Literature* (Philadelphia: University of Pennsylvania Press, 1993), p. 35. See also E. Jane Burns, 'Knowing Women: Female Orifices in Old French Farce and Fabliau', *Exemplaria*, 4 (1992), 81–104; 'This Prick Which is Not One', in *Feminist Approaches to the Body in Medieval Literature*, ed. by Linda Lomperis and Sarah Stanbury (Philadelphia: University of Pennsylvania Press, 1993), pp. 188–212.

[37] Burns, *Bodytalk*, p. 31.

[38] Kristeva, pp. 37–9.

vulva was 'associated with a wound in several medieval contexts'.[39] They continue: 'Any cut or tear in the body could be instinctively linked to the vulva; this association was profoundly important in a range of understandings of the significance of external female genitalia and the passage into and out of the body that is connoted.'[40] Peggy McCracken observes that 'late medieval images' make a clear association between Christ's wound and the vulva.[41] The link between the mouth and the vagina, each figured as a dangerous opening, is also obliquely apparent in certain interpretations of the Hippocratic treatises, in which the virginal vagina is understood as a pair of closed lips.[42] The folkloric motifs of *vagina dentata* and its lesser-known cousin, the *vagina loquens*, are further incarnations of the danger of feminine orifices which play respectively on the mouth's capacity both to ingest destructively and to exude excessively.

These motifs feed into the *fabliaux* corpus and appear in several different guises, each serving as a useful intertext for our examination of *Trubert*. The vagina-as-wound turns up most notably in the mid-thirteenth-century *Le Maignien qui foti la dame*, in which a woman, having fallen while getting into a bath, ends up straddling the edge of the tub and believes herself to be grievously wounded.[43] The woman's assessment of the situation is corroborated by both her maid and an opportunistic passer-by (who ends up 'curing' her by helpfully offering to push her entrails back inside her), and the text thus plays on the idea that the *con* as a terrible wound is not only a ruse used by the *Maignien* but is also a perfectly reasonable point of view for the women themselves. The *vagina dentata* is explored in relative depth in *Le Jugement des cons*: three women, in love with the same man, ask their uncle to decide who ought to be his wife.[44] The uncle's chosen method of adjudication is to ask the girls the same question and to give to the lucky bachelor the girl who comes up with the best answer. The uncle asks each girl

---

[39] Samantha Riches and Bettina Bildhauer, 'Cultural Representations of the Body', in *A Cultural History of the Human Body in the Medieval Age*, ed. by Kalof, pp. 181–201 (p. 190).

[40] Ibid.

[41] Peggy McCracken, *The Curse of Eve, the Wound of the Hero: Blood, Gender, and Medieval Literature* (Philadelphia: University of Pennsylvania Press, 2003), p. 108.

[42] Sarah Alison Miller, *Medieval Monstrosity and the Female Body*, Routledge Studies in Medieval Religion and Culture, 8 (New York: Routledge, 2010), p. 72. Katharine Park also notes that in what she describes as the first identification of the clitoris 'in a work of anatomy based on human dissection', this particular body-part is called a 'languette'. See 'The Rediscovery of the Clitoris: French Medicine and the Tribade, 1570–1620', in *The Body in Parts: Fantasies of Corporeality in Early Modern Europe*, ed. by David Hillman and Carla Mazzio (New York: Routledge, 1997), pp. 171–93 (p. 176).

[43] 440 (*NRCF*, VI, 73, pp. 301–11).

[44] 441 (*NRCF*, IV, 23, pp. 23–33).

which she thinks is older, her or her *con*, and the answers each play on the notion of the vagina-as-mouth: the first explains that her *con* is older than her since it has a beard; the second reasons that she is the eldest because she has teeth whereas her *con* does not yet; the third, and the one who wins the prize, tells her uncle that her *con* is younger than she because, while she has been weaned, it still has 'la goule baee' and 'veut aletier' (lines 150, 151) ['a gaping mouth' and 'wants to suckle'].

The mouth–anus connection is less well developed as a literary and folkloric motif than that between the mouth and the vagina, and seems to centre mainly on this broader hierarchical structure of purity and impurity.[45] The notion of the anus as a kind of improper mouth is often tied up in discussions of the genitals and/or the anus; in this sense, as part of the same bodily stratum they perform a more or less analogous symbolic function. James Paxson examines the medieval iconographic convention of figuring the devil with a face where his genitals would be, and considers the satanic connotation to be figured less by any orifice in particular than by these 'lower' orifices in general: 'That Hell Mouth had an analog in Hell Anus or Hell Cunt fits well the infernal semiotic economy of enticement, devouring, digestion, and excretion.'[46] Paxson goes on: 'Having an actual face instead of a backside, or vulva, or penis, the demonic body exists as a sign of the fallen, twisted, upside down mentality of the devil; it stands as physiologic and microcosmic emblem of the whole cosmos Satan had polluted and attempted to invert.'[47]

A similar model appears in another thirteenth-century *fabliau*, *Le Chevalier qui fist parler les cons*.[48] As the title suggests, the story is of a knight who gains the peculiar power of being able to make *cons* talk. The less obvious part of his power is that he can, in the event that a *con* is unable to answer him, make a *cul* speak in its stead. Here, then, the *con* and the *cul* can, albeit with a certain order of preference, both become improper mouths. In another *fabliau*, *Les Deux vilains*, the uncovered anus of a sleeping woman is mistaken for a mouth by a guest who has accidentally entered the hosts' room at night (*NRCF*, IX, 107, pp. 169–81).[49] Carrying a bowl of hot soup to his travelling companion, the man makes the mistake because of the darkness of the night. Probing around with his finger to make sure he has indeed found his friend, he feels that 'le trau ... estoit velus' [the hole ... was hairy] and is satisfied

---

[45] See Mary Douglas, *Purity and Danger: An Analysis of the Concepts of Pollution and Taboo* (London: Routledge, 1966; repr. 1992).

[46] James J. Paxson, 'The Nether-Faced Devil and the Allegory of Parturition', *Studies in Iconography*, 19 (1998), 139–76 (p. 148).

[47] Ibid., p. 152.

[48] 445 (*NRCF*, III, 15, pp. 45–173).

[49] 446 (*NRCF*, IX, 107, pp. 169–81).

since 'ses compaing estoit barbus' [his friend had a beard] (lines 78–80). He then proceeds to try to feed his 'friend' the soup, only to become increasingly frustrated at what he thinks is his friend repeatedly and unnecessarily blowing on the dish to cool it down.

Having established that there is a clear mouth–vagina–anus nexus in place both within the *fabliaux* that form *Trubert*'s immediate intertexts and in a wider cultural field, we must now turn back to *Trubert* to consider precisely how these precedents and conventions are drawn upon and how they serve as grist to the mill of *Trubert*'s radically disruptive programme. The first point to make is that a fourth term is added to this strange anatomy: the *cul* and the *con* are supposed to represent the *bouche* and the *narilles* of King Golias. Not simply a diabolical inversion, nor a violent counter to the threat of the orifice (the woman here is hardly threatening; she is, we note, both mute and anonymous), the *Trubert* episode forces us to consider the possibility of anatomical resemblance and, concomitantly, what is required to represent a face. Trubert needs to convince the duke that the woman's *cul* and *con* are parts of a king's face: why does he choose to pass them off specifically as a mouth and nostrils? Daron Burrows notes the usage of the word 'Golïas' as a euphemism for female genitalia. In which case, there is a further degradation of certain key distinctions that are also being played upon in the episode: between man and woman, between nobility and peasantry, between individuals, between, for James Simpson, the assertiveness of the masculine warrior and the passivity of the female body and, finally, between the ostensible anonymity of genitals and the identifying power of a name.[50] Simpson also points out that in the *cul/con* episode the longer form of the king's name, *Goulïas*, is used, and that it therefore also contains the word *goule*, the animalistic word for 'mouth'.[51] Citing Jeffrey Jerome Cohen's observation that this is a trope in sources about giants, Simpson posits this as part of the logic of the episode's bizarre recognition, whereby the duke sees the genitals as the face of his 'vanquished foe': 'the devouring maw [...] recurs in a number of sources as a [sic] image of the tyrant'.[52] Nonetheless, while a mouth may well be represented by or substituted for either of the two 'nether-orifices', to make someone believe that one of the two is a pair of

---

[50] Daron Burrows, '*Do con, do vet et de la soriz*: édition d'un texte tiré de Berne 354', *Zeitschrift für romanische Philologie*, 117 (2001), 23–49 (p. 35n18); James R. Simpson, *Fantasy, Identity and Misrecognition in Medieval French Narrative* (Oxford: Lang, 2000), p. 207. See also Sandy Feinstein's article about severed heads in which she draws on the idea that a key difference between the head and the genitals is that only the former plays a role in identification.

[51] Simpson, p. 208.

[52] Ibid., pp. 207–8.

nostrils is, in terms of anatomical credibility, beyond the pale (I am claiming that one of the few things that is quite clear in the episode is that the mouth and the nostrils are each represented by *one* of the two orifices). Indeed, we can take one step further back in the logic of the episode and ask why Trubert decides to cut off both the woman's *con* and her *cul* in the first place. The implicit answer, it seems, is that one orifice does not a face make. Trubert's other tricks are all explicitly based on minimal transformation or disguise, and so it may well be here: Trubert's trick is as undeveloped as possible. Even in a world in which it seems that the duke can be made to believe anything Trubert tells him, some concession appears to be being made to the need to have a certain degree of physical similarity between the body parts and what they are being presented as. That concession is, specifically, the presentation of *two* body parts rather than just one.

The notion of a 'real' physical similarity is, however, almost instantly called into question from within the narrative, and the idea that a face can be represented only by a minimum of two elements is complicated by a brief section of dialogue between Trubert and the duke. In this rapid exchange the logic upon which the trick is based shifts and falters as the duke first questions, then accepts, then again questions the identity of the body parts he is being shown. The trick draws upon both physical resemblance and naming as the basis of the deceit, but the text allows neither logic to complete fully. Immediately after Trubert has explained to the duke that what he is looking at are the 'bouche' and 'narilles' of the king, the duke makes two curious comments. Firstly, he affirms what he is being told:

— Par foi, je croi bien, dit li sires;
einsi faite bouche avoit il. (lines 1970–1)

['My faith! So it is', said the duke, 'his mouth was just like this']

He then asks: 'Et qu'est ce ci? est ce sorcil?' [And what is this? Is it an eyebrow?] (line 1972), to which Trubert replies, '— Ce sont les narilles, par foi' [Those are his nostrils, by my faith] (line 1973). The duke has no trouble seeing that he is being shown a mouth and goes as far as to say that it does indeed look like the king's. Where there is a very slight – one meagre line long – hesitation, it is concerning the *narilles*. Even here, however, the duke doesn't question that this is part of the king's face; the only momentary confusion is over which part. This rapid exchange is complex: on the one hand, it might be read as reinforcing my earlier proposition that the face can be evoked only by two or more elements together. It is no more anatomically credible to believe that a *con* or a *cul* is an eyebrow than it is to believe that either is a pair of nostrils; since both these individual comparisons are equally absurd, it seems that it is the combination that creates the effect.[53] The scenario suggests that, if the duke had been shown only one object, he would not have been deceived. On the other hand, however, a closer look at the order of the textual exchange reveals that it is precisely the fact that the mouth *can* be represented by a *con* or a *cul* that allows for the other comparison to work. In other words, the mouth can be represented on its own, but the nostrils – being less symbolically and culturally charged – cannot. The duke has trouble only with the latter; he accepts that he is being shown the king's mouth *before* he has established what the other object is. Indeed, this sense that the two body parts signify separately is reinforced by the duke's misreading of the second part, despite having been told what it is supposed to be. There are several shifts in logic packed densely and almost imperceptibly into the duke's reaction to the body parts, denying any one logic the chance to dominate. The intractability of how the duke reads what is being shown to him and, in turn, how we read what is being made into a face suggests that more is at work here and, perhaps more importantly, that more is at play. In other words, the narrative relies on, and describes in some detail, the possibility of other body parts being substituted for a face, but the text is such that no consistent mechanism for this substitution can be found. Further complicating the matter, we note that there is very little in the text to confirm which of the two body parts is supposed to represent which facial feature. *Cul* and *con* are always mentioned in this order, as are *bouche* and *narilles*, but there is only a single sequence in which the four features are all mentioned in relatively quick succession (lines 1958–68). While this repetition of the *cul–con/bouche–narilles* structure suggests that the *cul* is to be taken as the *bouche*, and the *con* as the *narilles*, it is inconclusive at best. Again we find the apparent precision of the starkly anatomical language (we note that *nez* is never used in place of *narilles*, for instance) undermined by the text's refusal to tell us precisely what is going on.

This moment is not just one among many tricks and disguises, it is the zenith of Trubert's, and of *Trubert*'s, transgression. It is incisively brutal and callous, and deeply disturbing in its impropriety. It plays on one of the most revered and hallowed signifiers of humanity – the face – and reveals how little there is to it; how little is required to make a face where there isn't one. There is, as I have discussed, a relationship between the face and the genitals; it is not this in itself that disturbs. Rather, it is taking this in vain, making it brutal, violent, humourless and, above all, literal. This is not a metaphor but a mutilation and inversion passed over without comment, left to speak for itself. Or, more accurately, left not to speak, not to explain, not to gloss, but

---

[53] The important question of which 'lower' orifice represents which facial feature will be addressed below.

as a mute and irreducible testament to the fragility of bodily signifiers. When we try to unpick its logic, we come unstuck. There is enough of a veneer of physiological plausibility in the trick at least to make us contemplate how far this resemblance might go. In the end, however, the text plays with and within the terms of signification, only to shut down the possibility of any coherent system. This revolves, it seems, around the crucial question of what is needed to represent a face. The *cul/con* episode suggests that certain criteria must be fulfilled for something to be read as a face, but it fails to pin these criteria down. What is radical about the text is perfectly condensed into this violent episode: as Bloch argues for the *fabliaux* as a group, behind the teleological, methodological pretence of Trubert's actions, there is a void. The 'degree zero of faciality' features in Trubert's decision to excise these body parts, in his decision to excise two instead of one and in the particular configuration of the duke's reading of these body parts. Crucially, when we try to locate the minimum facial representation, we find its absence. Similarly, throughout Trubert's incessant trickery, there is a lack of reference to any preconceived end-point. Indeed, at the end-point of the text Trubert disappears into the ether: he sends the serving girl to the unsuspecting king's bed and nothing more is said of him. In the *cul/con* episode itself, we learn simply that Trubert attacks the woman, and then that he will give the body parts to the duke as a 'present' (line 1929). Indeed, the first mention of the attack is as it happens; there is neither expression nor inference of any contemplation or premeditation on the part of Trubert. The first we learn of the trick Trubert is hoping to play is as he presents his gift to the duke (lines 1968–9).

In this I approach, though do not quite emulate, Cary Howie's highlighting the endless turning in *Trubert* that produces the protagonist's most fundamentally transgressive attribute: his being *nothing*.[54] Howie frames this in a way that is engaging in its recognition of the absence, in Trubert's character and behaviour, of outside referents. He tells us that Trubert enacts a 'solipsistic self-fashioning', by which he refuses the constituent outside that is the condition of the social and, therefore, the ethical.[55] I see this closed circuit enacted in the most brutal way in the episode of the *con* and *cul*. Trubert literally cuts the genitals off from their original signification, and pastes another onto them: another signification that is, while not totally arbitrary, not entirely based on the visual resemblance that is the conventional mode of deception. Trubert's uncanny ability to trick the duke forms one of the coexisting systems within which the body parts and the facial features can

[54] Cary Howie, 'Rude Theory: The Rough Trade of the Fabliaux', in *Comic Provocations: Exposing the Corpus of Old French Fabliaux*, ed. by Holly A. Crocker (New York: Palgrave Macmillan, 2006), pp. 163–74 (see p. 170 in particular).
[55] Ibid., p. 170.

be effectively exchanged. In his discussion of the role of genitals in various deceptions played out in the *fabliaux*, Simon Gaunt makes the point that tales in which a man is tricked by a woman are not telling us that all men are liable to be thus tricked but, rather, that 'one man's stupidity and credulity allows a clever woman to get the better of him'.[56] A similar thing is happening to the duke; it is not that the genitals are visually indistinguishable from a face, but that the duke is sufficiently gullible, and Trubert sufficiently *malin*, for the mistake to be made. With reference to a later trick in which Trubert gets the king to believe he is making love to a woman when in fact it is Trubert holding a purse, Gaunt explains: 'Any hole can become a *con*, provided it is being manipulated by someone clever enough for someone stupid enough.'[57] In other words, the deception depends in large part on the protagonists and not on the substance or resemblance of the body parts in question; these are more tricks of wit than of substance.[58] There is, nonetheless, a persistent material basis to these tricks; in the purse episode just alluded to, a minimum material resemblance is required, and in the background to the *cul/con* episode there remains the suggestion that the body parts have been chosen because of their similarity to the facial features for which they are substitutes. From the rather different perspective of a narratological analysis of the *fabliaux*, Roy Pearcy makes a similar point for the genre more broadly. He explains that narrative logic must interact with both 'character and circumstance' in order to produce the particular wit of the *fabliaux*.[59] Bringing this to bear on the *cul/con* episode, there is a logic to the deception that is then disrupted, but not eliminated, by the influence of the characters.

We have established that a variety of coexistent and yet broadly incompatible systems work in this text, and in particular in the *cul/con* episode, to effect absurd transformations and substitutions. That is, in the case of the *cul/con* episode, a substitution that hints at convention but which ultimately works outside the systems it evokes. This enacts on a small scale the inherent paradoxes of Trubert's life: for Simpson, the tale's 'moral weightlessness' derives precisely from the anti-hero's 'ability to sustain paradoxes at the expense of ontological consistency and integrity'.[60] In these terms, then, the 'degree zero of faciality' functions as a kind of myth, or as an

[56] Simon Gaunt, *Gender and Genre in Medieval French Literature*, Cambridge Studies in French, 53 (Cambridge: Cambridge University Press, 1995), p. 267.

[57] Ibid., p. 250.

[58] For an exploration of the role of wit in the destabilisation of social hierarchy in the *fabliaux*, see Gabrielle Lyons, '*Avoir* and *savoir*: A Strategic Approach to the Old French *Fabliaux*' (unpublished doctoral thesis, University of Cambridge, 1992).

[59] Roy J. Pearcy, *Logic and Humour in the Fabliaux: An Essay in Applied Narratology* (Cambridge: Brewer, 2007), p. 33.

[60] Simpson, pp. 199, 197.

untraceable origin, whereby it is manifest in ways that do not stand up to the kind of scrutiny they invite. The text plays on the ultimate impossibility of tracing the logic of Trubert's gruesome trick back towards a stable, originary understanding of precisely what a face is, and it does this through a troubled and inconsistent evocation of what it takes to make something look like a face. Sometimes it is a question of physical resemblance, as when Trubert decides to excise two body parts instead of one; sometimes it seems to be a question of calling upon the folkloric precedent of a link between the face and its lower equivalents, as when the duke accepts that he sees a mouth but briefly struggles to see nostrils, and sometimes it is a case of language and the power of naming, as when Trubert convinces the questioning duke by naming the body parts as facial features. In other words, the pivotal exchange between Trubert and the duke seems to call upon a series of what we might consider different origin stories of the human face. For instance, through successfully naming the body parts as facial features, Trubert hints at the notion of faciality as a linguistic construct; through choosing two body parts instead of one, he alludes to the idea of faciality as a case of pattern recognition. Each facial 'origin story' is disrupted by the simultaneous presence of several stories, and the basis of the trick is thus fragmented. What, we are left asking, does this trick tell us about the essence of faciality? What understanding of the face produces this deceit? What, finally, is the origin, or the degree zero, of faciality that allows for its reproduction? In this sense, the episode in question points towards the possibility that, if a *cul* and a *con* can become a face, what a face *is* becomes worryingly ungraspable. Jean Batany suggests that certain transformative episodes in *Trubert* show how the text reaches the limits of the impossible, and suggests by way of example that, while he can become a carpenter, Trubert 'ne peut pas devenir femme'.[61] What I hope to have shown in this analysis is that the text may well hint that there is an impossible, and that there are limits, but it fails to uphold the kind of logic Batany appeals to: Trubert is less a carpenter than the woman's genitals and anus are a face.

Le Chevalier qui fist parler les cons

I now move to a discussion of a tale more widely commented upon in modern times than *Trubert*. *Le Chevalier qui fist parler les cons* is the story of a knight given the gift of being able to make vaginas and anuses talk, and culminates in a woman trying and failing to prevent this power working on her own body. It is found in seven manuscripts, all dated, with varying degrees of certainty,

---

[61] Jean Batany, '*Trubert*: progress et bousculade des masques', in *Masques et déguisements dans la littérature médiévale*, ed. by Marie-Louise Ollier (Montreal: Presses de l'Université de Montréal, 1988), pp. 25–34 (p. 33).

to between c. 1250 and 1400. A (Paris, BnF fr. 837) contains an incomplete version of the text, while M (London, British Library, MS Harley 2253) contains an Anglo-Norman version of the text that differs considerably from the common version found in ABCDE and I. Indeed, these versions are considered sufficiently different to be classified separately in both Bédier's and Nykrog's inventories.[62] In each manuscript the text is attributed to 'Garin' (Gwaryn in I), and it is noted in the *NRCF* that the name itself is too common to be a useful clue as to the author's identity and that there is a dearth of other indicators.[63] The same volume also remains relatively circumspect as to the localisation of the text, noting that no linguistic clue can give any degree of certainty, but that the likelihood is that the story originated in the south-eastern region of the Île-de-France (excepting the *remaniement* found in I, which seems to have come from somewhere further north and/or further east).[64]

The primary goal of this analysis is to determine what kind of face is posited by this particular text's engagement with what might be its parodic other. In other words, if the talking vaginas and anuses effect a kind of subversion of the 'proper' face and its speaking role, how does this also assume and therefore uphold a particular image or conception of the 'proper' face? To couch the question in slightly different terms: what kind of original is posited by its (albeit partial) imitation? A second set of questions must then be asked: is this text really engaged in parodying the face? Indeed, is it even a question of imitation? What is the evidence for this notion that the talking genitals are a kind of second face? In pursuing this line of thought, we come across two apparently incompatible conclusions: on the one hand, we reduce the face to its speaking role. To understand the talking genitals as a kind of face is to imply that anything that speaks is a face. On the other hand, in emphasising the parodic or secondary status of the talking genitals, we claim that the 'true' face is much more than its speaking role and that, by implication, there exists a kind of originary 'whole' face of which the speaking role is an incomplete replica. To take this reasoning a step further, I suggest that the fact that we can conceive of these two possibilities, and that, as I will outline below, the text does not resolve the tension between the two, reveals and reflects an inherent instability in the very notion of the face. *Le Chevalier qui fist parler les cons* relies on both of these ostensibly incompatible models of replication or imitation to structure its presentation of talking genitals. Further, I hope to demonstrate that a close analysis of the text shows a refusal to admit the dominance of either model and that this is symptomatic of what I have

[62] *NRCF*, III, p. 47.
[63] Ibid., p. 48.
[64] Ibid., pp. 51–2.

observed throughout this book: that the notion of 'face' is at once foundational and ephemeral.

In the first section of this chapter I discussed the startling implications of body parts becoming or resembling faces through their physiognomy and examined how the breakdown of this framework reveals a deeply incoherent facial 'model'. Here I will use a different trope – the talking genital – as a way of further thinking through the problems of the notion of what I have been calling the 'degree zero of faciality', and how the traces and shadows of this concept belie its non-existence. My theoretical aid in this particular pursuit will be the work of Judith Butler, in which she examines the constitution of the subject through speech. In *Gender Trouble*, Butler asks a question about the human body that this whole book is asking about the face: what leads us to think of the body as an uncaused cause? Why do we assume that our conception of the body is a cause rather than an effect? She goes on to frame this question in terms of gender:

> How are the contours of the body clearly marked as the taken-for-granted ground or surface upon which gender significations are inscribed, a mere facticity devoid of value, prior to significance?[65]

Of the texts under consideration here, I am asking how they engage with the notion of the face as an origin. *Gender Trouble* begins with a discussion of the observable fact that certain bodies are ascribed certain meanings and that those meanings are then presented as innate or natural. Having recognised that these meanings do not originate in the body, it becomes possible to interrogate their cultural origins. Butler goes a step further, however, and interrogates the coherence of the body itself as a blank canvas. Why, she asks, is the body constructed in one particular way? Does the notion of 'stable bodily contours' not beg the same kinds of questions as that of a stable cultural body?[66] It is this kind of critical move that I have been attempting to apply to the idea of the face in medieval literature: having recognised that 'face' is a much less stable and coherent concept than we might think, I have tried to then ask what place the physiological face plays in this. In other words, if we can – and I think we can – prise apart the quality of faciality and the physiological face just enough to see that they are not entirely coterminous, why do they spring back together so readily? In Butlerian terms, what is it that firstly binds together the contours of the face and the meaning ascribed to it and that secondly causes us to recognise those particular contours as a face in the first place? Is it a

---

[65] Judith Butler, *Gender Trouble: Feminism and the Subversion of Identity*, 2nd edn (New York: Routledge, 1999; repr. 2008), p. 176.
[66] Ibid., p. 180.

question of the face having a value ascribed to its otherwise neutral features? Or is it a question of the face *being* those values? Is there something before the eyes–nose–mouth face? The intractability of this problem, demonstrated in the *fabliaux* that deal with non-face faciality on the human body, is precisely the point: there is no stable way in which we relate to the idea of the face as itself original faciality or as exemplar of a transcendent original faciality. We cannot undo this knot because it is, to mix metaphors, circular.

The interplay between the two scenarios I identified above in *Le Chevalier qui fist parler les cons* helps to structure this analysis. On the one hand, if anything that speaks is a face, there is a pre-existent faciality that is applied not only to the genitals but also to the 'eyes–nose–mouth'. This model is useful inasmuch as it strips away the specificity of the 'eyes–nose–mouth' face and offers a way of thinking about the possibility of this face as an effect of faciality rather than the originary cause. Here I will also turn to another of Butler's works that deals most explicitly with the power of speaking to make or break a particular subjectivity: *Excitable Speech*.[67] Butler examines how 'it is by being interpellated within the terms of language that a certain social existence of the body first becomes possible', as well as how the agency of spoken language is not necessarily the same as the agency of the speaking subject.[68] This raises curious questions in the context of the speaking vaginas and their agency which, in turn, raise questions about the supposed essence of faciality. Is the *con* a subject before it can speak? When it does speak, where can we locate its agency?

On the other hand, in the 'genitals are imitations of faces' model we see a much more explicit engagement with the idea of a facial 'essence' that originates in the 'eyes–nose–mouth'. In which case, the theoretical problem is more along the lines of that set out in *Gender Trouble*: why do we posit this body part (the face) as something to be given a particular value because of its 'contours'? Why do we stop, in Foucauldian terms, our genealogical investigation at the face? In the case of the talking vaginas in *Le Chevalier qui fist parler les cons*, I suggest that this problem turns around the hierarchy of face and pseudo-face; the text, in its two versions, presents a curious array of clues that construct the relationship between the *con* and the woman. Not only the ways in which the knight addresses the genitals, but also the discrepancies between what is said by the woman and what is said by her *con* are helpful ways of figuring how the text plays on the idea that one is a model for the other, and that there is a particular kind of hierarchy that positions the 'eyes–nose–mouth' face at the very top and, problematically, at the very beginning.

[67] Judith Butler, *Excitable Speech: A Politics of the Performative* (New York: Routledge, 1997).
[68] Ibid., pp. 5, 7.

Butler's analysis also outlines the idea of the impossible subject, which I find a helpful way of dealing with much of the contradiction in the textual portrayal of the speaking genital. It is, as we will see, a subject that ends up speaking its own impossibility, since its rebellious or subversive pretentions are always contingent and derivative. It is, of course, impossible to categorise certain textual or theoretical elements into one of two models, as they each feed into and influence each other. This is the point that the rest of this section will illustrate: as in *Trubert*, no coherent facial model can be discerned in a text that is nonetheless so heavily invested in and reliant upon the idea of faciality.

Broadly, the story is of a knight and his slightly wayward squire who, travelling to a tournament, come across three beautiful girls bathing in the forest. Desperately short of funds, the squire spies the girls' rich clothing and steals it. Of a nobler temperament, the knight reproaches the squire for his behaviour and replaces the clothing. Having noticed these antics, the girls decide that the knight deserves some reward for his actions, and they decide to grant him three gifts: the first is that the knight will be welcomed wherever he goes; the second is that *cons* will always answer him when he addresses them; and the third is that, in the event that a *con* is unable to respond to the knight's address, the *cul* will do so in its stead. Slightly bemused but grateful nonetheless, the knight continues on his way and meets a priest with a horse. Again egged on by Huet, his squire, the (unnamed) knight tests out his new ability to make *cons* talk by addressing the priest's horse's *con* and asking it about the priest's trip. The *con* dutifully replies and the terrified priest flees. Next, the two travellers find a beautiful castle and are lavishly welcomed (as per the terms of the girls' – we now know them to be fairies – first gift). After supper, the knight retires to his chamber, whereupon he is visited by a beautiful girl whom the lady of the castle has sent for his entertainment. The pair don't get very far in their encounter before the knight decides to test his new skill again, and addresses the girl's *con*, asking what he has already found out from the girl herself: why have you come here? The *con* corroborates the girl's story, but she is so frightened that she runs away and tells the countess what has happened. The countess's interest is clearly piqued by this bizarre tale and, at dinner the following day, she publicly offers a wager: she bets that the knight won't be able to make her own *con* talk. They agree on the terms, but the lady makes a quick visit to her chambers before the challenge begins, where she cheats by stuffing her *con* full so that it will be unable to speak. When she emerges and the knight calls to her *con* in his usual manner – 'Sire cons' – he is surprised to find that nothing happens. He calls again, but to no avail, and the knight believes that all is lost until Huet reminds him of the fairies' third gift to him: the ability to make a *cul* speak in the stead of an incapacitated *con*. He duly addresses the countess's *cul*, who answers and tells him why the *con* was unable to respond. The countess is humiliated, the knight wins the bet and everyone else falls about laughing.

As noted above, the text is found in two distinct versions; version I is reproduced in ABCDE and I, while the Anglo-Norman version II is found only in M. Version II is considerably shorter than version I: while all but one of the six witnesses to version I run to between 600 and 750 lines (A contains an incomplete version of the text), M is a mere 292 lines long. An examination of the two versions reveals that this is a question of what we might call economy of style; while both versions recount the same sequence of events, version II contains much less description and dialogue. It is noted in the *NRCF* that the Anglo-Norman manuscript contains traits that date it after the middle of the thirteenth century, but no comment is made on the relative date of the text.[69]

Two significant textual differences between the two versions are especially germane for the questions I am asking of the text(s) and so will be outlined here before proceeding. I want to highlight the differences here since these discrepancies very helpfully throw into relief some of the particular ways in which the agency, subjectivity and embodiment of the genitals in question are figured in the text. The first important thing to note is the nature of the gifts that the knight receives from the fairies in exchange for his virtuous behaviour. In version II, the first gift of hospitality remains the same, but the second differs; here the knight is told that any woman he deigns to love will be unable to refuse him. The third gift then combines what in version I are separate skills and explains that the knight has the power to make both vaginas and anuses talk. Crucially, the combination of the power to make both *cons* and *culs* talk elides the idea, present in version I, that the *cul* acts as a kind of backup. In version I it is clear that the *cul* can be made to speak only in the event that the *con* is incapacitated, whereas version II places the two orifices on an equal footing; whichever one the knight addresses is bound to answer him.

The second important discrepancy between the two versions comes in the form of the exchange between the knight, the girl at the castle and the girl's *con*. In version I the girl is sent by the countess to entertain the knight, she tells him this, then her *con* corroborates the story. The scandal is brought about by her surprise at the fact of her *con* speaking. In version II, however, the girl seduces the knight of her own accord. Once in bed, the knight decides to ask her *con* if the girl is a virgin or not, to which the *con* answers:

> Nanyl syre, certeignement
> Ele ad eu pl*us* que cent

---

[69] *NRFC*, III, p. 51.

Coillouns a soun derere
Que ount purfendu sa banere. (pp. 127, 129, lines 183–6)[70]

[Certainly not, sire. She has had more than a hundred balls in her behind that have broken through her banner]

Ashamed, the girl disappears, much like she does in version I. The question this particular divergent section raises is one of the possibility of contradiction between a subject and what is ostensibly 'their' body part. Why, we are prompted to ask, does the knight in version I feel it necessary to ask the *con* to corroborate what the girl has just told him? Why, we then wonder upon reading version II, does the girl's *con* betray her? Is it in fact a question of betrayal, since the girl is given no dialogue of her own in this scene? This moment of subject–body contradiction in version II vividly recalls the misogynist framework of stories such as Diderot's *Les Bijoux indiscrets* in which women are seen as fundamentally deceitful and in which, as a result, the only way to get to the truth is to ask their inherently truthful and, arguably, disloyal genitals. The notion that genitals can betray or contradict a subject is clearly tied up with a particular notion of womanhood or female nature, and I will bear this in mind throughout my analysis.

The first element of the text that I want to submit to close scrutiny is the interpellation of the *con* by the knight. I thus hope to shed some light on how the text – in its two versions – sets up the particular agency of the con and thus its relationship to the subject of which it is ostensibly a part. The first address to a *con* takes place when the knight and Huet come across a priest and his horse. Huet suggests that the knight try out his new gift and he obliges (version I):

Huez le saiche, si li dist:
'Sire, fait il, se Dieus m'aïst,
Les fees vos distrent tot voir!
Or le poez apercevoir,
Mais apelez delivrement
Le con de cele grant jument:
Vos l'orroiz ja parler, ce croi.'
Dist li chevaliers: 'Ge l'ostroi.'

---

[70] Line references for both version I and version II are to the critical edition and diplomatic transcription, respectively, found in the *NRCF*, vol. III (version I on pp. 158–73; version II on pp. 57–157). For version II I also give page numbers. Most analysis is of version I, and I hope that the context of my discussion makes it clear which version the quotation is from.

Maintenant li commence a dire:
'Sire cons, ou va vostre sire?
Dites le moi, n'en mentez mie!
– Par foi, il vait veoir s'amie,
Fait li cons, sire chevaliers!
Si li porte de bons deniers:
Dis livres de bone monnoie,
Qu'il a ceinz en une corroie
Por achater robe mardi.' (lines 273–89)

[Huet took him aside and said,
'See here, dear master, by my head,
all that the damsels said was true,
as I can see and so can you.
Now if you'll only speak, I swear,
to the cunt of his sturdy mare,
you're bound to hear the thing reply.'
The knight agrees, 'It's worth a try,'
and asks without hesitation,
'What is your master's destination?
Hide nothing, Mr. Cunt; tell all.'
'Sir knight, he's off to pay a call,'
the cunt says, 'on his concubine.
He's bringing her a gift of fine
new-minted money worth ten pounds
tied in a belt he's girded 'round
to buy a dress at Tuesday's fair.']71

A very particular set of relationships is established here. The knight addresses the *con* as 'Sire cons' (as he does in every other encounter in the text), suggesting at the very least that the *con* has a recognisable degree of autonomy from the horse to which it belongs, or of which it is a part. We might see this moment as the calling into subjectivity of the *con*. Butler entertains this possibility in relation to name-calling, and suggests that this kind of speech act is *productive* inasmuch as it designates a subject as such, a subject that did not exist prior to this designation.[72] Butler goes on to develop the idea that speech is not quite identical to agency, and that in the case of the speaking subject

[71] 'The Knight Who Made Cunts Talk', in *The Fabliaux*, trans. by Nathaniel E. Dubin (New York: Liveright Publishing Corporation, 2013), pp. 143–77 (lines 265–81). I will use this verse translation for longer quotations such as this.
[72] Butler, *Excitable Speech*, pp. 5–7.

(the knight, for the time being) there is always a part of speech that is beyond the volition of that subject, since the power of speech is always derivative: at some point in the past, the speaking subject had been 'initiated into linguistic competence'.[73] It is, therefore, not only the addressee who is at the mercy of another; the speaker, too, relinquishes any claim to full mastery of their own speech. What makes me think that this is a useful way of analysing this particular interpellation is that the text repeatedly emphasises the fact that the knight is the grammatical agent of the *con*'s speech. It is made clear in the fairies' declaration (in version I, at least) that it is the knight's address that will cause the miraculous speech:

> – Li miens dons ne riert pas petiz,
> Fait l'autre pucele en aprés.
> Ja n'ira mais ne loig ne pres,
> Por qu'il truisse feme ne beste
> Et qu'el ait deus elz en la teste,
> S'il daigne le con apeler,
> Qu'il ne l'escoviegne parler. (lines 216–22)

> ['Nor is the gift I'll make you slight,'
> the second lady says in turn.
> 'Whatever way your path may turn,
> every woman and female beast
> who've in their heads two eyes apiece
> whom you meet, if you call, their cunts
> will have to answer to you at once.'][74]

The knight's 'appel' is the prime condition for the *con*'s speech, and this format is repeated throughout the narrative. Indeed, the prologue offers a particularly good account of the knight's agency when it summarises the rest of the plot:

> Et ge vos di tot asseür
> Que il faisoit les cons paller
> Quant il les voloit apeler,
> Et li cus qu'iert en l'escharpel
> Respondist bien a son apel. (lines 16–20)

> [for be assured it was his portion
> to make cunts speak at his command

---

[73] Ibid., p. 33.
[74] Dubin, lines 208–14.

> whenever he would call them, and
> likewise the asshole in its nest
> had to make answer if addressed.][75]

In this segment, the knight is the subject of two out of three verbal phrases: he *makes* the vaginas talk when he *wants* them to. The *cul* is similarly only able to respond to his call rather than speak of its own volition. Indeed, the moments in the text when the *con*'s speech is expressed with the verb 'paller' instead of the contingent 'respondre' are almost always qualified by a verb of which the knight is the subject: when Huet tells the knight to address the priest's horse's *con*, he bets that 'Vos l'orroiz ja parler, ce croi' [you'll hear it speak, I'm sure] (line 279); later, the knight acquires a new epithet: 'Cil qui faisoit les cons paller' [he who makes cunts talk] (line 343); when the girl in the castle tells the startling incident to the countess she explains that 'Il prist mon con a apeler, | Assez l'a fait a lui paller' [he went to speak to my cunt, and thus made it speak to him] (lines 439–40).[76] Similarly, when the knight addresses the girl's *con* in the castle, he says: 'Sire cons, or parlez a moi!' [Sir Cunt, speak to me!] (line 419), reinforcing the idea that, while the body parts can indeed *paller*, they can do so only at the specific behest of the knight. It is also worth noting that the format of the gift means that the body parts must be addressed *each time* they are to speak; we therefore repeatedly come up against the idea that a subject is given the power of speech by another subject, and that this process continues *ad infinitum*. Indeed, the knight's power to incite speech in others is readily traced back to the second and third fairies' conferral of this power, whereby they perform the ultimate illocutionary speech act and give the knight this power at precisely the same time as they tell him about it.[77] The text even hints at the next step in the regression of linguistic agency; as fairies, the girls presumably draw their power from magical sources. Butler expresses the notion of always contingent speech thus:

> That linguistic domain over which the subject has no control becomes the condition of possibility for whatever domain of control is exercised by the speaking subject. Autonomy in speech, to the extent that it exists, is conditioned by a radical and originary dependency on a language whose historicity exceeds in all directions the history of the speaking subject.[78]

---

[75] Dubin, lines 16–20.
[76] These short translations are my own.
[77] In *Excitable Speech* Butler makes considerable use of J. L. Austin's distinction between an illocutionary speech act, in which the doing and the saying are identical, and a perlocutionary speech act, in which the saying causes later effects but is not itself an action.
[78] Butler, *Excitable Speech*, p. 28.

In this scenario, then, Butler's conception of always contingent speech allows us to frame the agency of the speaking body parts within a broader discursive system that takes into account the possibility that speech is not a marker of independent volition but only ever of a partial and derivative intentionality. The speaking genitals in this text are only partially autonomous, even before we get to the question of them being physically attached to another subject. They are already, by virtue of the condition of their speech, as emphasised repeatedly in the text, contingent beings *because* of this linguistic capacity. What Butler helps us to theorise is this idea that the talking genitals do indeed imitate the bodily act of speaking, properly attributable to the face, but also that the speech of the face itself – what we might call 'proper' speech – is also only ever a kind of imitation. In other words, the genitals seem to be acting out on a more literal level what the speaking face is always engaged in.

The next question to address is therefore that of the autonomy of the genitals relative to the women (or horse) to which they are attached. Brian Levy comments on the transformative power of speech, and notes that in the fable tradition it is this which causes animals to effectively become men. He then explains that, in *Le Chevalier qui fist parler les cons*, 'woman and animal are equated through their sexual parts', since the knight's power is effective on all *cons*, whether belonging to humans or animals, and suggests that this reverses the transformation from animal to man by transforming woman into animal.[79] The focus of my argument here, however, is on the transformative power effected on the sexual parts themselves, and on its implications. By interrogating the body parts' autonomy, we also consider the extent to which, and the mechanisms by which, these non-faces act like, imitate or become faces. It is this particular relation that is at the heart of this chapter and which is crucial to the project of elucidating the way in which the idea of 'face' is conceived and made use of in medieval texts. When addressing the priest's horse's *con*, the knight asks of it: 'ou va vostre sire?' [where is your master going?] (line 282). Since the 'sire' is clearly the priest, it seems that two possibilities arise here in relation to the status of the *con*. One the one hand, the knight is addressing the *con* as a discrete subject whose 'sire' is the priest. On the other hand, the knight is addressing the *con* as part of the horse, whose 'sire' is the priest. What makes this so intriguing is the fact that in version II the question is rephrased, as the knight asks, 'Ou va tu daun coun, ne le celez mie' [where are you going, Master Cunt? Don't hide it from me] (p. 95, line 125). Here the knight's question seems to confer on the *coun* a different status; the *coun* is going somewhere, and is able to tell the knight about this.

---

[79] Brian J. Levy, *The Comic Text: Patterns and Images in the Old French Fabliaux*, Faux Titre, 186 (Amsterdam: Rodopi, 2000), p. 56.

Ambiguity remains, however, as to the precise status of the interpellated *coun* in this exchange. While it is addressed as 'tu', the *coun* responds on behalf of the priest, explaining that 'je porte a mesoune le p*restr*e a s'amie' [I'm taking the priest home to his mistress] (p. 95, line 126); although addressed in the singular, and thus singled out from both the horse and the priest, the *coun* instantly collapses any autonomy it might have had in that moment of address.

We find further engagement with this kind of highly fluid anatomical and linguistic autonomy when the knight enters the castle and addresses the girl's *con*. In version I, he first asks the girl who she is and why she has come to his room. She explains that she has been sent by the countess for his entertainment, and they embrace. After having kissed her mouth and face and fondled her breasts, he places his hand on her *con* and says:

> Sire cons, or parlez a moi!
> Ge vos vueil demander por quoi
> Vostre dame est venue ci. (lines 419–21)

> [Now speak up, Mr Cunt, because
> I'm curious to know the cause
> that brought your lady here to me.][80]

In this scene there is a curious juxtaposition between the knight's sexual advances and his decision to talk to the girl's *con*. Apparently part of the knight's sexual exploration of and presumed desire for the girl's body, the gesture then retrospectively takes on the role of singling out this particular body part for interrogation. What might have been the most advanced sexual move in the sequence is in fact an entirely non-sexual gesture as it prefaces a question that clearly reveals the knight's distrust of the girl's own answer to his earlier question. Here, the *con* is addressed specifically as an *alternative* to the girl, and the possibility is raised that the two will have different and perhaps contradictory answers to the same question. In the event, the *con* corroborates the girl's story; again the gap between two distinct subjectivities – the girl and the *con* – is opened up slightly before being closed back down. Once again, I suggest that the differences between the two versions of the story serve to highlight certain moments as especially formative. In version II of *Le Chevalier qui fist*, the girl is not contradicted by her *coun*, since she does not say anything, but she is betrayed by its speech when it tells the suspicious knight that 'Ele ad eu p*lus* que cent | Coillouns a soun derere' [She has had more than a hundred balls in her behind] (pp. 127, 129, lines 184–5). Whereas

---

[80] Dubin, lines 395–7.

in version I the girl runs 'Quant cele oï son con paller, | Estrangement fu esperdue' [when she heard her cunt speak; she was uncommonly troubled] (lines 426–7), in version II it is because she has been 'honye' and 'engyné' [shamed; tricked] (p. 129, lines 189, 190). Clearly, the first scenario suggests that the girl is surprised by the fact of the *con* speaking at all, and the second that she is dismayed by the contents, rather than the fact, of its speech. In the first scenario, then, there is a much stronger sense that the *con*'s speech is considered miraculous and, therefore, to disturb an expected order. The *con* is figured as a rebellious voice by virtue of its very existence, and its impropriety is coterminous with its entrance into subjectivity. This calls to mind Butler's discussion in *Gender Trouble* of impossible subjectivity and sanctioned rebellion. While Butler maintains that there is in fact the possibility within language to subvert certain power structures, much of her analysis focuses on the oft-underestimated pervasiveness of those structures.[81] She notes

> the law's uncanny capacity to produce only those rebellions that it can guarantee will – out of fidelity – defeat themselves and those subjects who, utterly subjected, have no choice but to reiterate the law of their genesis.[82]

It seems that the *con* in version I enacts a similar kind of pseudo-rebellion, inasmuch as its speech – not the contents of that speech – at once marks it as a subject and marks it as impossible and therefore ineffectual. In version II, the *con*'s agency seems less contested. Here Butler's formulation is crucial: the version II *con* fits more easily into the established discursive structure, since the contents of its speech are understood and are effectual; it is therefore, paradoxically, the fact of betrayal that marks the *con* as a non-subversive and fully integrated speaker. I have already noted how the *con*, in both versions, is never fully autonomous, but here, in version II, it is temporarily subsumed, almost incognito, into normative discourse. While it is clear that this episode plays out against a background of the assumption of the duplicitous nature of woman – the literal enactment of her deceit, and the ultimate witness to her sexual voracity – the subtle comments the text makes on the near-agency of a speaking *con* are of greater interest to my project.

Finally, then, we arrive at the text's *dénouement*, in which the countess decides that she can stop her *con* from falling victim to the knight's power to incite speech. Having set the terms of the wager, she retires to her chambers, where she stuffs her *con* to prevent it from speaking (version I):

---

[81] Butler, *Gender Trouble*, p. 167.
[82] Ibid., p. 144.

> Plain son poig a pris de coton,
> Si en enpli tres bien son con;
> Bien en estoupa le pertus,
> A son poig destre feri sus.
> Bien en i entra une livre:
> Or n'est mie li cons delivre! (lines 531–6)
>
> [A basket full of cotton wad
> she took, and plugged her cunt up hard
> till the hole was completely choked;
> with her right fist she pushd and poked
> and stuffed inside at least a pound.
> There's no way Cunt can make a sound.][83]

The unspoken implication here is that the countess would not have taken these precautionary measures if she did not believe that the knight had these powers in the first place. While the girl has related her own story, the countess has no first-hand experience of this amazing gift and has little difficulty admitting its possibility. Already, then, the talking *con* has, to some extent, been admitted into the economy of the court – especially so since money has been bet on its performance and will eventually exchange hands. It is also clear that the antagonism between the woman in question and her *con* takes on a slightly different meaning when she seems to intuitively understand that the only way to prevent it speaking when spoken to is by what is described as a fairly comprehensive physical intervention. In other words, the *con* is seen by the woman as beyond her own subjective integrity. Physically part of her, it is nonetheless not under her sovereign control. Once again, the *con* enters a kind of no-man's land: it is not under the control of the woman as an integrated being, but it is nonetheless '*son* con' (line 532, emphasis added); the woman believes that she can, however, control it through external means and, while this in itself is true, she is betrayed by another part of her anatomy in what we might see as a kind of displaced semi-autonomy. Indeed, this scene corroborates the troubled subjectivity that I have been tracing throughout the text in a subtle yet arresting way: when the countess's *con* doesn't respond to the knight's first call, the narrative voice explains it thus:

> Mais li cons ne li pot respondre,
> Qui *la geule* avoit enconbree. (lines 548–9, emphasis added)
>
> [but the cunt couldn't reply, since its mouth was obstructed][84]

---

[83] Dubin, lines 509–14.
[84] Dubin's translation is based on a slightly different version, in which 'gueule' does

This is the most expansive description of the *con* in the whole text, since it adds a new dimension to its textual anatomy: 'la guele'. Suggesting that the *con* is a being of multiple parts, this apparently innocuous couple of lines, spread across two couplets, effects a kind of evolution on the previously single-cell *con*. Crucially, it opens up the notion that the organ is not simply a mouth, but that it *has* a mouth. While the implications are significant, they are never articulated; the *cul*, answering the knight in its stead, tells him that the *con*'s 'gueule' is 'tote pleine' [full up] (line 575), but when the uninhibited *con* is finally able to talk to the knight and explain itself, the emerging subject and its mouth collapse back into one another: 'Ge ne pooie, | Por ce que enconbrez estoie' [I couldn't, because I was obstructed] (lines 601–2). This final rhetorical moment of the rapid expansion and collapse of the *con*'s agency and subjectivity is, it seems to me, emblematic of the same movement happening throughout the text, and within the interplay between its two versions.

What I have been tracing, then, is a kind of bizarre semi-autonomy ascribed to the *con* in various different ways, and yet never fully articulated. My contention has been, as I hope is borne out in my analysis, that this reflects a particular kind of engagement with the relationship between the talking genital and the concept of 'face'. The common denominator between the two is, of course, speech, and I have been asking how the *con*'s speech and how, more broadly, its entrance into discourse structures a paradoxical relation of *both* imitating a face and being a face. I outlined at the beginning that these two possibilities have profound implications for our concept of what a face is, and it seems that this text entertains both at once and thus enacts what is emerging as the only essence of faciality: that it is at once foundational and ephemeral.

Conclusion: *Du vit et de la coille* and *Do con, do vet et de la soriz*

In a chapter examining the personification of body parts in the Middle Ages, Jean-Marie Fritz begins by briefly taking an inventory of different attributes given to a non-person in order to place it somewhere along the path towards 'la dignité' of personhood.[85] He notes that giving a voice to something, giving a face to something or giving that non-person a certain amount of agency are all ways of doing this.[86]

---

not appear here. This is my own translation.

[85] Jean-Marie Fritz, 'Personnifier les parties du corps: scandale ou carnaval?', in *La Personnification du Moyen Âge au XVIIIe siècle*, ed. by Mireille Demaules, Rencontres, 91 (Paris: Classiques Garnier, 2014), pp. 129–44 (p. 129).

[86] Ibid.

In this chapter I have been looking at this idea from a slightly oblique angle, inasmuch as I have analysed how certain texts explore the relationship between the human face and the genitals that seem to imitate, impersonate or parody it. Dealing first with a text that plays with the idea of genitalia resembling a specific face, and then with a text in which genitals are given the (albeit contingent) power of speech, this chapter has engaged with the possibility that the specific relationship thus set up is not in fact one of simple imitation, whereby a non-face acts like a face. It is imitation that seems to be at the heart of the notion of personification as outlined by Fritz. If a non-person is given certain attributes, the logic goes, that non-person will become more person-like, eventually attaining 'la dignité d'une personne' [the dignity of personhood].[87] Fritz's personification, however, restricts our understanding of what happens when genitals do person-like things, insofar as it maintains a strict difference between the two terms involved; between person and non-person. While on the one hand he concedes that, in some texts, 'le corps se fragmente pour donner naissance à plusieurs personnes' [the body splits, engendering multiple persons], he goes on to claim that, in *Du vit et de la coille*, 'le processus de personnification est complet' [the process of personification is complete], and that in *Le Chevalier qui fist parler les cons* it is incomplete, since the body part in question is given only one person-like attribute: the power of speech.[88] What I find problematic in this evaluation is not only that it denies the particularly powerful role of speech in subject creation (see above), but also that the possibility of complete personification is admitted only through qualitative analysis. That is to say, the body parts that are completely personified are considered thus because they exhibit a certain number of person-like traits (in this case, travelling independently, talking to each other without a human medium and being described using the attributes of very typical human literary types). Alison Moore observes a similar process when she explains that detached and/or talking genitals show a 'wholesale negation of the very possibility of fragmenting the human body, for every part that is cut off [...] becomes not a dead piece of discarded flesh but a person in its own right, *representing and replacing the person to whom it belonged*'.[89] Frustratingly close to what I'm arguing, Moore's statement nonetheless reinforces the idea that autonomous genitals are necessarily a derivation of an original, whole human being. The person is, in other words, maintained as an originary, knowable starting point from which the process of personification begins. Rather than thinking of the unified human as the end-point of this process, it is helpful to think of how this understanding places it

---

[87] Ibid.
[88] Ibid., pp. 131, 136, 140.
[89] Alison Moore, p. 278 (my emphasis).

firmly at the beginning; only through an apparently stable knowledge of what makes a person do we see these features in non-persons as precisely that: as non-persons being like persons. What I want to continue exploring, however, is the possibility that these autonomous genitals actually *are* persons.

The notion of personification is a useful starting point for this section that will deal, among others, with the text in which Fritz sees 'complete personification', and which will argue that what is actually happening is not personification, which relies always on imitation, but rather a destabilisation of the apparent difference between the 'model' and its 'imitator'. In these texts, then, genitals enact a far greater degree of autonomy than in any examined thus far, and so invite us more explicitly to reconsider their relationship to the 'person' from which they have become so comprehensively detached. If, I ask, a talking vagina can be shown not simply to act like a face but to become a face, and thus to abolish the notion of an originary physiological and conceptual model of faciality, what does a walking, talking, wine-making vagina do to this idea?

To end this chapter, I examine two complementary texts that have human genitals as their protagonists: the thirteenth-century *Du vit et de la coille* and *Do con, do vet et de la soriz*.[90] The first of these texts claims to explain the reason behind the antagonistic relationship between the *con* and the *coille*. The eighty-one-line tale is of a *vit* and a *coille* who go off in search of a *con*. As they find the *con*, a storm breaks, and the *vit*, who has offered its aid to the *con*, is allowed to shelter in the 'meson' of the *con*, while the less forthcoming *coille* is forced to wait outside until the storm passes, hammering at the door. *Do con, do vet et de la soriz* is a slightly longer text (124 lines), and tells the story of a *con* and a *vet* who, along with a mouse who joins them, go off to take part in the wine harvest. The *con* is especially useful as its great capacity makes it an excellent *cuve*, but during the labour the mouse is knocked into it by the *vet* and barely escapes with its life when it is helped out, owing to the forbidding dimensions of the hole in which it found itself.

In his study, Fritz notes that each of these apparently risqué texts is found in one of the two largest and most important *fabliaux* manuscripts that we know of: *Du vit et de la coille* is found in Berne, Burgerbibliothek 354, and *Do con, do vet et de la soriz* in Paris, BnF fr. 837. He claims that this is evidence for the fact that they are not in fact scandalous, as opposed to the truly subversive *Trubert* whose manuscript tradition – the only text in a unique manuscript – suggests a much more marginal existence.[91] Instead of the violence and

---

[90] I use Städtler's edition for the former, and Burrows' for the latter: Thomas Städtler, 'Du vit et de la coille', *Revue de Linguistique Romane*, 59 (1995), 131–5; Burrows, 'Do con, do vet et de la soriz'. Translations are my own.

[91] Fritz, 'Personnifier les parties du corps', p. 144. Translation my own.

transgression of *Trubert*, these texts engage rather in a 'jeu faussement naïf avec la littérature et le procédé de l'écriture allégorique'.[92] Fritz's assessment chimes with the idea that the Middle Ages were not a time of abject horror of body parts and bodily functions, but instead had a much more nuanced relationship with bodies and both their appearance and behaviours.[93] The horror of body parts was the preserve of the nineteenth-century scholars who first catalogued and edited these *dits* and *fabliaux*; it is notable that, while catalogued and used as sources in dictionaries, these texts were not edited until the late twentieth century and early twenty-first.[94] Indeed, the ways in which these and similar texts have been dealt with reveal much about the nature of the threat they are understood to pose, and therefore have an interesting bearing on our consideration of the role of the genitals. It is telling that much evidence for censorship focuses on the words themselves, as, for instance, when the hand that scratched out the words 'vit' and 'coille' from both the incipit and explicit of *Du vit et de la coille* in BnF fr. 837, but not from the body of the text. Later editors of similarly titled texts have taken the same approach; Méon's 1808 edition of the *fabliaux* omits the offensive words from both the title and the body of the text; Charles Livingston's 1951 edition of the work of Gautier le Leu omits the words 'con' and 'cons' in the contents page, but prints them in the main text.[95]

Burrows makes the salient suggestion that the lack of editions of one of the two texts I am examining here until relatively recently might be the result less of a concern over content and more of the linguistic concern we witness in the above examples. In other words, he states, publishing *Du vit et de la coille* with the offensive words missing 'ne ferait que rendre le texte presque incompréhensible' [would only make the text virtually incomprehensible].[96]

---

[92] Ibid., pp. 143–4.

[93] See, for instance, Caroline Walker Bynum's *Fragmentation and Redemption*, in which she explains that 'medieval artists and devotional writers did not either equate body with sexuality or reject body as evil'. Caroline Walker Bynum, *Fragmentation and Redemption: Essays on Gender and the Human Body in Medieval Religion* (New York: Zone Books, 1991), p. 116.

[94] Burrows, *Do con, do vet*, pp. 24–5, 38.

[95] See, for instance, the edition of *Le chevalier qui fist parler les cons* in *Fabliaux et contes des poètes françois des xi, xii, xiii, xiv et xve siècles*, ed. by Étienne Barbazan, 2nd edn, rev. by Dominique-Martin Méon, 4 vols (Paris: B. Warée, 1808), III, pp. 409–36; Charles H. Livingston, *Le Jongleur Gautier le Leu: étude sur les fabliaux*, Harvard Studies in Romance Languages, 24 (Cambridge, MA: Harvard University Press, 1951). Ross G. Arthur also notes that *Le Chevalier qui fasait parler les muets* is not a separate *fabliau* but is in fact Bédier's edited title for inclusion in the list of texts in his 1894 study. See Ross G. Arthur, 'On Editing Sexually Offensive Old French Texts', in *The Politics of Editing Medieval Texts*, ed. by Roberta Frank (New York: AMS, 1993), pp. 19–64 (pp. 27–8).

[96] Burrows, *Do con, do vet*, p. 25.

While Barbazan can reproduce a 'clean' version the story of *Le Chevalier qui fist parler les cons* without too much damage to the plot, texts in which the main – and, in the case of *Du vit et de la coille*, the only – protagonists are genitals must either be reproduced in all their offensive glory or not at all. This very brief excursus into the question of editing obscene texts underlines an obvious but important point: that the scandal of a particular text is a subjective and movable feature, one that reflects less on the text itself and more on the attitudes of those engaging with it. More specifically, it suggests that texts in which genitals are the main protagonists present a peculiar problem for the modern reader, a problem that finds its precursor in the apparent decision not to edit the two texts under consideration until recently: what is the status of the 'genital characters'? How, to put it simply, can they be both? How are we to respond to the apparent oxymoron presented by protagonists that walk, but which have no legs; that talk, but have no mouth; and that both own property (the *con*'s 'meson', for instance) and take part in economic activity (wine-making), but which are, of course, impossible legal persons? This might seem a terribly simplistic observation; the texts are, of course, allegorical. But they both present an unusually incoherent mixture of the literal and the metaphorical that begs further investigation. Burrows notes that this technique of 'les métaphores rendues littérales' [metaphors made literal] is a key part both of the humour of this kind of text and of its 'insaisissabilité' [ungraspability].[97] As with all the texts I look at in this chapter, further investigation reveals them to be much less straightforward than we might at first think.

In these texts in which body parts act both explicitly as those parts and as substitutes for the body whole, there is a clearly discernible play on the question of physical attributes, destabilising the possibility of a coherent morphology. It seems to me that in each of these two texts there is a distinct oscillation between ascribing physical attributes to the protagonists and describing the protagonists and the attributes as one and the same thing. I argue that this particular instability implicitly questions the idea that non-persons can become *like* persons through imitation. To take this a step further, I claim that these texts enact the possibility of a breakdown of the distinction between person (origin/model) and non-person (imitation/image). In *Du vit et de la coille*, for instance, we note that the *vit* is described as having a 'col' (line 14), and the *con* as having 'nus piez' (line 20). Similarly, when the *vit* offers help to the *con*, it is described thus:

> Le vit i cort sanz demorer,
> Mes la coille n'i vout aler.

---

[97] Ibid., p. 43.

> Le vit s'offri a son servise,
> A .ij. mains a la forche prise. (lines 25–8; my emphasis)

[The prick runs over without hesitating, but the ball doesn't want to go. The prick offers its help, taking the fork *with two hands*]

We also learn that, after taking shelter in the *con*'s 'meson', the *vit*

> S'en issi matez et honteus,
> Le chief enclin, tout vergondeus. (lines 57–8; my emphasis)

[left the house sad and ashamed, with *head* bowed, all contrite]

Finally, it is also intriguing to note that the text attributes to the *coille* '.ij. maillés' (line 44), which Städtler notes can be read as '"testicules"; emploi figuré de *maillet*' [testicles; the figurative use of *maillet*].[98] What is curious about this attribution of hands, feet, a head and even testicles to the genital protagonists is that it happens in conjunction with an awareness of the physical attributes of the genitals *as* genitals. The *con* is described in terms that, as Städtler notes, have elsewhere been used to describe female genitalia: 'blanc et gorgu et bien tailliez' [white and fleshy and well-built] (line 19).[99] The *vit* is, characteristically, 'Ausi roides comme .i. baston' [as stiff as a rod] before leaving the *con*'s house (line 56). I suggest that this attribution of body parts to body parts severely disrupts the possibility of a coherent relation between the genitals and the 'person' for which they partially stand. They are not simply parts of a whole, but nor are they scale 'versions' of the human body.

This phenomenon plays out in a more elaborate way in the longer of the two texts: *Do con, do vet et de la soriz*. Here we note several instances not only of the attribution of body parts to the genital protagonists, but also of the description of those protagonists *as* certain, non-genital, body parts. Specifically, we see the reappearance of the attribution of a 'gole' to the *con* that we first noted in version II of *Le Chevalier qui fist parler les cons*. In *Do con, do vet*, the *con* is initially described as:

> Molt orgoilleus et molt enflé;
> De la gole semble Rofé. (lines 9–10)

[So haughty and so puffed up; its mouth looked like Rofé's]

---

[98] Städtler, p. 134.
[99] Ibid.

As Burrows notes, Rofé is an unidentified, but presumably human, 'crieur de vin', and the comparison recalls the episode in *Trubert* analysed above, in which a *con* and *cul* are taken for the mouth and nostrils of a king.[100] A few lines later, the idea of the *con* having a 'gole' is reinforced, as we learn through another comparison that

> Vos cuideriez bien sanz fable
> Que sa gole fust de dëiable!
> Tant ele [fu] lee et parfonde. (lines 13–15)

[You'd believe this was the Devil's mouth, it was so wide and deep]

Towards the middle of the text, the *con* boasts of its great capacity and therefore its use in the grape-harvest:

> N'il n'a jusq'an Jerusalem
> De moi nule si bone cuve.
> De moi porroit l'an faire cuve
> A besoin por soi estuver.
> En moi se puet en encaver
> Sept folon, ce sai je bien. (lines 46–51)

[From here to Jerusalem there is no finer wine vat than me. You could make me into a tub for bathing. You can fit seven *folons* in me, that I know well]

Here the *con* explains both that it *is* a cuve (line 47) and also that it can be *made into* a cuve by somebody else (line 48), before immediately reverting back to it being a cuve (rather than potentially becoming one) when it states its precise capacity (lines 50–1). This instability is repeated in the rest of the text, as in line 80 when the 'borjois' offers to give the *con* 'six deniers' because 'grant tro *a*' (lines 78, 81, 80; my emphasis). Here the *con has* a 'tro', as opposed to being one. What this suggests to me is that, as with the addition of body parts in *Du vit et de la coille*, there is the sense that these genitals are not simply acting out the attributes they are said to have as part of the whole body (in the case of the *con*, sexual voracity), but that they are figures that have been given these attributes *in addition to* some kind of personhood or subjectivity. The *con* is not just a great devouring hole, but is a protagonist that *has* a great devouring hole, and which, moreover, is so aware of it that it knows its precise capacity. Later, however, the text describes the *con* in such a way as to reposition the *con* as the hole itself, rather than the possessor of

---

[100] Burrows, *Do con, do vet*, p. 32.

that hole: 'Et li cons tot maintenant *s'ovre*' [and the cunt opens *itself* up] (line 92; my emphasis). Here, the *con* opens *itself* 'por la vandange recevoir' [to receive the harvest] (line 93), suggesting that it *is* the hole or the receptacle.

What these two texts' engagement with the attribution of physical characteristics to body parts suggests to me is a fundamental instability vis-à-vis the status of the body parts in question. Sometimes the *con* is a hole or a mouth, sometimes it has a hole or a mouth. When Alexandre Leupin describes the rules of the art of *descriptio*, he notes that one of those rules is that the splitting of the whole body into parts for description is permissible only if those parts are eventually reunited in the description of the whole.[101] He argues that Gautier le Leu's *Du con* is a perfect inversion of this – and every – rule of *descriptio*, but concedes that, in a metonymic sense at least, the whole human body is described through the presentation of one of its parts. In the texts I have looked at above, however, this metonymic relationship is problematised to the extent that the morphology of the body parts is highly unstable. The import of this for the broader project of this chapter is that it suggests a less-than-simple relationship between the whole body and the 'microcosm' that ostensibly imitates some of its features (as in Fritz's model of personification, outlined above). These texts – as, indeed, do all the texts studied in this chapter – portray what I take to be the impossibility of a fixed and locatable facial model to be imitated. While these last texts are less obviously concerned with a facial model, their use in this chapter is to reveal how even what appears to be a greater degree of personification – and therefore imitation of a model – still ultimately does not uphold a distinct relation between original and model. As with my contention that that which imitates a face is no less a face than the 'eyes–nose–mouth', it seems that that which appears to imitate the face and other body parts cannot be said to be simply a false or a lesser version. The same conclusion can therefore be drawn: there is no stable originary face upon which all 'face-like' things are modelled. Or, more accurately, the 'eyes–nose–mouth' face is not that model. To return to the Butlerian question I evoke above: if the contours of the human body are themselves culturally constructed and thus identified, what comes before that identifiable body? Jane Gallop expresses these ideas in her defence of Irigaray's *Ce sexe qui n'en est pas un* in *Thinking Through the Body*.[102] Gallop explains what she sees as the central, and radical, tenet of Irigaray's writing, and offers a way of reading it that overcomes any accusation of biological essentialism. Gallop states:

---

[101] Alexandre Leupin, 'Le Sexe dans la langue: la dévoration: sur *Du c.*, fabliau du XIIIe siècle, de Gautier le Leu', *Poétique*, 12 (1981), 91–110 (p. 91).

[102] Jane Gallop, *Thinking Through the Body* (New York: Columbia University Press, 1988).

Modernity generally couples plurality with the credo that language is nonreferential. Polyvalence makes it impossible to know what a sign refers to, in any simple way. In Irigaray's text, however, a referential *illusion* stubbornly clings to plurality. And illusory though it might be – since this is only a texture of signifiers, as slippery as any – the *effect* of this *illusion* is to point the reader outside the text, extending the (post)modernist gesture to a realm normally considered to be at the antipodes of culture, the female genitals. Irigaray's *referential illusion* dislodges (post)modernism from its privileged station as 'culture' into a surprising, vulgar political *efficacy*. And in the process might just save (post)modernist poetics from the absurd appearance of asserting the nonreferentiality of language and move it into *a more complex encounter with the anxiety produced by the absence of any certain access to the referent*.[103]

In this chapter I have argued that the textual encounters we have with other body parts that do facial things or which exhibit faciality is also a kind of encounter in which, instead of the uncomplicated knowledge of that to which these body parts refer, a certain significatory anxiety is produced. What Gallop helpfully asserts here is precisely that this kind of signification is not annihilated by an investigation of the contours of the body, but that it becomes a possibility instead of a certainty and that our relationship to it must be understood differently once this is seen to be the case. This is what I have been arguing about the face: not that faciality is a meaningless concept, but that it is one that functions according to an idea that is much more ephemeral, and much less concrete than our engagement with it has heretofore suggested. It is this idea that is expressed by Derrida when he explains that false or imitation money functions in the same way as real money in any and all cases in which the possibility that the money is false have not been ruled out.[104] In other words, our engagement with faces is not based on whether they are 'real' or 'false', 'model' or 'imitation', but on their more immediate presentation of faciality, which includes the possibility of a referent as well as the possibility of meaninglessness. As Lesley Johnson explains with reference to the protagonists of the *fabliaux*, 'those who take the most irreverent view of language and conventional sign/referent relationships often hold the key to success'.[105] It is not quite 'success' that I have argued for here, but these protagonists do exhibit a liberating disregard for the face that demonstrates,

---

[103] Ibid., pp. 95–6 (my emphasis).

[104] Jacques Derrida, *Donner le temps 1: la fausse monnaie* (Paris: Galilée, 1991), pp. 124–5.

[105] Lesley Johnson, 'Women on Top: Antifeminism in the Fabliaux?', *MLR*, 78 (1983), 298–307 (p. 299).

through pushing the boundaries of similitude, the fragility and necessity of the tethers that nonetheless keep the face held up in its position at the top of the signifying chain.

Conclusion

This book is about faces in French literature of the High Middle Ages. Tracing a path through Arthurian verse (in its evolution from twelfth- to thirteenth-century modes), the *Roman de la Rose* and the *fabliaux*, with an excursus into drawn faces on fourteenth-century manuscript pages, my goal has been to elucidate the different ways in which the motif of the face performs complex and sometimes apparently contradictory interiority. The founding argument of the book has been that the literature of the French Middle Ages exhibits an illusion of a prioritised interiority. On the one hand, that is, these texts operate according to a model in which an interior and an exterior exist in hierarchical relation to each other, and in which this relation is mediated by a delimiting barrier between the two. This model is broadly Structuralist inasmuch as it posits a meaning – the referent – which is accessible only through a secondary sign. The meaningful interior is primary, and is valued over and above its external expression or representation. This linguistic model is translated into and reproduced in the notion of face and of faciality (which I have been using not as a translation of Deleuze and Guattari's *visagéité* but as denoting the broader quality of being a face, a quality which I have attempted to unpack in the course of this book, but which remains mutable and flexible) inasmuch as the face is understood and used in these texts as both a physiological and metaphorical phenomenon in which a prioritised – in terms of both temporality and value – inner kernel is accessible via its contingent outer expression. The classic physiological examples to which I have referred are those such as rising colour as an indication of love and the correlation between physical appearance and moral character. Widening the scope of 'face' to include its metaphorical use (although I query this distinction throughout the book, especially in Chapter 1), we note that other surfaces appear to perform a facial function: clothes, armour, shields, parchment and even walls all mediate access to a higher meaning beyond and, in spatial terms, behind themselves, whether it take the form of a subject (as individual identity or as a collection of attributes) or, as in the latter case, a whole value system (courtly love in the Garden of Deduit).

On the other hand, I argue that the medieval texts which form the object of my inquiry work within a broader hermeneutical model in which the model of interior and exterior is illusory – although not, crucially, deceitful. There is a Derridean/de Manian angle to this argument insofar as it recognises in the texts a dynamic of promise and refusal which centres precisely on the structure of invisible meaning made visible; the argument is that the visible, exterior part promises access to a meaning that, in the first instance, it is not necessarily able to provide and, secondly, which is not an entity on its own but, rather, an inference of the external sign itself.

It is indeed the case that medieval texts can and do enact slippage between external sign and internal meaning. In the broadest sense, this occurs when the stated purpose is at odds with what is actually expressed or performed. Perhaps the most famous example of this phenomenon is the promise at the beginning of the *Rose*:

> ce est li *Romanz de la Rose*
> ou l'art d'Amors est tote enclose. (lines 37–8)
>
> [it is the *Romance of the Rose*, in which the whole art of love is contained][1]

This narrator's promise is doubly broken: Guillaume's section breaks off before it can reveal its 'art', and Jean's wildly circuitous and telescopic continuation is an exemplary exercise in not getting to the point. These considerations are not lost on the texts at a smaller scale, of course; the debate between Amant and Raison on the proper and improper use of language is a proto-Structuralist case in point. Indeed, much medieval theory itself was concerned with this particular problem. Articulating the difference between what a text says and what it does is, of course, an important thread of modern medievalist scholarship, and takes a variety of different forms. Historically, it has taken the form of a kind of 'second guessing', whereby what appeared as anomalies – be that in relation to genre, to manuscript tradition or to narrative – were explained away or smoothed over. While it may seem counter-intuitive to see parallels between Derridean slippage and this kind of conservative scholarship, it is nonetheless the case that both are concerned with the possibility of a gap between the text in front of us and a higher meaning beyond. In the former, of course, this gap is a formative textual feature and its recognition and reproduction are highly productive, whereas for the latter it presents an interpretative problem whereby the text's obfuscation of meaning is considered an unfortunate hurdle to overcome. It remains the case, however, that in both scenarios there is a mismatch between appearance and its meaning. The Derridean line goes further, and uses this gap to undo the

---

[1] *The Romance of the Rose*, p. 3.

notion of an originary meaning in the first place, expressing discontent with the idea of writing itself as a secondary sign, and attempting to excise from critical textual enquiry what it sees as a vain and distorting attempt to uncover an immutable structure of meaning.

Medieval scholarship has long engaged with the disconnect between meaning and its presentation in ways that do not seek to recuperate an originary meaning but, rather, to decentre it, to articulate it differently from the model of interior and exterior, of sign and referent. Not something 'within' or 'behind' the text that can be sought, a text's meaning is found rather in its effect and in its performance of ideas and dynamics. Indeed, the goal for much work in the last quarter-century or so has been to tread the fine line between nineteenth-century positivism and what Keith Busby semi-seriously called 'Dubiotics' in a 1993 conference paper asserting his own doubts about the then new trend of 'doing theory' to medieval texts.[2] In other words, the aim has been to move beyond deconstruction and the perceived risk of obliterating the possibility of meaning and to enter a phase of scholarship that decentred rather than destroyed the meaning of the medieval textual object.

In my book, the notion of 'reading at face value' takes on slightly different connotations from those of the conventional meaning of 'not looking deeper than the visible surface'. In line with the critical history that has sought to deal adequately with the destabilising possibilities of deconstruction, I have tried to articulate another way of decentring meaning while recognising that there is an active surface–depth structure in the texts in question. The face is a motif that enacts this, and it is with the aid of a number of critical theories that I have tried to demonstrate how the face is both a motif and a model for reading. The face is neither an unambiguous representation of and therefore access point to a meaning behind, nor is it a disingenuous mask, deceiving us into thinking we know something that we cannot and which, ultimately, does not exist. Rather, the face is a synthesis of these erstwhile contradictory positions. Or, to put it more accurately, the face is a concept that encompasses both. Not only does it reveal and conceal (the mirror is the archetypal model for this) but it is both surface and depth. The face, as I have tried to articulate it, is a conceptual nexus which allows for the coexistence of representative and non-representative signification. The face is not simply a model I have applied to these texts, but a model used within them, and which we can, following the texts' lead, trace firstly in the motif itself and, secondly, in objects, surfaces and images that echo its role.

There is a discernible gap between the general claims I make for literature from a fairly broad period and across a spectrum of genres, and the very

---

[2] Keith Busby, 'Doin' Philology While the -isms Strut', in *Towards a Synthesis? Essays on the New Philology*, ed. by Keith Busby (Amsterdam: Rodopi, 1993), pp. 85–95 (pp. 85–6).

particular and precise examples which I give. This may require some explanation. The primary goal of my book is not to present incontrovertible evidence for a literary trend but, rather, to analyse in detail certain instances of its functioning. The kind of engagement with interiority and its representation that I pick out in the texts under examination is symptomatic of broader literary and cultural trends, much as the modern discussions of the face that I look at are symptomatic of their historical moments. It is these symptoms that are the object of my study; by characterising precise moments, I hope primarily to shed some light less on what is behind them (although I do of course consider this), and more on what they are, how we read them and how they are embedded in the texts. Reading on a small scale has inherent merits that I hope to have brought to bear in this book, and it is not the quantity of such instances that interests me but their quality, intensity, depth and embeddedness. It is from this that I judge the face to have great importance as a literary motif, a cultural model and a philosophical concept.

The face as literary motif and philosophical concept is, in both guises, mutable and unstable. I have attempted not to pin it down, but to trace some of its incarnations and implications. One of the key points about the face that I hope to have demonstrated, both in medieval examples and in more modern philosophical writing, is that it is both recognisable and indefinable; both universal and unrepeatable. Faciality in the *Rose* is wildly different from faciality in *Yvain*, and yet it is indeed faciality which is exhibited in each. This is a large part of my interest in the face; it is identifiable in a series of discrete and differently intricate manifestations. To see this fully, then, it is useful to look at a small series of examples and to look at them in depth, engaging with and preserving their intricacy and complexity. We thus also preserve the gaps among different modes of faciality, and avoid the risk of flattening out their difference and of returning to this enquiry's point of departure, where the face was coherent, legible and stable. To trace a phenomenon that is so diverse, two options are possible: to undertake to survey a broad spectrum of its manifestations, illustrating its scope and diversity quantitatively, or to home in on a small body of discrete examples, highlighting the quality of their diversity and, as is central to this book, focusing on this as a foundational feature of the phenomenon itself. Both approaches are valid; I have chosen the latter.

Through the face I explore the notion that the literature of this period of the Middle Ages worked according to the illusion of a prioritised interior: not just that there was always a prioritised interior, but that it was a non-deceitful illusion. In the texts I have examined with this in mind, there is a discernible interplay between the notion of representation (by which the interior is represented on an outside surface) and what I have been calling non-representational signification. In the first chapter I looked at how the face of a duelling knight is not limited to his physiological features but in fact extends to his outer, facing surface, including not only his helmet but also his shield. Both objects constitute the facing surface of the knight in battle and, therefore, his face. In parallel to the structure by which a knight can be identified through both his physiological face and his shield and armour, another system is at play: these latter objects also serve to express simply the presence of a knight. Instead of saying simply that they sometimes fail to identify (as when a shield is too battered to show adequately a knight's arms), the facial model in this instance proposed by Levinas allows us to see how they sometimes don't serve this purpose at all. The face of the Arthurian knight as he evolves into his thirteenth-century iterations thus goes some way towards tracing the complex status of the concept of the individual. Evoking the Janus-like notion of a two-faced figure, I have tried to go beyond this and to suggest that the two faces of the knight are not opposed but, rather, come in and out of focus as he traverses the various intersubjective encounters in which his individual identity is more or less at stake. When it is less at stake, his face is the Levinasian kind, which expresses nothing but its own presence. When the knight acts in his capacity as a named and unique individual, the face is the (not always successful) marker of that individuality. Indeed, often the interplay between the two modes is complex and the two overlap; this again provides a useful commentary on how interiority is problematised, not to be undone or destroyed but to be explored.

In the second chapter the goal has been to move temporarily outside narrative in order to reinforce the notion of problematised interiority with reference to the marks on the manuscript page that carry the narrative. Looking at a series of doodles of faces, all attached in different degrees to letter forms, this chapter has tried to demonstrate how the graphic face is exceptional in its capacity to promise legibility. The point is not simply that it then refuses it, but that this refusal is not conclusive; in the same dynamic with which the two faces of the knight in Chapter 1 come in and out of focus, switching places sometimes imperceptibly, so the face doodle is constantly oscillating between legibility and its refusal. Rather than take a purely Derridean line, however, I read these faces in terms of their irruption into the order of the manuscript page and of how they draw attention to the surface–depth dynamic as precisely that: the reader moving back and forth between recognition of a human face and the promise of a depth – a subject – behind it, and the recognition that this is precisely a face without a subject. I turn here to Lacan and articulate the graphic face in terms of the dynamic between the symbolic and the real orders: with one metaphorical foot in each, the graphic face is a paradoxical marker of its own impossibility insofar as it expresses the absence of precisely what it represents. In this respect, however, it disturbing to the reader not just in terms of that reader's recognition of his or her fragile contingency but also in terms of the face itself: the subject behind the face is concentrated and distilled into the two-dimensional image.

The third chapter returns to narrative, but discusses it with relation both to ekphrasis and to manuscript illumination. Looking at Guillaume de Lorris's opening section of the *Roman de la Rose*, I have traced the surface–depth dynamic again, this time in an examination of the garden wall that delimits the space within which the value system of courtly love reigns supreme. Focusing on Amant's encounter with the portraits on the outer edge of the wall, on the wall itself and, finally, on facial surfaces within the garden, I have tried to show how the text again functions according to the 'open secret' of the priority of interiority. In this case, spatial and narrative dynamics are exploited by the text in order to present a complex system of surface–depth interaction. On the face of it, the narrative works according to a relentless forward movement, whereby Amant moves from one conceptual and physical space to another, and from which he cannot return. Drawing on Deleuze and Guattari's concept of *visagéité*, we might see the garden wall and Amant's movement through it as an enactment precisely of the stultifying codification of meaning that the term purports to describe. However, reading Deleuze and Guattari more closely, it becomes possible to see that theirs is a facial dynamic which, once again, admits the possibility of an interaction between codified meaning and its undoing. *Visagéité* is a notion that allows for its own perpetual undoing, and it is this that is enacted in Guillaume's garden wall: not subversion or antagonism but, rather, a space opened up between, on the one hand, representation and, on the other, its movement from ignorance to knowledge, and non-representation and its surface movement. Indeed, what is subverted is any modern expectation that the text accidentally undoes its own premise.

The final chapter turns to the human body in its exploration of the face and interiority. Looking at the *fabliaux*, the chapter has sought to explore the limits of the face when interwoven with its ostensible opposite number: the genitals. In a series of stories in which the genitals are mistaken for or play the role of the face, I have argued that what passes for a face is a relative concept and that, as such, slides over the surface of subjectivity, forming a loose but coherent connection.

I briefly evoked above the debate in the early 1990s over the role of theory in medieval literary scholarship and the concern for the safeguarding of academic rigour in the face of what was seen as the opening up of a hitherto highly specialised and technical discipline. With the advent of digital imaging and digital communication, it seems that we are now at another pivotal moment in the discipline, and that some of the same questions are again being asked. Manuscripts, specifically, are increasingly accessible outside specialist libraries in digital format and the ability to see – literally – medieval texts differently in fact also provokes a set of new questions. What, for instance, should the role of emotional attachment be in the study of medieval texts, if they now permeate our lives not just outside the library but on our computers, tablets and phones?[3] In asking this, we also ask precisely about what we are looking at when we look at the various different components of a medieval text; what is it to look at an out-of-context manuscript image? And what of a digital edition versus a high-resolution image of the manuscript? This all, to my mind, can be articulated in the question of faciality that I have attempted to answer in this book: when we look at a face, not what, but *how* does it tell us? The answer I have tried to trace is that it communicates through a mixture of representation and affect and of symbolism and pure expression.

I have been arguing that the face articulates a medieval illusion of interiority. This is what we seem to be partially reproducing in the increasing dissemination of digitised and sometimes dismembered medieval texts: a heady mix of texts and images to be seen as much as interpreted, and to be seen and reacted to not in ignorance but in full knowledge that these texts and images also, in different encounters, point behind or beyond themselves. In much the same way, we might smile at a face doodle in one encounter, and ask what's behind it in another. If the answer is 'nothing', this has not made the question any less valid.

Finally, if any recuperating has been done in this book, it is of the face itself. I have tried not just to draw together these two aspects – by turns a metaphor for clarity and for deception – but also to see the face outside this dichotomy and in different terms. For the Levinasian knight it does not simply cover and/or reveal but expresses his presence outside epistemological terms; in the case of the manuscript doodle it similarly expresses its own presence, this time through repeating the paradox that it is hiding nothing; in the *Rose* the face is by turns a permeable barrier and a Möbius strip, disrupting the opposition between revelation and concealment; in the *fabliaux*, the face embodies the possibility of a legible 'otherwise'.

---

[3] On the role affect and emotional attachment play in modern medievalism, see Carolyn Dinshaw, *How Soon is Now? Medieval Texts, Amateur Readers, and the Queerness of Time* (Durham, NC: Duke University Press, 2012).

Bibliography

Manuscript Sources

Guillaume de Lorris and Jean de Meun, *Le Roman de la rose*, London, British Library, MS Harley 4425, consulted at British Library Digitised Manuscripts <http://www.bl.uk/manuscripts/FullDisplay.aspx?ref=Harley_MS_4425> [accessed 5 November 2013]
—— *Le Roman de la rose*, Los Angeles, J. Paul Getty Museum, MS Ludwig XV 7, consulted at The *Roman de la rose* Digital Library <http://romandelarose.org/#book;LudwigXV7> [accessed 5 November 2013]
—— *Le Roman de la rose*, Oxford, Bodleian Library MS Douce 195, consulted at The *Roman de la rose* Digital Library <http://romandelarose.org/#book;Douce195> [accessed 5 November 2013]
—— *Le Roman de la rose*, Oxford, Bodleian Library, MS Douce 371, consulted at <http://bodley30.bodley.ox.ac.uk> [accessed 5 November 2013]
—— *Le Roman de la rose*, Paris, Bibliothèque de l'Arsenal, MS 5226, consulted on Gallica <http://gallica.bnf.fr/ark:/12148/btv1b60002983> [accessed 6 November 2013]
—— *Le Roman de la rose*, Paris, Bibliothèque nationale de France (BnF), MS fonds français 12595, consulted on Gallica <http://gallica.bnf.fr/ark:/12148/btv1b60002167> [accessed 6 November 2013]
—— *Le Roman de la rose*, Paris, Bibliothèque nationale de France (BnF), MS fonds français 19153, consulted on Gallica <http://gallica.bnf.fr/ark:/12148/btv1b60003548> [accessed 6 November 2013]
Guillaume de Saint-Pathus, *Vie et miracles de saint Louis*, Paris, Bibliothèque nationale de France (BnF), MS fonds français 5716, consulted on Gallica <http://gallica.bnf.fr/ark:/12148/btv1b8447303m> [accessed 25 March 2014]
Jean de Joinville, *Vie de saint Louis*, Paris, Bibliothèque nationale de France (BnF), MS fonds français 13568, consulted on Gallica <http://gallica.bnf.fr/ark:/12148/btv1b8447868p> [accessed 25 March 2014]
La Quête du saint graal et la mort d'Arthus, Paris, Bibliothèque nationale de France (BnF) MS fonds français 343, consulted on Gallica <http://gallica.bnf.fr/ark:/12148/btv1b84584343> [accessed 25 March 2014]

Primary texts

Barbazan, Étienne, ed., *Fabliaux et contes des poètes françois des xi, xii, xiii, xiv et xve siècles,* 2nd edn, rev. by Dominique-Martin Méon, 4 vols (Paris: B. Warée, 1808)

Burrows, Daron, '*Do con, do vet et de la soriz*: édition d'un texte tiré de Berne 354', *Zeitschrift für romanische Philologie*, 117 (2001), 23–49

Chrétien de Troyes, *Arthurian Romances*, trans. by Carleton W. Carroll and William W. Kibler (London: Penguin, 1991)

—— *Le Chevalier au lion; ou, Le Roman d'Yvain*, ed. by David F. Hult (Paris: Livre de Poche, 1994)

—— *Le Chevalier de la charrette; ou, Le Roman de Lancelot*, ed. by Charles Méla (Paris: Livre de Poche, 1992)

—— *Cligès*, ed. by Charles Méla and Olivier Collet (Paris: Livre de Poche, 1994)

—— *Le Conte du graal; ou, Le Roman de Perceval*, ed. by Charles Méla (Paris: Livre de Poche, 1990)

—— *Erec et Enide*, ed. by Jean-Marie Fritz (Paris: Livre de poche, 1992)

Douin de Lavesne, *Trubert: fabliau du XIIIe siècle*, ed. by G. Reynaud de Lage (Geneva: Droz, 1974)

Guillaume de Lorris and Jean de Meun, *Le Roman de la rose*, ed. by Félix Lecoy, 3 vols (Paris: Champion, 1965–70)

—— *The Romance of the Rose*, trans. by Frances Horgan (Oxford: Oxford University Press, 1999)

Guillaume de Saint-Pathus, *Les Miracles de saint Louis*, ed. by Percival B. Fay (Paris: Champion, 1931)

—— *Vie de saint Louis*, ed. by Henri-François Delaborde (Paris: Picard, 1899)

Jean de Joinville, *Vie de saint Louis*, ed. by Jacques Monfrin, 2nd ed (Paris: Classiques Garnier, 1998)

Le Chevalier as deus espees, ed. and trans. by Paul Vincent Rockwell, Arthurian Archives, 13 (Cambridge: Brewer, 2006)

Le Roman de Balain: A Prose Romance of the Thirteenth Century, ed. by M. Dominica Legge (Manchester: Manchester University Press, 1942)

Le Roman de Gliglois, ed. by Marie-Luce Chênerie, Classiques français du Moyen Âge, 143 (Paris: Champion, 2003)

Noomen, Willem, and Nico van den Boogaard, eds, *Nouveau recueil complet des fabliaux*, 10 vols (Assen: Van Gorcum, 1983–1998)

Ovid, *Metamorphoses*, trans. by Frank Justus Miller, 3rd edn, rev. by G. P. Goold, 2 vols (Cambridge, MA: Harvard University Press, 1977)

Raoul de Houdenc, *Meraugis de Portlesguez*, ed. by Michelle Szkilnik, Champion Classiques: Moyen Âge, 12 (Paris: Champion, 2004)

—— *La Vengeance Raguidel*, ed. by Gilles Roussineau (Geneva: Droz, 2004)

Renaud de Beaujeu, *Le Bel Inconnu*, ed. by Michèle Perret, Champion Classiques: Moyen Âge, 4 (Paris: Champion, 2003)

The Fabliaux, trans. by Nathaniel E. Dubin (New York: Liveright Publishing Corporation, 2013)

The Romance of Yder, ed. by Alison Adams, Arthurian Studies, 8 (Cambridge: Brewer, 1983)

Städtler, Thomas, ed., 'Du vit et de la coille', *Revue de Linguistique Romane*, 59 (1995), 131-5

Secondary texts

Armstrong, Adrian and Sarah Kay, *Knowing Poetry: Verse in Medieval France from the 'Rose' to the 'Rhétoriqueurs'* (Ithaca: Cornell University Press, 2011)

Arthur, Ross G., 'On Editing Sexually Offensive Old French Texts', in *The Politics of Editing Medieval Texts*, ed. by Roberta Frank (New York: AMS, 1993), pp. 19-64

Avril, François and Marie-Thérèse Gousset with Jean-Pierre Aniel, *Manuscrits enluminés d'origine italienne: xive siècle, Lombardie-Ligurie* (Paris: Bibliothèque nationale de France, 2005)

Avril, François and Nicole Reynaud, *Les Manuscrits à peintures en France: 1440–1520* (Paris: Flammarion, 1993)

Bakhtin, Mikhail, *Rabelais and His World*, trans. by Hélène Iswolsky (Cambridge, MA: MIT Press, 1968), p. 21

Banks, Kathryn, 'The Ethics of "Writing" Enigma: A Reading of Chrétien de Troyes' Conte du Graal and of Lévinas's Totalité et infini', *Comparative Literature*, 55 (2003), 95-111

Batany, Jean, '*Trubert*: progress et bousculade des masques', in *Masques et déguisements dans la littérature médiévale*, ed. by Marie-Louise Ollier (Montreal: Presses de l'Université de Montréal, 1988), pp. 25-34

Baumgartner, Emmanuèle 'Chrétien's Medieval Influence: From the Grail Quest to the Joy of the Court', in *A Companion to Chrétien de Troyes*, ed. by Norris J. Lacy and Joan Tasker Grimbert, Arthurian Studies, 63 (Cambridge: Brewer, 2005), pp. 214-27

Beckett and the Phenomenology of Doodles, University of Reading (2006-9) <https://www.reading.ac.uk/ftt/research/ftt-beckettdoodles.aspx> [accessed 5 May 2015]

Bedos-Rezak, Brigitte Miriam, 'Medieval Identity: A Sign and a Concept', *The American Historical Review*, 105 (2000), 1489-533

Bibliothèque nationale de France catalogue, Gallicalabs <http://gallicalabs.bnf.fr/ark:/12148/btv1b8447303m/f2.item> [accessed 5 March 2015]

Birge Vitz, Evelyn, *Medieval Narrative and Modern Narratology: Subjects and Objects of Desire* (New York: New York University Press, 1989)

Bloch, R. Howard, *The Scandal of the Fabliaux* (Chicago: University of Chicago Press, 1986)

Bonheim, Helmut, 'The Acromegalic in Chrétien's *Yvain*', *French Studies*, 44 (1990), 1-9

Brown, Penelope and Stephen C. Levinson, *Politeness: Some Universals in Language Usage*, Studies in Interactional Sociolinguistics, 4 (Cambridge: Cambridge University Press, 1987; repr. 1996)

Brody, Saul N., 'Reflections of Yvain's Inner Life', *Romance Philology*, 54 (2001), 277-98

Bruckner, Matilda Tomaryn, 'The Lady and the Dragon in Chrétien's Chevalier au lion', in *From Beasts to Souls: Gender and Embodiment in Medieval Europe*, ed. by E. Jane Burns and Peggy McCracken (Notre Dame: University of Notre Dame Press, 2013), pp. 65–86

Burns, E. Jane, *Bodytalk: When Women Speak in Old French Literature* (Philadelphia: University of Pennsylvania Press, 1993)

—— 'Knowing Women: Female Orifices in Old French Farce and Fabliau', *Exemplaria*, 4 (1992), 81–104

—— 'This Prick Which is Not One', in *Feminist Approaches to the Body in Medieval Literature*, ed. by Linda Lomperis and Sarah Stanbury (Philadelphia: University of Pennsylvania Press, 1993), pp. 188–212

Burrows, Daron, '*Trubert*: Transgression, Revolution, Abjection', *Reinardus*, 19 (2006), 37–52

Busby, Keith, *Codex and Context: Reading Old French Verse Narrative in Manuscript*, Faux titre, 221, 222, 2 vols (Amsterdam: Rodopi, 2002)

—— 'The Diabolic Hero in Medieval French Narrative: *Trubert* and *Wistasse le Moine*', in *The Court and Cultural Diversity*, ed. by Evelyn Mullally and John Thompson (Cambridge: Brewer, 1997), pp. 415–25

—— 'Doin' Philology While the -isms Strut', in *Towards a Synthesis? Essays on the New Philology*, ed. by Keith Busby (Amsterdam: Rodopi, 1993), pp. 85–95 (pp. 85–6)

—— *Gauvain in Old French Literature*, Degré Second, 2 (Amsterdam: Rodopi, 1980)

Butler, Judith, *Bodies That Matter: On the Discursive Limits of 'Sex'*, 2nd edn (New York: Routledge, 2011)

—— *Excitable Speech: A Politics of the Performative* (New York: Routledge, 1997)

—— *Gender Trouble: Feminism and the Subversion of Identity*, 2nd edn (New York: Routledge, 1999; repr. 2008)

Caie, Graham D., 'An Iconographic Detail in the *Roman de La Rose* and the Middle English *Romaunt*', *Chaucer Review*, 8 (1974), 320–3

Camille, Michael, *Image on the Edge: The Margins of Medieval Art* (Cambridge, MA: Harvard University Press 1992)

Chiesa, Lorenzo, *Subjectivity and Otherness: A Philosophical Reading of Lacan* (Cambridge, MA: MIT Press, 2007)

Cobby, Anne Elizabeth, *Ambivalent Conventions: Formula and Parody in Old French*, Faux Titre, 101 (Amsterdam: Rodopi, 1995)

Colby, Alice M., *The Portrait in Twelfth-Century French Literature: An Example of the Stylistic Originality of Chrétien de Troyes* (Geneva: Droz, 1965)

Cole, Jonathan, *About Face* (Cambridge, MA: MIT Press, 1998)

Conklin Akbari, Suzanne, *Seeing through the Veil: Optical Theory and Medieval Allegory* (Toronto: University of Toronto Press, 2004)

Copjec, Joan, *Read My Desire: Lacan Against the Historicists* (Cambridge, MA: MIT Press, 1994)

Darwin, Charles, *The Expression of the Emotions in Man and Animals*, ed. by Paul Ekman, 4th edn (Oxford: Oxford University Press, 2009)

Davis, Colin, *Levinas: An Introduction* (Cambridge: Polity, 1996)
Dean, Carolyn, 'Beyond Prescription: Notarial Doodles and Other Marks', *Word & Image*, 25 (2009), 293–316
Delestre, J.-B., *De la physiognomonie: Texte-Dessin-Gravure* (Paris: Ve Jules Renouard, 1866)
Deleuze, Gilles, *Francis Bacon: logique de la sensation* (Paris: Seuil, 2002)
Deleuze, Gilles and Félix Guattari, *Capitalisme et schizophrénie: l'anti-Œdipe* (Paris: Minuit, 1972)
—— *Capitalisme et schizophrénie 2: mille plateaux* (Paris: Minuit, 1980)
—— *Anti-Œdipus: Capitalism and Schizophrenia*, trans. by Robert Hurley, Mark Seem and Helen R. Lane (Minneapolis: University of Minnesota Press, 1983)
—— *A Thousand Plateaus: Capitalism and Schizophrenia*, trans. by Brian Massumi (London: The Athlone Press, 1988)
de Man, Paul, 'The Resistance to Theory', *Yale French Studies*, 63 (1982), 3–20
——*The Rhetoric of Romanticism* (New York: Columbia University Press, 1984)
Derrida, Jacques, *De la grammatologie* (Paris: Minuit, 1967)
—— *Donner le temps 1: la fausse monnaie* (Paris: Galilée, 1991)
—— 'Violence et métaphysique: Essai sur la pensée d'Emmanuel Levinas', *Revue de Métaphysique et de Morale*, 69 (1964), 322–54
de Saussure, Ferdinand, *Cours de linguistique générale*, ed. by Tullio de Mauro (Paris: Payot, 1972)
Didi-Huberman, Georges, 'Face, proche, lointain: l'empreinte du visage et le lieu pour apparaître', in *The Holy Face and the Paradox of Representation*, ed. by Herbert line Kessler and Gerhard Wolf, Villa Spelman Colloquia, 6 (Bologna: Nuova Alfa, 1998), pp. 95–108
Dinshaw, Carolyn, *How Soon is Now? Medieval Texts, Amateur Readers, and the Queerness of Time* (Durham, NC: Duke University Press, 2012)
Douglas, Mary, *Purity and Danger: An Analysis of the Concepts of Pollution and Taboo* (London: Routledge, 1966; repr. 1992)
Duggan, Joseph J., *The Romances of Chrétien de Troyes* (London: Yale University Press, 2001)
Edelman, Lee, *Homographesis: Essays in Gay Literary and Cultural Theory* (New York: Routledge, 1994)
Ekman, Paul, ed., *Darwin and Facial Expression: A Century of Research in Review* (New York: Academic Press, 1973)
—— and others, eds, *Emotions Inside Out: 130 Years After Darwin's 'The Expression of the Emotions in Man and Animals'*, Annals of the New York Academy of Sciences, 1000 (New York: The New York Academy of Sciences, 2003)
Evans, Dylan, *An Introductory Dictionary of Lacanian Psychoanalysis* (London: Routledge, 1996)
Feinstein, Sandy, 'Losing Your Head in Chrétien's *Knight of the Cart*', *Arthuriana*, 9 (1999), 45–62
Fink, Bruce, *Lacan to the Letter: Reading 'Écrits' Closely* (Minneapolis: University of Minnesota Press, 2004)

Fleming, John V., *The 'Roman de La Rose': A Study in Allegory and Iconography* (Princeton: Princeton University Press, 1969)

Frank, Adam, *Transferential Poetics, from Poe to Warhol* (New York: Fordham University Press, 2015)

Frappier, Jean, *Étude sur 'Yvain ou le chevalier au lion' de Chrétien de Troyes* (Paris: Société d'Édition d'Enseignement Supérieur, 1969)

Fritz, Jean-Marie, 'Personnifier les parties du corps: scandale ou carnaval?', in *La Personnification du Moyen Âge au XVIIIe siècle*, ed. by Mireille Demaules, Rencontres, 91 (Paris: Classiques Garnier, 2014), pp. 129–44

Füg-Pierreville, Corinne, 'Le Déguisement dans *Trubert*: l'identité en question', *Moyen Age: revue d'histoire et de philologie*, 114 (2008), 315–34

Gallop, Jane, *Thinking Through the Body* (New York: Columbia University Press, 1988)

Gates, Kelly A. *Our Biometric Future: Facial Recognition Technology and the Culture of Surveillance* (New York: New York University Press, 2011)

Gaunt, Simon, 'Bel Acueil and the Improper Allegory of the *Romance of the Rose*', *New Medieval Literatures*, 2 (1998), 65–93

—— *Gender and Genre in Medieval French Literature*, Cambridge Studies in French, 53 (Cambridge: Cambridge University Press, 1995)

Gilbert, Jane, '"I am Not He": Narcissus and Ironic Performativity in Medieval French Literature', *MLR*, 100 (2005), 940–53

Godefroy, Frédéric-Eugène, ed., *Dictionnaire de l'ancienne langue française et de tous ses dialectes du ixe au xve siècle*, 10 vols (Paris: Vieweg, 1880–1902)

Gombrich, E. H., *Art and Illusion: A Study in the Psychology of Pictorial Representation* (New York: Pantheon, 1960)

Goriunova, Olga, 'Face Abstraction! Biometric Identities and Authentic Subjectivities in the Truth Practices of Data', *Subjectivity*, 12.1 (2019), 12–26

Gravdal, Kathryn, *'Vilain' and 'Courtois': Transgressive Parody in French Literature of the Twelfth and Thirteenth Centuries* (Lincoln: University of Nebraska Press, 1989)

Griffin, Miranda, *The Object and the Cause in the Vulgate Cycle* (London: MHRA and Maney, 2005)

—— *Transforming Tales: Rewriting Metamorphosis in Medieval French Literature* (Oxford: Oxford University Press, 2015)

Groebner, Valentin, *Defaced: The Visual Culture of Violence in the Late Middle Ages* (New York: Zone Books, 2004)

Haidu, Peter, *Lion-queue-coupée: l'écart symbolique chez Chrétien de Troyes*, Histoires des idées et critique littéraire, 123 (Geneva: Droz, 1972)

—— *The Subject Medieval/Modern: Text and Governance in the Middle Ages* (Stanford, CA: Stanford University Press, 2004)

Helfand, Jessica, *Face: A Visual Odyssey* (Cambridge, MA: MIT Press, 2019)

Heller-Roazen, Daniel, *Fortune's Faces: The 'Roman de la Rose' and the Poetics of Contingency* (Baltimore: Johns Hopkins University Press, 2003)

Hole, Graham and Victoria Bourne, *Face Processing: Psychological, Neuropsychological, and Applied Perspectives* (Oxford: Oxford University Press, 2010)

Howie, Cary, 'Rude Theory: The Rough Trade of the Fabliaux', in *Comic Provocations: Exposing the Corpus of Old French Fabliaux*, ed. by Holly A. Crocker (New York: Palgrave Macmillan, 2006), pp. 163–74

Hult, David F., *Self-Fulfilling Prophecies: Readership and Authority in the First 'Roman de La Rose'* (Cambridge: Cambridge University Press, 1986)

Hunt, Tony, 'The Dialectic of "Yvain"', *MLR*, 72 (1977), 285–99

Huot, Sylvia, *Dreams of Lovers and Lies of Poets: Poetry, Knowledge, and Desire in the 'Roman de la Rose'*, Research Monographs in French Studies, 31 (London: MHRA and Maney, 2010)

—— *From Song to Book: The Poetics of Writing in Old French Lyric and Lyrical Narrative Poetry* (Ithaca: Cornell University Press, 1987)

Jaeger, C. Stephen, *Enchantment: On Charisma and the Sublime in the Arts of the West* (Philadelphia: University of Pennsylvania Press, 2012)

Johnson, Joseph R., 'Flying Letters and Feuilles Volantes: Symptoms of Orality in Two Troubadour Songbooks', *Exemplaria* 28 (2016), 193–211

Johnson, Lesley, 'Women on Top: Antifeminism in the Fabliaux?', *MLR*, 78 (1983), 298–307

Kalof, Linda, ed., *A Cultural History of the Human Body in the Medieval Age* (Oxford: Berg, 2010)

Kay, Sarah, *Courtly Contradictions: The Emergence of the Literary Object in the Twelfth Century* (Stanford, CA: Stanford University Press, 2001)

—— 'Legible Skins: Animals and the Ethics of Medieval Reading', *Postmedieval*, 2 (2011), 13–32

—— 'Original Skin: Flaying, Reading, and Thinking in the Legend of Saint Bartholomew and Other Works', *Journal of Medieval and Early Modern Studies*, 36 (2006), 35–73

—— *The Romance of the Rose*, Critical Guides to French Texts, 110 (London: Grant & Cutler, 1995)

—— *Subjectivity in Troubadour Poetry* (Cambridge: Cambridge University Press, 1990)

—— 'Surface and Symptom on a Bestiary Page: Orifices on Folios 61v–62r of Cambridge, Fitzwilliam Museum, MS 20', *Exemplaria*, 26 (2014), 127–47

Kemp, Sandra, *Future Face: Image, Identity, Innovation* (London: Profile Books, 2004)

Kendrick, Laura, *Animating the Letter: The Figurative Embodiment of Writing from Late Antiquity to the Renaissance* (Columbus: Ohio State University Press, 1999)

Köhler, Erich, 'Observations historiques et sociologiques sur la poésie des Troudabours', *Cahiers de civilisation médiévale*, 6 (1964), 27–51

Kristeva, Julia, *The Severed Head: Capital Visions*, trans. by Jody Gladding (New York: Columbia University Press, 2012)

—— *Visions capitales* (Paris: Réunion des musées nationaux, 1998)

Kwakkel, Erik, *Medieval Books Blog*, <https://medievalbooks.nl/> [accessed 15 May 2015]

—— *Tumblr* account, <http://erikkwakkel.tumblr.com/> [accessed 15 May 2015]

Lacan, Jacques, *Écrits* (Paris: Seuil, 1966)
—— *Le Séminaire, livre xi: les quatre concepts fondamentaux de la psychanalyse*, ed. by Jacques-Alain Miller (Paris: Seuil, 1973)
—— *The Four Fundamental Concepts of Psycho-Analysis*, trans. by Alan Sheridan (London: Karnca Press, 2004)
—— *The Seminar of Jacques Lacan, Book ii: The Ego in Freud's Theory and in the Technique of Psychoanalysis* (Cambridge: Cambridge University Press, 1988)
Lacy, Norris J., 'Fabliaux and the Question of Genre', *Reading Medieval Studies*, 13 (1987), 25–34
—— 'Medieval McGuffins: The Arthurian Model', *Arthuriana*, 15 (2005), 53–64
—— 'On Armor and Identity: Chrétien and Beyond', in *'De Sens Rassis': Essays in Honor of Rupert T. Pickens*, ed. by Keith Busby, Bernard Guidot and Logan E. Whalen, Faux Titre, 259 (Amsterdam: Rodopi, 2005), pp. 365–74
Laqueur, Thomas, *Making Sex: Body and Gender from the Greeks to Freud* (Cambridge, MA: Harvard University Press, 1992)
Laurie, Helen C. R., 'The Psychomachia of *Yvain*', *Nottingham French Studies*, 30 (1991), 13–23
Le Breton, David, *Des visages: Essai d'anthropologie* (Paris: Métailié, 2003),
Le Goff, Jacques and Pierre Vidal-Naquet, 'Lévi-Strauss en Brocéliande: Esquisse pour une analyse d'un roman courtois', in *Textes de et sur Claude Lévi-Strauss*, ed. by Raymond Bellour and Catherine Clément (Paris: Gallimard, 1979), pp. 265–319
Leupin, Alexandre, 'The *Roman de la Rose* as a Möbius Strip (on Interpretation)', in *The Medieval Author in Medieval French Literature*, ed. by Virginie Greene (New York: Palgrave Macmillan, 2006), pp. 61–75
—— 'Le Sexe dans la langue: la dévoration: sur *Du c.*, fabliau du XIIIe siècle, de Gautier le Leu', *Poétique*, 12 (1981), 91–110
Levinas, Emmanuel, *Autrement qu'être ou au-delà de l'essence* (The Hague: Nijhoff, 1974)
—— *Difficile liberté: essais sur le judaïsme* (Paris: Albin Michel, 1963)
—— *Difficult Freedom: Essays on Judaism*, trans. by Seán Hand (Baltimore: Johns Hopkins University Press, 1990)
—— 'La Réalité et son ombre', *Les Temps modernes*, 4 (1948), 771–89
—— 'Reality and its Shadow' in *The Continental Aesthetics Reader*, ed. by Clive Cazeaux (London: Routledge, 2000), pp. 117–28
—— *Le Temps et l'autre* (Paris: Presses Universitaires de France, 1983; repr. 2012)
—— *Time and the Other*, trans. by Richard A. Cohen (Pittsburgh: Duquesne University Press, 1987)
—— *Totalité et infini: essai sur l'extériorité*, (Paris: Livre de poche, 1990; repr. 2012)
—— *Totality and Infinity: An Essay on Exteriority*, trans. by Alphonso Lingis (The Hague: Martinus Nijhoff, 1979)
Levy, Brian J., *The Comic Text: Patterns and Images in the Old French Fabliaux*, Faux Titre, 186 (Amsterdam: Rodopi, 2000).

Lewis, Charlton T. and Charles Short, eds, *A Latin Dictionary*, (Oxford: Clarendon Press, 1879; repr. 1955)

Liggett, John, *The Human Face* (London: Constable, 1974)

Livingston, Charles H., *Le Jongleur Gautier le Leu: étude sur les fabliaux*, Harvard Studies in Romance Languages, 24 (Cambridge, MA: Harvard University Press, 1951)

Loomis, Roger Sherman, 'Arthurian Tradition and Folklore', *Folklore*, 69 (1958), 1–25

Lyons, Gabrielle, '*Avoir* and *savoir*: A Strategic Approach to the Old French *Fabliaux*' (unpublished doctoral thesis, University of Cambridge, 1992)

Maddox, Donald, *The Arthurian Romances of Chrétien de Troyes: Once and Future Fictions*, Cambridge Studies in Medieval Literature, 12 (Cambridge: Cambridge University Press, 1991)

—— *Fictions of Identity in Medieval France*, Cambridge Studies in Medieval Literature, 43 (Cambridge: Cambridge University Press, 2000)

Marion, Jean-Luc, *L'Idole et la distance: cinq études* (Paris: Grasset & Fasquelle, 1977)

Massumi, Brian, *A User's Guide to 'Capitalism and Schizophrenia': Deviations from Deleuze and Guattari* (Cambridge, MA: MIT Press, 1992)

McCracken, Peggy, *The Curse of Eve, the Wound of the Hero: Blood, Gender, and Medieval Literature* (Philadelphia: University of Pennsylvania Press, 2003)

Meaningful Scribbles: Children's Drawings as Psychological Instruments 1880–1950, Max Planck Institute for the History of Science <https://www.mpiwg-berlin.mpg.de/en/research/projects/deptiii_wittmann_meaningful_scribbles> [accessed 5 May 2015]

Medieval Francophone Literary Culture Outside France, (2011–2015), <http://www.medievalfrancophone.ac.uk/browse/mss/222/manuscript.html> [accessed 20 September 2016]

Miller, Sarah Alison, *Medieval Monstrosity and the Female Body*, Routledge Studies in Medieval Religion and Culture, 8 (New York: Routledge, 2010)

Moore, Alison, 'The Medieval Body and the Modern Eye: A Corporeal Reading of the Old French *Fabliaux*', in *Worshipping Women: Misogyny and Mysticism in the Middle Ages*, ed. by John O. Ward and Francesca C. Bussey, Sydney Studies in History, 7 (Sydney: University of Sydney, 1997), pp. 237–82

Moore, Michael Edward, 'Meditations on the Face in the Middle Ages (with Levinas and Picard)', *Literature & Theology*, 24 (2010), 19–37

Morris, Colin, *The Discovery of the Individual 1050–1200* (London: SPCK, 1972)

Nancy, Jean-Luc, *Noli me tangere: essai sur la levée du corps* (Paris: Bayard, 2003)

—— *Noli me tangere: On the Raising of the Body*, trans. by Sarah Clift, Pascale-Anne Brault and Michael Naas (New York: Fordham University Press, 2008)

Newman, Barbara, *Medieval Crossover: Reading the Secular against the Sacred* (Notre Dame: University of Notre Dame Press, 2013)

Nichols, Stephen G., 'Ekphrasis, Iconoclasm, and Desire', in *Rethinking the 'Romance of the Rose': Text, Image, Reception*, ed. by Kevin Brownlee and Sylvia Huot (Philadelphia: University of Pennsylvania Press, 1992), pp. 133–66

Nickel, Helmut, 'About the Knight with Two Swords and the Maiden under a Tree', *Arthuriana*, 17 (2007), 29–48

—— 'Arthurian Armings for War and for Love', *Arthuriana*, 5 (1995), 3–21

Nouvet, Claire, 'An Allegorical Mirror: The Pool of Narcissus in Guillaume de Lorris' *Roman de la Rose*', *Romanic Review*, 91 (2000), 353–74

O'Sullivan, Simon, *Art Encounters Deleuze and Guattari: Thought beyond Representation* (Basingstoke: Palgrave Macmillan, 2006)

Otter, Monika, '*Vultus Adest* (The Face Helps): Performance, Expressivity and Interiority', in *Rhetoric Beyond Words: Delight and Persuasion in the Arts of the Middle Ages*, ed. by Mary Carruthers (Cambridge: Cambridge University Press, 2010), pp. 151–72

Park, Katharine, 'The Rediscovery of the Clitoris: French Medicine and the Tribade, 1570–1620', in *The Body in Parts: Fantasies of Corporeality in Early Modern Europe*, ed. by David Hillman and Carla Mazzio (New York: Routledge, 1997), pp. 171–93

Paxson, James J., 'The Nether-Faced Devil and the Allegory of Parturition', *Studies in Iconography*, 19 (1998), 139–76

—— 'The Personificational Face: *Piers Plowman* Rethought through Levinas and Bronowski', in *Levinas and Medieval Literature: The 'Difficult Reading' of English and Rabbinic Texts*, ed. by Ann W. Astell and J. A. Jackson (Pittsburgh: Duquesne University Press, 2009), pp. 137–56

Payen, Jean-Charles, '*Trubert* ou le triomphe de la marginalité', in *Exclus et systèmes d'exclusion dans la littérature et la civilisation médiévales*, Senefiance, 5 (Aix-en-Provence: Cuer, 1978), pp. 119–33

Pearcy, Roy J., *Logic and Humour in the Fabliaux: An Essay in Applied Narratology* (Cambridge: Brewer, 2007)

Perkinson, Stephen, *The Likeness of the King: A Prehistory of Portraiture in Late Medieval France* (Chicago: University of Chicago Press, 2009)

Perrett, David, *In Your Face: The New Science of Human Attraction* (New York: Palgrave Macmillan, 2010)

Picard, Max, *The Human Face*, trans. by Guy Endore (London: Cassell, 1931)

Porter, Martin, *Windows of the Soul: Physiognomy in European Culture, 1470–1780*, (Oxford: Clarendon Press, 2005)

Randall, Lilian M. C., 'Frontal Heads in the Borders of Parisian and South Netherlandish Books of Hours, ca. 1415–60', in *Tributes to Jonathan J. G. Alexander: The Making and Meaning of Illuminated Medieval and Renaissance Manuscripts, Art and Architecture*, ed. by Susan L'Engle and Gerald B. Guest (London: Harvey Miller, 2006), pp. 249–68

Riches, Samantha and Bettina Bildhauer, 'Cultural Representations of the Body', in *A Cultural History of the Human Body in the Medieval Age*, ed. by Linda Kalof (Oxford: Berg, 2010) pp. 181–201

Rivers, Christopher, *Face Value: Physiognomical Thought and the Legible Body in Marivaux, Lavater, Balzac, Gautier, and Zola* (Madison: University of Wisconsin Press, 1994)

Robbins, Jill, *Altered Reading: Levinas and Literature* (Chicago: University of Chicago Press, 1999)

Rockwell, Paul V., '*Appellation Contrôlée*: Motif Transfer and the Adaptation of Names in the *Chevalier as deus espees*', in *'Por Le Soie Amisté': Essays in Honor of Norris J. Lacy*, ed. by Keith Busby and Catherine M. Jones (Amsterdam: Rodopi, 2000), pp. 435–52

—— 'The Failed Embrace of the Father: Historical Continuity in *Le Chevalier as deus espees* and *Le roman d'Eneas*', *Romance Quarterly*, 51 (2004), 2–14

—— 'The Promise of Laughter: Irony and Allegory in *Le conte dou graal* and *Li chevaliers as deus espees*', in *Courtly Arts and the Art of Courtliness*, ed. by Keith Busby and Christopher Kleinhenz (Cambridge: Brewer, 2006), pp. 573–85

Root, Jerry, 'Marvelous Crystals, Perilous Mirrors: *Le Roman de la Rose* and the Discontinuity of the Romance Subject', *The Romanic Review*, 102 (2011), 65–89

Rouse, Richard H. and Mary A. Rouse, *Manuscripts and Their Makers: Commercial Book Producers in Medieval Paris, 1200–1500*, 2 vols (Turnhout: Harvey Miller, 2000)

Rudy, Kathryn M., 'Kissing Images, Unfurling Rolls, Measuring Wounds, Sewing Badges and Carrying Talismans: Considering Some Harley Manuscripts through the Physical Rituals They Reveal', *Electronic British Library Journal*, 2011, article 5 <http://www.bl.uk/eblj/2011articles/article5.html> [accessed 30 January 2015]

Sartre, Jean-Paul, *Les Écrits de Sartre*, ed. by Michel Contat and Michel Rybalka (Paris: Gallimard, 1969)

Sauerländer, Willibald, 'The Fate of the Face in Medieval Art', in *Set in Stone: The Face in Medieval Sculpture*, ed. by Charles T. Little (New Haven: Metropolitan Museum of Art and Yale University Press, 2006), pp. 2–17

Schmolke-Hasselmann, Beate, *The Evolution of Arthurian Romance: The Verse Tradition from Chrétien to Froissart*, trans. by Margaret and Roger Middleton, Cambridge Studies in Medieval Literature, 35 (Cambridge: Cambridge University Press, 1998)

Scott, Kathleen, ed., *An Index of Images in English Manuscripts: From the Time of Chaucer to Henry VII, c.1380–c.1509,* (Turnhout: Harvey Miller, 2000-)

Sedgwick, Eve Kosofsky and Adam Frank, eds, *Shame and Its Sisters: A Silvan Tomkins Reader* (Durham, NC: Duke University Press, 1995)

Simmel, Georg, 'Sociology of the Senses: Visual Interaction', in *Introduction to the Science of Sociology*, ed. by Robert E. Park and Ernest W. Burgess, 3rd edn (Chicago: University of Chicago Press, 1972), pp. 356–61

Simpson, James R., *Fantasy, Identity and Misrecognition in Medieval French Narrative*, (Oxford: Lang, 2000)

Skoda, Hannah, 'Representations of Disability in the Thirteenth-Century *Miracles de Saint Louis*', in *Disability in the Middle Ages: Reconsiderations and Reverberations*, ed. by Joshua R. Eyler (Farnham: Ashgate, 2010), pp. 53–66

Soler, Colette, *Lacanian Affects: The Function of Affect in Lacan's Work*, trans. by Bruce Fink (London: Routledge, 2016)

Stearns Schenck, Mary Jane, *The Fabliaux: Tales of Wit and Deception*, Purdue University Monographs in Romance Languages, 24 (Amsterdam: John Benjamins, 1987)

Steimatsky, Noa, *The Face on Film* (Oxford: Oxford University Press, 2017)

Stevenson Stewart, Jessica, 'Toward a Hermeneutics of Doodling in the Era of *Folly*', *Word & Image*, 29 (2013), 409–27

Synnott, Anthony, 'Truth and Goodness, Mirrors and Masks – Part I: A Sociology of Beauty and the Face', *The British Journal of Sociology*, 40 (1989), 607–36

Tasker Grimbert, Joan, *'Yvain' dans le miroir: une poétique de la réflexion dans le 'Chevalier au lion' de Chrétien de Troyes* (Amsterdam: Benjamins, 1988)

Taussig, Michael, *Defacement: Public Secrecy and the Labor of the Negative* (Stanford, CA: Stanford University Press, 1999)

Thompson, Jennifer A., 'Reading in the Painted Letter: Human Heads in Twelfth-Century English Initials' (unpublished doctoral thesis, University of St Andrews, 2000)

Thrift, Nigel, *Non-Representational Theory: Space, Politics, Affect* (London: Routledge, 2008)

Tomkins, Silvan, 'The Phantasy Behind the Face', in *Exploring Affect: The Selected Writings of Silvan S. Tomkins*, ed. by E. Virginia Demos (Cambridge: Cambridge University Press, 1995), pp. 263–78

—— 'What and Where Are the Primary Affects? Some Evidence for a Theory', in *Exploring Affect: The Selected Writings of Silvan S. Tomkins*, ed. by E. Virginia Demos (Cambridge: Cambridge University Press, 1995), pp. 217–62

Tracy, Larissa, 'The Uses of Torture and Violence in the Fabliaux: When Comedy Crosses the Line', *Florilegium*, 23 (2006), 143–68

Trigg, Stephanie, 'Introduction: Emotional Histories – Beyond the Personalization of the Past and the Abstraction of Affect Theory', *Exemplaria*, 26 (2014), 3–15

Usborne, Simon, 'Medieval Doodles Prove that it's Goode to Scribble in ye Margins', *The Independent*, 9 December 2014 <http://www.independent.co.uk/arts-entertainment/books/news/medieval-doodles-prove-that-its-goode-to-scribble-in-ye-margins-9774982.html> [accessed 2 May 2015]

Vanian, Jonathan, 'Microsoft follows IBM and Amazon in Barring Police from Using its Facial-recognition Technology', *Fortune*, 11 June 2020 < https://fortune.com/2020/06/11/microsoft-ibm-amazon-facial-recognition-police/> [accessed 11 June 2020].

Verhuyck, Paul, 'Guillaume de Lorris ou la multiplication des cadres', *Neophilologus*, 58 (1974), 283–93

von Wartburg, Walther, ed., *Französisches Etymologisches Wörterbuch*, 25 vols (Basel: Zbinden, 1925–2002)

Waldenfels, Bernhard, 'Levinas and the Face of the Other', in *The Cambridge Companion to Levinas*, ed. by Simon Critchley and Robert Bernasconi (Cambridge: Cambridge University Press, 2002), pp. 63–81

Walker Bynum, Caroline, *Fragmentation and Redemption: Essays on Gender and the Human Body in Medieval Religion* (New York: Zone Books, 1991)

Wittgenstein, Ludwig, *Philosophical Investigations*, trans. by G. E. M. Anscombe, 2nd edn (Oxford: Blackwell, 1958; repr. 2000)

Žižek, Slavoj, *Enjoy Your Symptom: Jacques Lacan in Hollywood and Out*, 2nd edn (Abingdon: Routledge, 2008)

—— *Organs without Bodies: On Deleuze and Consequences*, 2nd edn (Abingdon: Routledge, 2012)

—— 'Smashing the Neighbor's Face' <http://www.lacan.com/zizsmash.htm> [accessed 23 February 2016]

Index

acheiropoieta   93 n.28
affect theory   82, 99–103, 115
allegory   120, 129, 134, 142, 150, 152, 155, 197
Arthur, King   44, 45, 46, 68, 77

Bacon, Francis   94
Bakhtin, Mikhail   170
beauty   4, 9, 17, 29, 56, 126, 133, 157,
beheading *see* decapitation
Bel Inconnu   1
biometrics   2, 22
Butler, Judith   181–3, 186–9, 191, 200

Capgras Syndrome   92 n.24, 104, 116
charisma   95, 111
Chevalier as deus espees   24, 35, 51 n. 66, 57–67, 77
Chrétien de Troyes   24, 29, 33 n.13, 34–6, 43–4, 50–3, 77
  Chevalier au Lion   24, 28–36, 43–51, 53–7, 63, 75, 77, 206
  Chevalier de la charrette   35, 70
  Cligès   30–1
  Conte du graal   31 n.10, 36, 51, 51 n.66, 52–3, 58, 116, 132
  Erec et Enide   43, 52, 70 n.96

de Man, Paul   6, 11–12, 13, 132 n.43
decapitation   69–72, 74–5, 76, 174 n.50

Deleuze, Gilles   94
Deleuze, Gilles and Félix Guattari   12–13, 25, 116–21, 126–32, 134–5, 137–41, 148, 150, 154–5, 158–9, 203, 208 *see also visagéité*
disfigurement   17, 32, 84, 106–8, 165
disguise   35, 55, 57, 59–60, 61, 73, 166–7, 169–70, 175
doodles *see under* face

ethics   10, 34, 36, 54, 56, 57, 62, 76–7, 177
expressions *see under* face
eye/eyes *see under* face
eyebrows *see under* face

fabliaux   26, 58, 203, 208, 209, 160–201
  Chevalier qui fist parler les cons   26, 160, 173, 179–94, 197, 198
  Deux vilains   173
  Do con, do vet et do la soriz   26, 160, 195, 198–200
  Du vit et de la coille   26, 160, 194, 195–8, 199
  Jugement des cons   172–3
  Maignien qui foti la dame   172
  Trubert   162, 164–71, 174–9, 183, 195
face
  doodles   25, 80 n.1, 82–112, 114–5, 207, 209

face (*cont'd*)
  etymology of 7
  expressions 9, 21, 84, 91, 99, 103, 104–5
  features 8, 15, 20, 39
    cheek 47
    chin 84
    eye/eyes 8, 15, 50, 84, 101, 109, 111, 112, 131, 134, 159
    eyebrows 84, 168–9, 175
    forehead 47
    mouth 8, 32, 74, 160, 165, 168–76, 179, 190, 192–3, 197–200
    nose 47, 171
    nostrils 160, 165, 168–70, 174–6, 179
    teeth 124, 172–3
  letter-face 82, 96–8, 100, 107–9
  pattern recognition 8, 179
  picture-face 80 n.1, 82, 91–2, 96, 100, 109, 115
  Sainte face 25, 82, 90–3
  saving face 18, 19
face-to-face 10–11, 18, 36, 38, 40–3, 46, 52–77, 100, 120
Facial Recognition Technology 2, 20–2, 26
forehead *see under* face
Frank, Adam 103, 115

Gauvain 1, 24, 28, 32–3, 44–6, 51, 54–77
gaze 110–2, 155
Guattari, Félix *see* Deleuze, Gilles and Félix Guattari
Guillaume de Saint-Pathus 25, 87

Holy Face *see under* face
Hunbaut 1

icon 37, 38, 94–5
idol 93

Jaeger, Stephen C. *see* charisma

Jean de Joinville 25, 88

Kristeva, Julia 94, 171

Lacan, Jacques 25, 82–3, 99, 104, 105–6, 108–12, 114, 115, 118, 119, 158, 207
Levinas, Emmanuel 10, 13, 28, 36–57, 59–62, 65, 66, 67, 75, 76, 80, 207, 209
Louis, Saint (Louis IX) 86, 88, 91, 107

Marion, Jean-Luc *see* idol
mask 28, 203
Meraugis de Portlesguez 32
mirror 4, 93, 121, 142–3, 144, 146, 157–9, 205
misrecognition 2, 4, 33, 35, 44, 52, 55, 58, 59, 61, 63, 64, 66, 68–9
mouth *see under* face

Nancy, Jean-Luc 78–9
Narcissus 3–5, 121, 142–3, 158
nose *see under* face
nostrils *see under* face

personification 136, 142, 149, 153, 193–5, 200
physiognomy 11, 13–17, 20, 23, 37
Picard, Max 9–10
portrait (portraiture) 23, 24, 29, 37, 84 n.9
  vice-portraits 120, 121–34, 138, 140–2, 143–4, 149–50
prosopagnosia 92 n.24

recognition 2, 8, 13, 29, 43, 52, 53, 55, 58, 67, 73, 132 n.43, 174, 207
relic(s) 70, 95
Roman de Gliglois 66 n.85
Roman de la Rose 5, 26, 116–7, 119–59, 203, 204, 206, 208, 209
Roman d'Yder 32

Sainte face see under face
Sartre, Jean-Paul   2, 70–1, 111
Simmel, Georg   10, 18, 39
speech   180–93

teeth *see under* face
Tomkins, Silvan   25, 82, 99–103, 115
Trubert see under fabliaux

vagina
   dentata   172–73
   loquens   172
Vengeance Raguidel   24, 33, 67–75, 76, 77

visagéité   12–13, 25, 116–21, 128–35, 137–41, 146–8, 150, 154–9, 203, 208

Wittgenstein, Ludwig   80 n.1, 82, 91, 92, 98

Yvain (protagonist)   24, 28–34, 44, 45, 46, 51–7, 63, 77

Žižek, Slavoj   56–7, 83, 104, 108, 114

Gallica

Already Published

1. *Postcolonial Fictions in the* Roman de Perceforest: *Cultural Identities and Hybridities*, Sylvia Huot
2. *A Discourse for the Holy Grail in Old French Romance*, Ben Ramm
3. *Fashion in Medieval France*, Sarah-Grace Heller
4. *Christine de Pizan's Changing Opinion: A Quest for Certainty in the Midst of Chaos*, Douglas Kelly
5. *Cultural Performances in Medieval France: Essays in Honor of Nancy Freeman Regalado*, eds Eglal Doss-Quinby, Roberta line Krueger, E. Jane Burns
6. *The Medieval Warrior Aristocracy: Gifts, Violence, Performance, and the Sacred*, Andrew Cowell
7. *Logic and Humour in the Fabliaux: An Essay in Applied Narratology*, Roy J. Pearcy
8. *Miraculous Rhymes: The Writing of Gautier de Coinci*, Tony Hunt
9. *Philippe de Vigneulles and the Art of Prose Translation*, Catherine M. Jones
10. *Desire by Gender and Genre in Trouvère Song*, Helen Dell
11. *Chartier in Europe*, eds Emma Cayley, Ashby Kinch
12. *Medieval Saints' Lives: The Gift, Kinship and Community in Old French Hagiography*, Emma Campbell
13. *Poetry, Knowledge and Community in Late Medieval France*, eds Rebecca Dixon, Finn E. Sinclair with Adrian Armstrong, Sylvia Huot, Sarah Kay
14. *The Troubadour* Tensos *and* Partimens: *A Critical Edition*, Ruth Harvey, Linda Paterson
15. *Old French Narrative Cycles: Heroism between Ethics and Morality*, Luke Sunderland
16. *The Cultural and Political Legacy of Anne de Bretagne: Negotiating Convention in Books and Documents*, ed. Cynthia J. Brown
17. *Lettering the Self in Medieval and Early Modern France*, Katherine Kong
18. *The Old French Lays of* Ignaure, Oiselet *and* Amours, eds Glyn S. Burgess, Leslie C. Brook
19. *Thinking Through Chrétien de Troyes*, Zrinka Stahuljak, Virginie Greene, Sarah Kay, Sharon Kinoshita, Peggy McCracken
20. *Blindness and Therapy in Late Medieval French and Italian Poetry*, Julie Singer
21. Partonopeus de Blois: *Romance in the Making*, Penny Eley
22. *Illuminating the* Roman d'Alexandre: *Oxford, Bodleian Library, MS Bodley 264: The Manuscript as Monument*, Mark Cruse
23. *The* Conte du Graal *Cycle: Chrétien de Troyes'* Perceval, *the Continuations, and French Arthurian Romance*, Thomas Hinton
24. *Marie de France: A Critical Companion*, Sharon Kinoshita, Peggy McCracken

25. *Constantinople and the West in Medieval French Literature: Renewal and Utopia*, Rima Devereaux
26. *Authorship and First-Person Allegory in Late Medieval France and England*, Stephanie A. Viereck Gibbs Kamath
27. *Virgilian Identities in the French Renaissance*, eds Philip John Usher, Isabelle Fernbach
28. *Shaping Courtliness in Medieval France: Essays in Honor of Matilda Tomaryn Bruckner*, eds Daniel E. O'Sullivan, Laurie Shepard
29. *Violence and the Writing of History in the Medieval Francophone World*, eds Noah D. Guynn, Zrinka Stahuljak
30. *The Refrain and the Rise of the Vernacular in Medieval French Music and Poetry*, Jennifer Saltzstein
31. *Marco Polo's* Le Devisement du Monde: *Narrative Voice, Language and Diversity*, Simon Gaunt
32. *The* Pèlerinage *Allegories of Guillaume de Deguileville: Tradition, Authority and Influence*, eds Marco Nievergelt, Stephanie A. Viereck Gibbs Kamath
33. *Rewriting Arthurian Romance in Renaissance France: From Manuscript to Printed Book*, Jane H. M. Taylor
34. *Unsettling Montaigne: Poetics, Ethics and Affect in the* Essais *and Other Writings*, Elizabeth Guild
35. *Machaut and the Medieval Apprenticeship Tradition: Truth, Fiction and Poetic Craft*, Douglas Kelly
36. *Telling the Story in the Middle Ages: Essays in Honour of Evelyn Birge Vitz*, eds Kathryn A. Duys, Elizabeth Emery, Laurie Postlewate
37. *The Anglo-Norman Lay of* Haveloc: *Text and Translation*, eds Glyn S. Burgess, Leslie C. Brook
38. *Sacred Fictions of Medieval France: Narrative Theology in the Lives of Christ and the Virgin, 1150–1500*, Maureen Barry McCann Boulton
39. *Founding Feminisms in Medieval Studies: Essays in Honor of E. Jane Burns*, eds Laine E. Doggett and Daniel E. O'Sullivan
40. *Representing the Dead: Epitaph Fictions in Late-Medieval France*, Helen J. Swift
41. *The* Roman de Troie *by Benoît de Sainte-Maure: A Translation*, translated by Glyn S. Burgess and Douglas Kelly
42. *The Medieval Merlin Tradition in France and Italy: Prophecy, Paradox, and* Translatio, Laura Chuhan Campbell
43. *Representing Mental Illness in Late Medieval France: Machines, Madness, Metaphor*, Julie Singer
44. *The Logic of Idolatry in Seventeenth-Century French Literature*, Ellen McClure